1.

WITH ENGLAND IN AUSTRALIA

M. W. JEFFELS.
25. SWALEDALE AVE.
DARLINGTON.
AUGUST. 1947.

Mrs Jeffels.
167 Clifton Road
Darlington.

The Duke and Duchess of Gloucester at Melbourne during the third Test Match. The Duke—whose farewell visit as Governor-General this was—is shaking hands with Hardstaff, and the Duchess with Evans. On the right near camera is Hammond; on the left, Edrich and Compton.

WITH ENGLAND IN AUSTRALIA

The Truth About the Tests

by

BRUCE HARRIS

Cricket Correspondent "Evening Standard"

With 17 Illustrations

HUTCHINSON'S
LIBRARY OF SPORTS AND PASTIMES
London   New York   Melbourne   Sydney   Cape Town

To
ONE WHO STAYED AT
HOME

Printed in Great Britain at
The Fleet Street Press
East Harding St., EC4

CONTENTS

ILLUSTRATIONS

CHAPTER I

CONFESSION

ONCE more the Ashes of cricket lie undisturbed in Australia. If the late Sir Nevile Henderson had not chosen the title for a weightier disappointment, I should have liked to call this book on the recent M.C.C. tour there "Failure of a Mission."

After failure, inevitably, came the inquests.

"Blame Hitler," say many—and the Dear Departed certainly did take our eye off the ball for six almost cricketless years. But Hitler is beyond our displeasure.

"Blame Hammond," one or two critics have said, alleging maldistribution of the field or mismanagement of bowling, or lack of inspiration and drive. Well, I am not saying that Hammond is the best captain who ever led an English side on and off the field, but had he been a combination of M. A. Noble, A. C. Maclaren, D. R. Jardine and—for that matter—Don Bradman, he still could not have brought the Ashes from Australia. He had not the resources at his command.

"Blame the umpires," is a cry not unheard. Judging from evidence nearer than the Press box, we have suffered what the Australians call a "rough spin" or two—notably that l.b.w. decision against Bill Edrich when century-bound in the third test at Melbourne. It was annoying, perhaps even demoralising, to our men. But the most accurate of umpiring—if it exists in Australia or anywhere else—would not have brought us the Ashes.

"Blame bad luck," is the last of these aliases. We certainly had it. The rains did not fall equally on just and unjust. Brisbane in the first test provided our batsmen with two "stickies"—although the uncomfortable fact should not be forgotten that the Australians had already scored 645 against us. Twice, later, when Australia was batting or about to bat, Sydney's Sunday sun dried a wicket which in all probability would have provided our bowlers on a working day with a harvest. Injury put Voce almost out of the third test and deprived us of Edrich's bowling for a day. Finally Len Hutton, after an incomplete 122 in the last test, spent the rest of the match in hospital.

But when all is said and done the best reason for defeat lies in the words "Blame ourselves." We did not win because our cricket was not good enough. Other causes were merely contributory. Australia, recovering more quickly from the effects of the war than we could, found a collection of young, or youngish, players equal at least in batsmanship and fielding to our own and more varied and menacing in their bowling. We feared it before the tour began, so why the pained surprise?

No, I am not specially alarmed or disappointed at this failure of this particular mission. But there is cause for concern at the continued failure of a succession of missions at home and overseas. Before I go fully into the story of this latest tour allow me—single-garmented on a sticky Indian Ocean homeward-bound—to suggest that all is not well with English cricket.

It is important to realise this, in the present sackcloth-and-ashes mood, if we are to hold our own in the future. Look at this:

Since Jardine brought home the Ashes in 1933—and ran into a lot of trouble—we have either lost, or failed to win, three test series.

In 1934 at home the England teams led first by C. F. Walters and then by R. E. S. Wyatt, lost the rubber by two matches to one, with two draws.

In 1936-7 G. O. Allen's side in Australia lost by three to two—after winning the first two matches.

In 1938 England, captained by W. R. Hammond, drew the series one all, with two matches drawn and one abandoned without a ball bowled. So Hammond has been rather more successful than the others.

Now, in the series just over, we have lost decisively by three to nil, with two drawn, both heavily in favour of our opponents.

Yet Australia has a population roughly equal only to that of London.

Don't let us sit back and say "By the time the Australians arrive next year all will be well—our cricket will have recovered." That is to live in a fool's paradise. Australian superiority—sixty matches to fifty-five since the tests began though England still leads eighteen to seventeen in test series—is due to more than questions of captaincy or war conditions. The causes lie deeper, are worth examining before I take you round Australia on my third tour there.

"Climate" say the excusers glibly in explaining why the Australians produce about half a dozen times as many fine cricketers as we per thousand of population. Don't you believe them. In my last two tours in Australia we have had as many, and as long, interruptions from rain as in a normal English summer. They have more sunshine and fewer clouds than we, but we in England have the priceless advantage of long, light evenings denied to countries like Australia, which lie nearer the Equator. Here we have fine opportunities of training young players.

No, we shall go on losing against the Commonwealth more often than we win until we display the same zeal for organisation and enthusiasm for the game as they manifest out there. From the time when boys first take confident strike on the excellent concrete and matting wickets of their public parks—pitches never seen in England—to the days when they become adult cricketers they are watched and encouraged. They are at the bottom of the ladder, but the ladder is there complete. In England it must often seem to the youngster that a rung or two of his ladder are missing.

In Australia the clubs, in grade competition against each other, have a link with first-class cricket much closer than in England. The test match star of one weekend may be setting, the following Saturday, a standard for his young colleagues in his club. Don Bradman, with the captaincy of Australia to think about, yet turned out last season for the Kensington Club in Adelaide.

I know that in the South of England the idea of "league cricket" is distasteful. In the North the leagues thrive, which is a reason why Yorkshire and Lancashire, handicapped though they are by weather, give us southerners so many lickings. Undoubtedly something of the pleasant atmosphere of "friendly" cricket may be lost when league tables and championships take its place. But that such competitive play develops the best cricketers is obvious in the North of England—and in Australia. There it builds up big reserves of good young players, capable of making a show in the best company. In nearly all our so-called minor matches down there our full-time cricketers bumped into far-from-negligible opposition. Did not J. Gardiner down in Tasmania, for example, come within six of scoring against England bowlers the first century of his life in first-class cricket? If Bradman, Miller, Lindwall, McCool, Morris and Dooland were to go out of cricket to-morrow, successors from the Unknowns would soon fill their places.

In cricket, as in other sports, leagues are the anvil on which natural talent is hammered into shape. We can go on playing "pleasant" cricket if we like—there is very much to commend it. But it will not produce enough of the greatest players to beat Australia.

It would pay M.C.C., or for that matter the Club Cricket Conference, to send someone out to Australia next southern summer to look into club organisation out there. He would be given every assistance and would come home with an idea or two.

In Middlesex R. W. V. Robins is doing his best to strengthen the link between county and club. It ought to happen everywhere.

Reform of first-class cricket in England—to make it really live up to its name instead of being merely "second-class first-class"—is outside the scope of this book about one tour. But there is one urgent digression concerning army cricket. Everywhere I go among thinking players I hear the lament that, since boys will be going into the Services at eighteen, they will inevitably be lost to the first-class game just when they should be developing into cricketers. That is, or ought to be, a fallacy. A boy in any of the Services has much more time for sport than civilian occupation allows. Given proper co-operation with Whitehall a regular Services side could be developed to contain the cream of our up-and-coming players. That side should receive exactly the same encouragement as the universities. Counties should be asked to give it regular fixtures, so that when the soldier or airman of promise discarded uniform he could step straight into a county side a "made" player. The Services are usually sympathetic towards sport. Lots of cricket is played in every military centre. But a permanent All-Services side is needed to give the best cricketers the best practice.

Reforms like this, however, are long term. They will not enable us to beat the very strong Australian side due in England next year. That is going to be "some job." Of our seventeen players now home from the front very few are reasonably certain of a place in the 1948 England side, which means it will have to be rebuilt, from the captaincy downwards. I should say that the nucleus of the eleven will be Godfrey Evans—the most conspicuous success of the late tour as wicketkeeper and useful batsman; Denis Compton, who opened his test contributions poorly but ended them brilliantly; Len Hutton, of whom much the same can be said; W. J. Edrich, our best all-rounder in Australia; and the two bowlers Alec Bedser and Douglas Wright, both likely to do better at home than in Australia. Six men, with, quite possibly, Norman Yardley as captain and all-rounder.

Our conspicuous needs are a fast bowler, for Australia has two; a slow left-hander of the Verity type able to keep batsmen quiet on good wickets and cascade them out on bad ones; another right-hand leg-spinner to relieve Wright; and two or three more top-class batsmen. Cyril Washbrook may be Hutton's opening partner again, but his place is not assured. John Ikin may be a man we want, for his fielding is so whole-hearted that we await eagerly centuries from him instead of useful fifties and sixties.

Time will be beginning to tell next summer against nearly all the others who went to Australia under Hammond, himself retiring at forty-three from international play.

English cricket will indeed have to be combed in the summer of 1947 for the men we need, especially the fast bowler. Time was when every county had one as a matter of course; now the race of great amateur fast bowlers—the Brearleys, the Knox's, the Kortrights and the like—has died out, and the young professional, with his living to earn, thinks twice before cultivating a branch of the game where his cricketing life is short and arduous. But to have any chance of regaining the Ashes we must have an express bowler next year. Sometimes talent shows itself quickly. The tests against South Africa may yield a pleasant surprise or two.

Australia's problems have almost solved themselves. Fifteen men played in one or more tests against us recently. If the whole party, unchanged, were packed off to England next April they would be a formidable side, capable, on present evidence, of holding the Ashes. Only one of them, their captain, would have reached the veteran stage—Bradman by then will be nearly forty. He is his usual non-committal self about coming to England again; somehow I think he will be here. If he does come you will see a still great batsman not quite his old self, and a first-rate captain, whom the young members of the side regard almost with veneration. There is no doubt that Bradman built a happy as well as a magnificent team in Australia.

I shall write in more detail later of the individual Australians likely to be with us soon. Two factors, more than any others, brought them victory with lots to spare. One was the variety of their bowling —fast, medium right and left, right-hand leg-spin, slow left-hand, right-hand off-spin—the whole battery was there at Bradman's command. The other factor was their "all-roundness." Toshack was the only bowler to whom Bradman could not look for runs at a pinch; when a fast bowler can score a century like that of Lindwall at Melbourne his captain may well sleep sound o' nights.

Note that of the eight Australians chosen primarily for their bowling or wicketkeeping McCool had an average of 54, Lindwall 32, Tallon 29, Johnson (despite "spectacles" at Melbourne) 21, Tribe 17, Dooland 16, Toshack 4 and Freer infinity—one innings of 25 not out. Think also of the all-round qualities of Miller (averaging 76 with the bat and sixteen wickets for 21 each with the ball) and you realise that Bradman had, in effect, several more than eleven cricketers in his command. We have indeed some leeway to make up. Note also that of the fifteen only three—Bradman, Barnes and Hassett—had ever played in a test match before the war.

Which all leads naturally to the shortcomings of our much more experienced side—of the party of seventeen players, eight had been chosen before the war for tests against Australia and others against other countries. Undoubtedly the early disappointment was our batting, for the men on whom we had relied for runs in plenty either were slow off the mark in the series or hardly got off it at all. Remember, by way of palliation, that on the Brisbane dual "sticky" in the first test 20 or 30 runs were worth a century. But even taking this into account it was disappointing to everyone, including the players concerned, that in the first three tests Hammond, Hutton and Compton, with six innings each, scored only 369 runs between them. The only score of more than 50 by these players in these matches was Compton's 54 in the second test at Sydney. Everyone knows that in the later tests Hutton and Compton struck top form, but by then two test matches of the five had been lost and recovery was impossible. Batsmen like Edrich, Ikin, Yardley and Washbrook who came earlier into their own were always having to fight a losing battle at this period of the tour.

Several times our bowlers were entitled to argue that the batting let the side down. Our inability to turn a strong position into something better was conspicuous. In the second test at Sydney our batsmen, chasing a very hostile 659 for eight, were all out for 255, but at 219 for two in the second innings looked like making a good job of the follow-on. Yet the whole side were out for 371.

In the third test at Melbourne a wonderful chance went astray of heading the moderate Australian first innings total of 365. With 150 on the board we had only one wicket down; yet our total fell short of Australia's by 14. At Adelaide a month later our middle batting broke down again; although Hammond was eventually able to declare the opportunity of setting the Australians a real problem for the fourth innings was sacrificed. On that occasion 100 for one wicket became 215 for six—and then Compton and Evans came to the rescue.

The fifth test at Sydney provided the last of the examples of uneven batting. From 150 for no wicket the rot set in—and though Hutton was still there the total became 225 for six. With Hutton absent ill when the innings was resumed we were all out for 280 Consistency was never a feature of our batting. Someone or other always "came off," but there were never enough big scores to make high totals. Only once did we exceed 400—460 in our first innings at Adelaide. Our average for ten innings was a mere 280, though one of these ten attempts ended with seven and another with eight wickets down. Here are not nearly enough runs for winning test matches on Australian wickets. These have lost their old speed and tend all the time to become easy. Such totals will not win matches even in England.

How much the Australian bowling had to do with all this record of batting failure is a matter of opinion. The just answer probably is that, competent though the bowling was, it was not as good as all that.

We knew all about the limitations of our bowlers before the side sailed last August. We were not disappointed. Australia needed to bat only eight times against our ten, and on three of these occasions only eight, one and five wickets fell. Yet their aggregate was 3,374 against our 2,800, and their average 422 an innings. Worked out on the basis of runs per wicket the disparity would be even greater. They had two innings of over 600—645 at Brisbane and 659 for eight at Sydney, each in turn a record for tests in Australia. We feared that our bowlers would "get some stick." They certainly got it.

Our trouble was not so much the individual bowlers themselves as the lack of reserves and the unsuitability to Australian wickets of the fast-medium type of bowler. The wickets which made Maurice Tate so deadly no longer exist. Two sorts of bowlers succeed in Australia to-day—the fast sort like Lindwall and the leg-spinners of the McCool type.

Douglas Wright was probably the best spin bowler on either side. He was the only man who took more than twenty wickets in the series, and Alec Bedser, with sixteen, was exceeded only by Wright (twenty-three), Lindwall and McCool (eighteen each), and Toshack (seventeen). That Wright's wickets cost 43 runs each and Bedser's 54 is largely explainable by the number of overs they had to bowl—Wright 240 and Bedser 246. On the Australian side Toshack, often filling the position of a stock bowler, bowled most overs with 178. That their bowlers finished the series with averages in the twenties is explained by the fact that six of them were able to share the burden. Wright and Bedser too often had to "bowl themselves into the ground." But for the unexpected relief given by Yardley they would probably have bowled themselves under ground. Think of their sending down 43 and 41 overs respectively during that huge Australian innings at Brisbane; of their forty-six each during the even greater aggregate in Sydney. Eight-ball overs, at that. Wright, too, often found himself bowling without the least luck.

In the fourth test match we faced the music with only three regular bowlers—Bedser, Wright, Edrich—plus Yardley and an occasional over or two from Ikin and Compton. It is not nearly enough, especially in the humid February heat of Adelaide. Yet in the circumstances at the time, and with the list of injuries, it was difficult to see what else the selectors could do.

Hammond himself in previous tours used to be a valuable breaker of stubborn partnerships. This tour he put himself on for three overs against South Australia in October—and then gave up the experiment. He was afraid that bowling would stir up the latent trouble in his back.

Like our batting, our bowling could not turn to account winning opportunities. In the first test Morris and Barnes were out with the score 46: yet Australia totalled 645. In the second, Morris, Johnson, Hassett and Miller were gone with 159 up, but only four more wickets fell before the declaration at 659 for eight. In the fourth test Harvey and Bradman were both out in the first innings with 18 on the big board; yet the total was 487. Let me emphasise again that the captain had not enough reserves to nurse his best bowlers.

Fielding comparisons are less easy to draw. When we left for Australia it was feared that the side would look "old" in the field. I do not think it did. I should say that there was little in it between the two sides. Certainly a better cover-point than Washbrook does not exist in England or Australia to-day, or a more whole-hearted and efficient gully than Ikin, who could field elsewhere with equal trustworthiness. Edrich—despite the dropping in the slips of Bradman at a crucial moment of the last test—had as safe a pair of hands as anyone and had unbounded enthusiasm and energy. Hammond at forty-three was still a menace to any batsman at first slip. Yardley had a consistently good record as an in-fieldsman.

We were rather short of outfielders, but Compton, despite a certain casualness in some of his returns to the wicketkeeper, used his speed near the boundary unstintingly and was a safe catch. There was not a man in the side whom it was necessary to "hide."

As for captaincy, Bradman's leadership was always more apparent from the ringside than Hammond's. The Australian captain took longer than Hammond over his field-placings at each change of bowlers, had more to say to his bowlers between overs, often between balls. Bradman certainly can claim that the care he took produced results. Hammond's methods were less obvious to any but the players: sometimes, indeed, the stranger might go on wondering awhile who was directing the attack. This quietness of leadership sometimes brought the criticism that Hammond was just "letting the game go on." The impression was probably quite erroneous. Some of the most successful captains of cricket have been the least demonstrative.

In any event I do not believe that Hammond had under him the makings of a successful side. Too many holes existed in the English armament. There were no criticisms that I can remember of Hammond's captaincy at home in 1938; he is obviously no less experienced and knowledgeable a leader now than then. An Australian off-the-field criticism that Hammond liked to go about eastern Australia in his car, rather than in trains, seems to be beside the point.

There were, however, two errors of judgment for which Hammond and the selectors must bear responsibility. More important of these was the failure to recognise that Evans was the predestined wicket-keeper for the tests. The result of this was that he did not get the early batting practice he needed—and it was evident later that Evans was a valuable acquisition with the bat. He would have been still more valuable after earlier opportunities. Until he was given his place in the second test match at Sydney just before Christmas he played only three innings—not much more than one a month—and one of these was against the Queensland Country side at Gympie.

The second error was the non-recognition of James Langridge as a likely all-rounder for the tests. After a home season in which he scored his customary "double" with bat and ball he did some useful bowling in early matches and played an innings of 30 not out against the strong Combined Eleven at Perth. He is a better bat than Ikin—though perhaps not so active in the field—and his bowling would have been invaluable when we needed more bowlers during the huge Australian innings of the first and second tests. But he was not given a chance until selected among the twelve for the third match at New Year. On the eve of this test he was injured at practice and had to be omitted. Later, with the injury still bothering him, he made 100 against South Australia. Langridge is not a Hedley Verity, but when we sorely needed bowlers it was a mistake to leave him out. "Too old at forty," say some. If that were so why take him to Australia? How absurd it is to send him there and give him only three innings in first-class cricket throughout the tour.

CHAPTER II

SEND A TRAINER

OUTSIDE the actual cricket two or three reforms and innovations appear to me, as a close observer of the tour, to be necessary in future. The first concerns the physical fitness of our touring sides. I believe that the M.C.C. should place our touring cricketers in charge of a trainer, with full powers in his own domain. It is as necessary in cricket as in football, though obviously methods would be different for a tour lasting seven months. You cannot train a cricketer with a long programme of matches before him as fine as a footballer before a cup final, or a boxer before a fight, or a university boat race crew before a certain big day in March.

I wonder, for example, whether anyone thought what the result would be of the sudden change from spartan English diet to the abundance of the voyage out and the still greater abundance of that land of plenty, Australia. What exercises were needed to counteract it? And so on. About this time there was an outbreak of boils among the men. It may have had something to do with more liberal feeding.

At Perth soon after landing the team were met by Tom Langridge, a Sydney physical culture expert, who remained with the party for the whole Australian tour. His record in bringing English and other football sides up to victory pitch is an outstanding one. He took over, with great satisfaction to our players, the treatment of injuries. With the enthusiasm for his work which he always shows he arranged early morning classes for anyone who would go along. But—and it is a bit but—he was not given complete authority to *order* this or that.

To some men—usually the youngsters of a party—physical exercise is a joy. Denis Compton, for example, could never have too much of it; running round cricket grounds, playing squash rackets and any other brisk work that came along were a delight to him. There was no fitter man in the side; he exuded health and good spirits. But not all men are spontaneously eager for exercise, and I do not believe that all our men were 100 per cent fit.

Do not read between these lines what is not there. In their manner of life these cricketers were as abstemious a party as any I have known. They enjoyed life, of course. So do the Australians when they tour England. So do any bunch of young men on tour anywhere. They would not be human, especially after the restrictions

18

of wartime, if they did not appreciate some of the parties "thrown" for them everywhere. There is nothing against such enjoyment, for too strict a training would lead to staleness. But I saw no inclination to late nights, or joyous parties, at test match time. Rupert Howard, the manager, in answering a journalist who suggested that one of the reasons for failure in the tests was that the side were having a good time socially, said he had never known a more careful-living set of players. Nor have I.

My argument, without casting reflections on the men, amounts simply to this—that training athletic and games teams these days must be a specialist business if maximum fitness is to be achieved. Seventeen players ought not to be left without direction in such matters. Hence the need of a trainer with full power to act.

Another question affecting the morale and success of any side is that of adequate practice for the "reserves"—the men who do not look immediate probables for the tests. We send seventeen men to Australia, each of them presumably a potential test player; yet under the present one-match-a-week system about half a dozen of them cannot hope to get into top form. On the other hand Australians, in England, with two matches a week, have every opportunity— even those apparently right out of the running for the tests.

The case of Joe Hardstaff is a flagrant illustration. That great batsman played, before the first test on 29th November, just three innings against first-class sides and two against minor ones. A club cricketer playing only at weekends gets more match play than this. Between 2nd November, when he batted against Victoria, and 9th December, when he reappeared against Queensland Country at Gympie, he did not have an innings at all. His next first-class match was the Combined Eleven one in Tasmania at Hobart on 10th-13th January. The only test match for which he was chosen was the fourth. A moderate start had put him out of the running for the first test and he had no real chance of recovery.

I have already mentioned the case of Evans. Now take that of Langridge. His total innings before the first test were four, two of them against minor opposition. Consider a bowler, Dick Pollard, who, like Langridge, did not play in any test match. In the seven weeks before the first test he bowled, in six innings, 108 overs in all. Think how many he would bowl for Lancashire in seven weeks and then consider how any man can keep at his peak on such an allowance.

Paul Gibb on the other hand had plenty of practice until he was dropped for the second test match on 13th December. Thereafter until the Australian tour ended on 5th March his appearances were limited to Newcastle, Bendigo, two Tasmanian matches, Ballarat and the return match against Victoria at Melbourne— the only one of the lot that is more than nominally first-class. He did not always keep wicket even in these. If Evans had been injured, and Gibb had been recalled to the test team at a moment's notice, what then?

All this, be it noted, was not the fault of the selectors. They have to give their prospective test side, especially the batsmen, as much practice as they need. The fault lies in the fact that a cricket team has only eleven players and that long distances between Australian grounds make it impossible to play more than one match weekly. Something ought to be done about this problem before the next side goes out. Maybe, if the Australians were asked, they would arrange some scratch matches for our spare men. Not an ideal solution, admittedly, for such games would not be fought keenly. But almost any match play is better than none. It is no use sending seventeen cricketers to Australia if they cannot be kept in practice. Some of the men left out of the early tests might have done well in them if they had had opportunities. I have omitted the case of Fishlock, because injury at Adelaide early in the tour put him out of the running for six matches in a row, including the first test.

Another unsatisfactory feature of the tour was the inordinate number of drawn games. Look at this record:

	Played	Won	Lost	Drawn
Test matches	5	0	3	2
Other first-class matches ..	12	1	0	11
Minor matches	8	3	0	5
Total	25	4	3	18

Yet six days were allotted to the tests; four to the other first-class matches except those at Perth and in Tasmania; two days to the minor matches apart from the one-day fixtures at Fremantle and Bendigo. Eleven draws in twelve first-class matches other than the tests is a farcical state of affairs, even though we are able to boast that the side was unbeaten except by the full strength of Australia. Be it noted that the only first-class side we found time to beat was Victoria, strongest of the States.

Yet a definite result was reached in by far the greater number of the Sheffield Shield matches, in which Australian sides were playing each other. They, too, are four-day fixtures.

Certainly if eleven matches out of twelve are to be drawn the Australian public will lose their keenness for them. Australians will be reluctant to support any cricket which appears to them to be a predestined draw from the word "Go."

Rain, about which I will say more presently, had undoubtedly much to do with this record of inconclusiveness. But not everything. I believe that other influences were our bowling weakness and the growing tendency to regard matches against the Australian States as a mere preparation for the test matches ahead. Time was when

a match against Victoria or New South Wales ranked as an event
of importance almost comparable with one against Australia. Now
it is not so. The tendency among modern touring sides is to make
sure not to lose such fixtures and to give batsmen plenty of practice.
This is the way of futility. Better lose a match or two against the
States—and win two or three—than draw them all. Certainly the
most ardent cricket enthusiast may be pardoned if his zeal is blunted
because eighteen matches in the entire programme of twenty-five
are left unfinished. He is apt to prefer football or speedway racing,
with assured results.

I agree that nearly everywhere we went we took rain with us.
In remote parts of Australia, where sheep were dying in thousands
during drought, station-owners longed for a visit by Hammond's
men. Of the twenty-five matches fourteen were more or less affected
by rain; in some cases whole days were washed out.

Manchester could teach Sydney very little in its summer rainfall·
Bill Ferguson, our scorer, whose diligence in taking records is
phenomenal, has given me all the rain-history of the two tests
there, as follows:

SECOND TEST:
Friday fine and hot.
Saturday hot, sultry. Off the field 12.55, bad light and rain.
Resumed 4 p.m. Off the field 4.54 bad light. Play limited that day
to under two hours.
Other days fine and hot.

FIFTH TEST:
Friday fine but close.
Saturday no play, heavy rain.
Monday, Tuesday, Wednesday, fine and cool.

In the two matches against New South Wales rain was more
troublesome still. During the first it drove the players off the field
at 3.10 on the Friday and there was no resumption until the following Tuesday. Play in the whole four days was limited to about five
and a half hours, and no one could be blamed for that draw.
During the second of these State matches there was forty minutes
of "bad light stopped play" on the Saturday, thirty-five minutes of
rain interruption on the Monday and an end to the game at 4 p.m.
on the Tuesday, when we looked like winning a thrilling match
against the clock.

Two of the four Sydney Saturdays of the tour therefore were
washed out, the third was limited to less than two hours' cricket
and the fourth escaped with only a brief interruption.

During the terrifying Great Storm on the fourth afternoon of the first test in Brisbane—the greatest I have ever seen during a cricket match—one could almost have rowed a boat across the ground. It speaks astonishingly for the recuperative powers of the turf that rain interruptions during that match were limited to something over five hours.

Adelaide, hot and humid, spared us rain during its test match except for one brief shower lasting 23 minutes—the tail end of a great storm in the neighbourhood. Melbourne was fine except for the fourth day, when four brief interruptions totalling three-quarters of an hour took place.

"An exceptional summer," I was told. So it was the previous tour.

Don't imagine that in Australia, any more than in England, cricket is always played in a land of sheer dry delight. The only difference is that usually the Australians wait for their cricket in warm rain while we shiver in cold. We in England cannot often point proudly to a series of five test matches every one of which suffered in greater or less degree from the clouds.

CHAPTER III

NEXT YEAR'S VISITORS

NEXT summer we shall see in England a very strong and attractive Australian side, able, I believe, to bear comparison with any fore-runners. Not even the Olympic Games should keep us away from their matches. I will combine a review of their achievements in the tests they have now won with anticipation of what we may expect from them. First, in alphabetical order, the fifteen who have played against us in the recent series, although there are others strongly in the running for a visit home.

First *S. G. Barnes*, then, whose name, read first at the announce-ment of the Australian side for the opening test, made us news-papermen think for a fraction of a second that Bradman had jettisoned himself. He is one of the three men of the 1946-7 tests who played against us in 1938 at home—the others being Bradman and Hassett. Then his test appearances were limited to one, for on the way over he hurt an arm and was out of the early matches.

Since those days Barnes has filled out, until now at nearly thirty-one he is a sturdy pony-like figure conspicuous in the field for his liking for the "silly" leg positions—where Godfrey Evans gave him what the curate in the "Private Secretary" would have described as "a good hard knock"—and at the wicket for his ability to stay much longer than we liked. He stayed during the second test for ten hours, forty-two minutes, scoring 234 and adding with Bradman 405. Bradman whose individual score was the same, took only six hours thirty-one minutes—and in the old days would have covered the ground quicker than that. Barnes used not to be an opening batsman, but when W. A. Brown, of Queensland, hurt his thumb he took over the position and made quite a job of it with Arthur Morris.

In Australia he is regarded, from sundry mannerisms in the field, as the "comedian" of the New South Wales side. Comedian or not Barnes is a competent cricketer of the older school—and in Australia anyone over thirty belongs to that.

Occasionally he bowls a few overs of leg-spinners.

Barnes came to England immediately after the fifth test. Whether he will be available for selection next year remains to be seen; if so he is a pretty certain choice.

Performances in the recent series. First test 31 and 1, as a bowler, 1—0—1—0; second 234 and 3—0—11—0; third 45 and 32; fourth ill, did not play; fifth 71 and 30 and 3—0—11—0. Third in Australian test averages with 73.8.

When we arrived in Australia last September cricketing journalists there told us that *Don Bradman* was a very uncertain starter. Had he not been ill? Was he not out of practice? Was he not thirty-eight and a busy man? All these things were true; yet here I read in my records that the little man is at the head of the test averages again, with 680 runs for eight innings, one of them uncompleted, an average of 97.1. In 1938 in England it was 108.50; in Australia, 1936-7, 90.00; in 1934 in England 94.75; in Australia, 1932-3 (the "bodyline" tour) 56.57; in England, 1930, 139.14; in Australia, 1928-9, 66.85.

So far as figures go then, Bradman shows little or no falling from grace. He made the runs, even though he did not make them with his old dare-devilry.

When we arrived at Adelaide, Bradman, discussing with me the still-doubtful question whether he could play, confirmed that he had indeed been ill—and it was obvious from his appearance that he spoke the truth. Business, he added, might make it difficult or impossible for him to leave Adelaide, and what, anyhow, was the use of saying he would play several weeks before the decision was necessary? He scouted the notion that he was making an unnecessary mystery.

Much the same position seems to prevail to-day concerning a farewell tour in England by Bradman next year. Bradman has carefully refrained from ruling out such a visit: like Brer Fox he lies low and says nuffin. But just as I thought all along that he would play in 1946-7, so I think he will do so, if form remains good, in 1948. His health certainly improved during the tour just over—at the end of it he was looking a different man, with clearer skin and sprightlier step. Despite one or two strains early in the tour he stuck it in the field remarkably well. A man who can score 234 runs, as Bradman did in the Sydney test, is hardly near the end of his physical resources. Yes, I think we shall see the Don in command in England again next year. "Fear" would probably be a better word, for he is to be feared as captain as much as batsman. Yet I don't know: the supreme performers of cricket ought to be immortal as well as international.

I have no doubt that Bradman, if he chose, could come to England in a more lucrative role than that of cricketer. For the asking he could obtain £2,000 or £3,000 plus expenses for one tour as a writer on the game. If and when that ever happens the

Empire Cricket Writers' Club will obtain a recruit of some brilliance. But Bradman is fond of his cricket and will be reluctant to exchange too early bat for typewriter—if he ever does, for his stockbroking business in Adelaide is a tax on his attention.

Bradman made the runs against us all right in our recent tour, but it would be false to say he made them as attractively as of old. There was too much uncertainty early in his innings, too many mistimed and misdirected strokes then. One often felt that our bowlers could do everything except get him out. Not even, when he did settle down, did he score with the same old freedom.

His centuries were two—the Sydney 234 and the Brisbane 187—an innings which aroused one of the umpiring controversies of the tour. Several of our fieldsmen, including Ikin, who took the ball, thought he was caught in the slips off Voce when he had made no more than 28. Umpire Borwick said no—apparently on the ground that the ball had come off the floor. The decision was viewed with disfavour on the English side. Getting Bradman out once is difficult enough; twice is heartbreaking. Umpire Scott has told us that we in the Press box are quite out of position for judging nice points. He is right, so I won't take sides. Our men believed one thing; Borwick and, obviously, Bradman himself, the contrary.

"Why bring it all up again?" you may inquire. Because the decision, right or wrong, changed the whole run of the match. Sticky wickets came later, and if the Australian innings had been shortened by Bradman's early departure his batsmen would have had their share of them.

In the field Bradman, while still not to be taken lightly by batsmen trying sharp singles, does not get down to the ball with quite his old quickness. But as a captain he seems to be cuter than ever. It was often desperately difficult for our hardest-hitting batsmen to pierce the field he set, and he showed generally an aggressive leadership which contributed enormously towards the three Australian victories. The chief criticism levelled against him was that he did not go flat out for victory in the Adelaide test after Hammond had declared just after lunch on the last day and left Australia 314 to make to win that afternoon.

In all first-class matches of the season Bradman scored 1,032 runs, with an average of 79.3. One batsman, S. Loxton of Victoria, stood above him with 107.7, but played only five innings against Bradman's fourteen. Now Bradman has 97 centuries to his credit in first-class cricket; if he does not complete his century of centuries in the next Australian season we may see him achieve it in England next summer.

Bradman's test match performances were: First test 187; second 234; third 79 and 49; fourth 0 and 56 not out; fifth 12 and 63.

Bruce Dooland at twenty-three is the youngest, as Bradman is the oldest, of the fifteen who played against us. He is a leg-break bowler and stubborn late batsman, able to hold up an end well. Our men did not find him as devastating as Colin McCool, but they had an even greater respect for his powers. He is probably the more consistent of the two and seldom bowls a ragged length. He is faster through the air than McCool—though not so quick as Douglas Wright—and as a rule does not toss the ball up like his Queensland colleague. But he makes one "float" now and then.

We saw much of Dooland in matches other than the tests, for he came to West Australia to meet us and played in the Combined team at Perth. There he had the wickets of Washbrook, Compton, Edrich and Yardley for 88 runs. He played twice against us for South Australia and bore the brunt of the bowling each time. A bank clerk in Adelaide.

Test performances: appearances restricted to two. Third 19 and 27—5—69—4; 1 and 21—1—84—1; fourth 29 and 33—1—133—31; did not bat and 17—2—65—0. Averages 16.3 and 43.8.

Fred Freer's bowling in the tests was limited to twenty overs for 74 runs and three wickets; his batting to one incomplete innings of 25. He was always on the fringe of the Australian side, but played in only one of the five matches—the second at Sydney, when Lindwall was away with chicken-pox. He is a tall medium-fast bowler with a nice action and a puzzling swing and our batsmen were not at all displeased when he was crowded out of the side. Washbrook, Ikin and Compton were his victims in his one match. Freer twice played against us for Victoria and once with the Australian Eleven at Melbourne with fair success. He is a reasonable batsman and often a brilliant field. In England he would do well as a stock bowler.

Mervyn Harvey—one of six cricketing brothers—is the sort of opening batsman one likes to see succeed —there is something of the dasher about him. But he did not quite come off in several games against us. His only test appearance was as opener in the fourth match at Adelaide in place of the sick Barnes, then he scored 12 and 31. For Victoria he had 21, 57, 22 and 10. Yet in Sheffield Shield cricket he had a good season. One felt that all he needed against us was one good innings to set him going. Harvey is a fine outfield. One of his brothers, Neal, a left-hand bat, showed quite exceptional promise against us for Victoria, only eighteen though he is. These two Harveys may find each other competing for a place in the side for England.

In cricket you must make your runs at the right time if you are to be chosen for test matches, and it is preferable to make them under the noses of the right people. *Ron Hamence*, the young South Australian batsman, was unlucky in the former requirement. When we passed through Adelaide in October his innings for South Australia against our men were 0 and 7. So he passed out of consideration for the early tests. But when we returned his way in January he produced a 145 which was as good an innings as any against us all the tour. This, and good performances in Sheffield Shield cricket, won him a place in the last test match. He made 30 not out in the first innings when runs mattered a lot to Australia and 1 in the second when they mattered less. The first effort, which came after his side had lost four wickets for 187, was a "sheet anchor" innings when everyone except his first partner Hassett was getting out in a hurry. It pared the England first innings lead to a mere 27 and helped Australia to recover much lost ground. Not bad for a first appearance.

Hamence is a delightfully stylish batsman to watch and has a strong chance of inclusion in next year's party.

Lindsay Hassett is thirty-three—next to Bradman the oldest member of the Australian side. But these light, dapper men often wear better than the big fellows, and there seems no reason why Hassett should not be welcomed back to England next summer. No one could be more welcome, for Hassett plays cricket as a game, and off the field is the most cheerful, friendly fellow imaginable. He is captain of Victoria and if Bradman does not come next year Hassett may well step from the vice-captaincy of the Australian side to the captaincy.

In England in 1938 he was third in the tour averages, with 1,607 runs at 50.21. With the Services side in England in 1945 he showed us batting more spirited than he permitted himself in the recent series, in which too often he played the part of "sticker." He and Bradman together put on 256 for the third wicket in the first test match, but Hassett's 128 on that occasion took the laborious time, for him, of 392 minutes. This, I know, went all against the grain with him.

If there is a better outfield than Hassett now playing cricket I have yet to discover him; his gathering and return of the ball are model actions. Out there he reminds me of Eddie Paynter: he could not do an ungraceful thing if he tried.

In Australian cricket last season Hassett scored 1,203 runs at 70.7. His test performances were: First 128; second 34; third 12 and 9; fourth 78; fifth 24 and 47. Average 53.7.

Ian Johnson, of Victoria, shared with Jack Ikin the distinction of acquiring "spectacles" in a test match. Like Ikin, he has greater claims to distinction than this. He is one of the most useful all-rounders his country possesses—a sound batsman and, rather unfashionable in his own country, an off-break bowler who would be more useful on an English than on an Australian "sticky," where the fast bowlers achieve the slaughter. On any wicket he bowls accurately, as shown by the fact that of 124 overs he bowled against us in tests thirty-five were runless.

When he came to Perth to play against us for the Combined Eleven in the second match of the tour, wise men drew the inference that he was unlikely to be chosen for the tests: otherwise the selectors would not have been keen to show him to our batsmen thus early. In fact he played in four of the five matches and missed the fifth only because of a broken finger. By occupation he is a wine merchant.

Test performances: First 47, did not bowl. Second 70—1. With the ball 30.1—12—42—6 (including a wicket with his first over in a test match) and 29—7—92—2. Third 0 and 0; with the ball 6.5—1—28—1 and 12—4—24—0. Fourth 52; with the ball 22—3—69—0 and 25—8—51—1. Fifth, did not play. Averages 21.2 and 30.6, with ten wickets.

When we first landed in Australia we heard of the name and fame of *Ray Lindwall*, aged twenty-five, a Sydney clerk who had established a reputation as a fast bowler, with the physique and stamina of a first-class Rugby League full-back. We did not see him until the New South Wales match and then, in the damp gloom, he was used so sparingly that he bowled only four overs—for 20 runs and the capture of Washbrook's wicket. But it was obvious even then that Lindwall was really fast and not just fast-medium. What we did not realise then was that he was a century-making batsman as well.

Lindwall is no more than medium height, but of sturdy build, with plenty of muscle in back and shoulders. His run-up is easy but his arm still goes over at about the angle of ten or eleven o'clock. He opened the Australian attack in all but the second test match, during which he was in hospital with chicken-pox. Thrice he did the real job of a fast bowler by breaking our opening partnership in his first spell—his quick victims being Hutton in the third test and Washbrook and Fishlock in the fifth. On the first day of the last test he shipwrecked our whole first innings with seven for 63.

As a batsman in test number three, he scored 100 exactly and by advancing, with Tallon, the score from 341 to 495 for the eighth wicket turned a moderate total into a formidable one. He is a good fieldsman too. From all of which it will be seen that Australia has in him a first-class all-rounder. As a batsman he is a hitter, but he is no slogger; he makes strokes.

Test performances: First 31 and 12—4—23—0 (here we see the chicken-pox bug at work). Second did not play. Third 9 and 100; 20—1—64—2 and 16—2—59—1: Fourth 20, and with the ball 23—4—52—4 and 17.1—4—60—2. Fifth 0, and with the ball 22—2—63—7 and 12—1—46—2. Average eighteen wickets for 367 at 20.4 and with the bat 32 per innings.

Is Lindwall really fast compared with bowlers of past generations? Vain inquiry, for comparisons are nearly impossible. Probably not as fast as Larwood, or as accurate, but quite certainly one of the royal line of fast bowlers. He is young enough to improve and will get many wickets in England next year.

Colin McCool, of whom we had never heard except as a vague rumour before we arrived in Australia, shared with Lindwall the biggest bag of wickets—eighteen—on their side. When I first saw him bowling against us in an Australian Eleven match at Melbourne, where he took the wickets of Hutton, Washbrook, Edrich, Compton, Hammond, Yardley and Voce—seven of them—for 106 runs, I thought of the dismal early progress through the Eastern States of our side of ten years before. Then anyone who would toss the ball high and innocently enough was assured of a good haul. There was a bowler named Frederick, and another named Mudge, who bamboozled our best batsmen in those days. I wondered whether McCool and other leg-spinners were going to take our wickets cheaply all through this tour. Gradually our batsmen, pioneered by Edrich, got his measure in some degree, although he remained dangerous to the end and will be dangerous again in England next summer.

McCool is a slow, slow bowler—nearly as slow as Clarrie Grimmett—relying on flight and spin—and a judicious use of the wrong-'un, but he can push one through faster now and then.

He is one of those accommodating cricketers easily identifiable by any spectator at any time—a smallish, alert, fair man with high shoulders and perkily aggressive manner who when he is not bowling stands very competently in the slips. In our earlier matches against him he had a habit, when batsmen returned the ball to him, of flourishing it in an "I'll run you out" gesture—even when there was no the faintest chance of bringing it off. Cumulatively the habit became rather irritating, creating a false impression of "cockiness" and we were glad when McCool dropped it in later games.

McCool, with Tallon, has been a mainstay of the rather weak Queensland side, though he is from New South Wales and learned his early cricket in one of the Sydney parks. I heard before leaving Australia that his business as a salesman was taking him back to New South Wales, which state will welcome him with open arms.

McCool is almost as dangerous with the bat as the ball, as test innings of 95 and 104 not out show. He is an extraordinary good number six or seven.

Test performances: First 95 and 1—0—5—0 (on the sticky wickets Bradman had no need of him). Second 12 and, with the ball, 23—3—73—3 and 32.4—4—109—5, including the wicket of Hammond in both innings. Third 104 not out and 43; 19—3—53—2 and 24—9—41—1. His century, during which he survived four partners, caused the Australian total to move from a meagre 192 for six to 365. Fourth 2 and, with the ball, 29—1—91—1 and 19—3—41—0. Fifth 3 and 13 not out; 13—0—34—1 and 21.4—5—44—5. Average 54.4 and eighteen wickets for 27.3 each.

There are no personalities in cricket now, say the old-timers. There never were. Yet big *Keith Miller*, who when going sweetly is nearly the best bat in the world to watch to-day, is a creditable imitation of one. He used to enliven some of our wartime Saturday afternoons at Lords when on leave from the R.A.A.F. He enlivened us Englishmen more than we wanted at times in Australia.

Keith, aged twenty-seven, ruddy-complexioned, six feet or thereabouts, is a happy warrior of cricket, wielding a bat that really swings to the ball handsomely in approach and follow-through. Physically he is a man whom no one in his senses would want to inflame, and he gets enormous power into his drive. Of Frank Woolley it used to be said that he did not hit the ball so much as "persuade it to go away." There is no nonsense of this sort about Miller. Compulsion, not persuasion, is his method; yet it is a compulsion graceful to admire.

To watch Miller bat is to see ardent youth thoroughly enjoying itself in expending strength and skill liberally. No half-measures about Keith—full measure, pressed down, shaken together and running over.

To see him bowl is fun also—except sometimes for the batsman. It is said that Miller is not fond of bowling; that he would prefer to devote all his time to batting. If so he conceals his preference well. He is not as great a fast bowler as he is a fast batsman, but he is undeniably quick, and if he is not entirely accurate, his way of letting an occasional ball fly makes him an awkward customer. He used to give Hutton a liberal share of "bouncers," apparently taking the view that if Hutton ducked—as he often did—instead of venturing the hook shot such a policy justified itself. But Miller as a bowler has his bad moments, notably an occasion in Sheffield

Bow-tie that startled Australia. In M.C.C. touring colours of red, yellow, and blue, it had to be worn every Monday morning under pain of fine (often incurred). Smith and Compton show their colours.

Photo: *Telegraph, Sydney.*

Barbecue at Northam, Western Australia. Rupert Howard (centre) and Walter Hammond (right) try
chops straight from the embers.

Shield cricket last season when Morris hit him for twenty-five in one over.

In test cricket against us he took sixteen wickets, only two fewer than Lindwall, the number one fast bowler of the side, and came second to him in the averages with figures little inferior, though nine of his wickets fell on the Brisbane stickies. As he was second also in the batting averages Miller has done as much as anyone to keep the Ashes in Australia.

Off the field he and Hassett—the big and the little man—are as cheerful a pair as any tourist of cricket would wish to meet anywhere. Miller now has a traveller's job in Sydney, which will mean that New South Wales will take him from Victoria next season. A big gap his departure from Melbourne will cause in the side of the champion state; but even Melbourne will prefer him to go to Sydney rather than the Lancashire League—a transfer which at one time seemed possible. He will at least be available to play for Australia again. For the tour in England he must be about the first to be picked after the captain.

Test performances. First 79 and, with the ball, 22—4—60—7 and 11—3—17—2. Second 40 and, with the ball, 9—2—24—0 and 11—3—37—1. Third 33 and 34 and, with the ball, 10—0—34—0 and 11—0—41—2. Fourth 141 not out and, with the ball, 16—0—45—1 and 11—0—34—1. Fifth 23 and 34 not out and, with the ball, 15—.3—2—31—1 and 6—1—11—1.

Averages: Batting 76.8, bowling 20.9.

I have mentioned that as a batsman Miller often moves swiftly. He was specially swift in patches of his Adelaide century. His 141 not out took him 270 minutes, which is quick by test standards, and he and Johnson added 150 in 118 minutes.

Hutton was out eight times during the tests; thrice he fell to Miller, but the last time they were in conflict Hutton, 122 not out in the fifth test, got his measure. Then unhappily Hutton had to retire through illness.

Nowadays in a test match I would rather see the back of *Arthur Morris* than that of any other Australian batsman, not excluding Bradman—or Miller, whose attractive sense of adventure is liable to get him into trouble. Morris, aged twenty-four and a clerk in Sydney, scored 148 and 111 for New South Wales against Queensland six years ago in his first first-class match. Now he has taken his place in the forefront of the world's opening batsmen. He is a left-hander, phenomenally safe in defence, for no one gets over the ball better than he. Yet he can hit as hard as anyone, and when he lets go his hook the deep leg fieldsman is apt to see the ball soar over his head and over the fence. He is a quiet, likeable young man,

C

of medium build and with the physique of a first-class Rugby player.

His first two test matches against us were unpromising, for he contributed insignificant scores towards the great Australian totals at Brisbane and Sydney. But, like Compton, he finished the series triumphantly, going one better than Compton with three centuries in a row. It was remarkable that these two, with a century in each innings of the Adelaide match, emulated at the same time a feat performed only three times previously in England v. Australia cricket—by Bardsley, Sutcliffe and Hammond.

Curiously it was not until the fourth test that an Australian opening pair ran up a three-figure partnership, for in the first three matches Morris and Barnes never came off together. When three figures did come it was Harvey, not Barnes, who was Morris's partner. In the fifth test Morris and Barnes achieved the century together at last.

One piece of useful information is thrown up by the records. In test matches Morris was out seven times—once run out, once bowled by Edrich, and the other five times dismissed by Bedser. He is apt to move rather far across in attempting to turn the ball round the corner.

Morris is a fine slip fieldsman and has the reputation in club cricket of being a good left-hand slow bowler.

Test match performances: First 2. Second 5. Third 21 and 155. Fourth 122 and 124 not out. Fifth; 57 and 17.

By many good judges in Australia the strong opinion is held that *Don Tallon*, the Queensland wicketkeeper, now transferring to South Australia, ought to have been in the side visiting England in 1938. He was left at home, with the result that this outstanding wicketkeeper did not play his first test match until thirty. But he is young enough to visit us next year and there is no one in the field, except perhaps Saggers of New South Wales, liable to displace him as the number one keeper of his country. Australia is rich indeed in this branch of the game; otherwise how could so good a keeper as S. G. Sismey, with the Services side in England in 1945, have passed into cricket obscurity last season?

Tallon is an aggressive wicketkeeper. I have heard our batsmen say that the knowledge that he is behind the stumps to his fellow Queenslander McCool is always in their minds. In our first innings of the second test there were two "caught Tallon b McCool" (the wickets of Hammond and Compton) and two "caught Tallon b Johnson" (Hutton and Yardley).

Tallon equalled a wicketkeeping record in the Australian

season of 1938-9 by securing twelve dismissals in a match against New South Wales at Sydney.

He has the reputation of being a first-class batsman, and certainly his strokes are of the classic type. He used them to best purpose in his 92 against us in the third test.

Test match performances: First 14—caught three. Second 30— caught five, stumped one. Third 35 and 92—caught one. Fourth 3—caught four. Fifth 0—caught three, stumped three.

Australians habitually bisect each others' Christian names. So it comes about that *Ernest Toshack* is "Ern" in newspapers and dressing-rooms. He is by no means least interesting among the new crop of post-war cricketers.

Toshack, like McCool, always picks himself out on any cricket field—a tall, swarthy left-hander of thirty, not one of the sprightliest fieldsmen of the side, though he is no dolt, and certainly not one of the best batsmen. But his bowling won him seventeen of our wickets in the test matches, in which he bowled more overs— 178—and more maidens—fifty—than any other Australian. The figures illustrate his value as a defensive bowler, though he can be an attacking one as well.

He is a seam, not a finger-spin, medium-paced bowler and "cuts" the ball for any turn he achieves. Over the wicket he bowls the ball which goes away from the batsman, and he can make one do the opposite too. Defensively he bowls accurately to a strong leg-side field, and is very difficult to get away on a full-sized test match ground. On our smaller county grounds batsmen will be able to lift the ball with more impunity. Washbrook during the Melbourne test undertook the job more completely than anyone else.

His supreme virtue lies in his command of length, which is apt to make the most patient batsman forget himself and do something fatally foolish. His wickets, costing 25.9 runs each, were obtained more cheaply than any except those of Lindwall and Miller, the shock bowlers, and Freer, who bowled in only one match. But Toshack was helped in this respect by his nine wickets on the Brisbane stickies. Six of these came in the second innings, and it was said that sage advice from Bradman had much to do with the improvement. Certainly on the fourth day of this match he could take no wicket at all while Miller was collecting four; but next day Toshack achieved nine out of the fifteen which fell under very similar conditions.

Not even his closest friends would say that Toshack was a batsman. Indeed, I doubt whether he would lay claim to the distinction himself. In five innings during the tests his top score was 6 and his aggregate 14. But Australia has solid batting right down to number ten, and a weak number eleven can be carried easily enough.

Test performances: First 1 not out: 15.5—11—17—3 and 20.7—2—82—6. Second did not bat, 7—2—6—0 and 6—1—16—0. Third 6 and 2 not out; 26—5—88—1 and 16—5—39—1. Fourth 0 and, with the ball, 30—13—59—1 and 36—6—76—4. Fifth 5 and, with the ball, 16—4—40—0 and 4—1—14—1. Bowling average 25.7.

George Tribe came to England recently in the same ship as myself to take up a professional job in the Lancashire League. Which fact will not necessarily rule him out of the tests next summer—so long as he goes home for the Australian season in the meanwhile. Quite possibly he will be in the Victorian side again next November.

Here is another left-hander, but of a different type and appearance from Toshack. He is a smallish, fair, quick-moving man, who bowls on Fleetwood-Smith principles—the left-hander's finger-spin off-break to a right-hand batsman varied by the googly going the other way.

Some of our batsmen regarded him as the most dangerous of the Australian spin bowlers, even though his test figures do not bear out that opinion. His two wickets, both taken in the same innings at Brisbane, cost him during the three matches for which he was chosen 165 runs each in the ninety-five overs he bowled. But in the Australian first-class averages for the season he was third, with forty-eight wickets at 25.9 each. Too often against our batsmen his length was erratic. Yet the selectors must have seen great possibilities in him and in England he may be destructive.

He is no mean batsman—the sort of number nine or ten liable to irritate tired bowlers by helping to put on 50 runs late in the innings. His 25 not out in the second test, share of a partnership of 41 with Freer, was an example. It raised the Australian score to the monumental 659 for eight at which the innings was closed.

Test performances: First 1 run, 9—2—19—0 and 12—2—48—2. Second 25 not out, 20—3—70—0 and 12—0—40—0. Third and fourth did not play. Fifth 9 runs, 28—2—95—0 and 14—0—58—0.

Tribe, alphabetically is the last of the fifteen. Of those unchosen for tests last season, the most conspicuous is W. A. Brown, the Queensland opening batsman, well known in England already. He hurt a thumb in a club match early in the season and did not play except for a charity match at the end. Before I left Australia he told me that the thumb is now well and he will be returning to cricket next November. If he confirms his before-the-war form he will assuredly open the Australian innings with Morris. A formidable pair they will be. During the 1938 tour in England Brown was second only to Bradman in the batting averages, with 73.14 for eight innings, chief of which was his 206 not out at Lord's, and his 133 at Trent Bridge. As Brown is no more than thirty-four he must be regarded as a probable selection—and indeed as a possible captain.

A second wicketkeeper must be sent. The probable choice is R. Saggers of New South Wales. He is in the Tallon class as a wicketkeeper and is a fair batsman.

But I am not going to be inveigled into forecasting the Australian side a year before the event. So quickly does talent develop out there that quite possibly two or three men will arrive of whom we have barely heard. It is bound to be a powerful team, for, unlike ourselves, numbers of young players have already proved themselves.

When the Australians come to England they may find that our rations may beat them even when English batsmen and bowlers cannot. We don't want that sort of false victory. Ways must be found of giving them a diet not too much of a contrast from their own abundance which I have recently been sharing. Even if we cannot beat our opponents we don't want to starve them into surrender. Perhaps they will bring their own basic rations.

CHAPTER IV

OUR SEVENTEEN VANQUISHED

ALEC V. BEDSER, of the twin Woking brotherhood of Bedser and Bedser, comes first alphabetically in the M.C.C. party, which is just as well, because he deserves some special prominence. He and Godfrey Evans were the only men among them not established first-class cricketers before the war. Both showed that up to a point youth can overcome lack of the biggest experience.

Alec had another handicap to overcome. Australian wickets, slower now than in the days of Maurice Tate, no longer encourage the fast-medium type of bowling; the old nip off the pitch is deadened. That Alec succeeded well enough in the tests to take sixteen wickets, as well as often doing the job of a stock bowler, is proof of his doggedness and skill. On the greener wickets of England, and in our heavier atmosphere, his swingers will not cost his side 54.7 runs each as in Australia.

Bedser, despite that high toll of runs against him—the result largely of insufficient support—had his high moments. For example, he broke the Australian first wicket partnership in the first innings of the first test at Brisbane by having Morris caught in the slips with the total only 9; this was the first of the five occasions on which he took the wicket of this dangerous opener. That his analysis at the end of that innings was two for 159 did not cancel the memory of this performance, which was capped by his capture of Hassett's wicket after that batsman had added 276 with Bradman. In the only Australian innings of the second test he took, at long last, the wicket of Barnes, though to be sure by that time Barnes, after scoring 234, was not altogether reluctant to depart. By that time his side had runs and to spare.

The third test—with six wickets—was his best. They included those of both Australian openers in the first innings, and of Morris again in the second. In the fourth he bowled Harvey for 12 and Bradman for a duck with the score only 18. In the fifth he accounted for Barnes and Morris after these two had put on 126 for the first wicket.

If only it had been possible to bowl Bedser in shorter bursts, how different his figures. As it was he bowled twice as many overs in the series as either of the Australian openers, Lindwall and Miller.

Bedser is a first-class tourer—a big, strong, good-tempered

fellow willing to go on bowling until he drops. Wandering about Australia with him, giving moral support, was brother Eric. No, they are not quite as alike as two peas; after long observation I can tell one from the other at close range. When they stand far off on a cricket field it is different. But why should twins always choose to dress alike? When they were due to meet in Melbourne for the first time in Australia they exchanged sartorial details in advance, right down to which of the numerous club ties they sport.

In England we had become used to stories about the Bedsers To Australians they were new, and the newspapers made the most of them. Both were lionised, invited here and there, to sheep stations and fishing expeditions. Brother Eric, like Alec in temperament as well as face and giant build, found Australia a very pleasant place for wintering.

I should have said that Alec at times proved his usefulness as a batsman. In the first innings of the third test his 27 not out and 25 were specially valuable. His partnership of 45 with Yardley on the last evening saved the match.

Test performances: First 0 and 18, with the ball, 41—4—159—2. Second 14 and 3 not out, with the ball, 46—7—153—1. Third 27 not out and 25, with the ball 31—4—99—3 and 34.3—4—176—3. Fourth 2 and 3, with the ball, 30—6—97—3 and 15—1—68—0. Fifth 10 not out and 4, with the ball, 27—7—49—2 and 22—4—75—2.

Test averages: Batting (ninth): innings 10, not out 3, highest score 27 not out. Aggregate 106, average 15.1. Bowling (fourth): 246.3—34—876—16—54.7.

All first-class matches: Batting (fourteenth): 17—3—51—214—15.2. Bowling (eighth): 391.3—54—1,359—29—46.8.

When, last October, *Denis Compton* went to the gay country town of Northam, in Western Australia, and scored 84 in his first innings in that country, everyone regarded it as a prelude to many other big ones against better bowling than Northam's. When in his next our innings, against varied bowling, he scored 98,100, 71 and 143, the happy impression was confirmed that whatever other batsmen might do Denis at least was all right.

So indeed he was, judging alike by figures, by the value of his performances to our side and by the happy impression he created all through Australia. His, and our, only regret must be that his innings in the first three test matches were a moderate 17 and 15 on the Brisbane stickies, 5 and 54 at Sydney and 11 and 14 at Melbourne. We could have done with many more runs from Compton, as from others, on those occasions. We had many more in the fourth and fifth tests—147 and 103 not out at Adelaide, 17 and 56 at Sydney.

He and Hutton are at the head of our test averages. If you regard the Yorkshireman's 122 in the last test as a completed innings—as technically I suppose it is—then Compton leads. But if you credit Hutton with a "not out" then he goes to the top. The working out of averages is an unofficial business not covered by rule, and you can take your choice. Morally, I suppose, Hutton "has it." It was not his fault that tonsilitis laid him low before any Australian bowler could get him out.

Of the two, Compton was on the whole the better to watch, as he ought to be, seeing he went in at number four and not number one. But Hutton had his moments. I don't think anything throughout the tour was more pleasing than that 37 by Hutton in twenty-four minutes in the second innings of the second test—an innings ended when the thumb of his batting glove slipped off and caused him to hit his wicket. Here was a gem innings indeed, full of the most delightful strokes at the expense of fresh fast bowling. There was hardly a spectator who did not lament the untimely end.

I thought that Compton was at his delightful best in his 143 against Victoria, which took him only three hours and ten minutes with three test bowlers, Freer, Tribe and Johnson, in action against him. In the tests his natural genius was too often masked because of failures by earlier batsmen. Undoubtedly his outstanding effort against Australia's full strength was his 103 not out at Adelaide—his second hundred of the match, in which he and Evans scored 85 together—Evans 10 of them—without being defeated. The story of that tremendous effort I shall tell later in describing the game. Enough now that Compton that day proved that he is a sound strategist with a wise head, as well as about the most gifted batsman in England.

Who else, by the way, could run out of his crease to fast bowling, as Compton does in his more impertinent moods, and produce a deft cut from it?

Compton, in addition to his two test centuries at Adelaide, gave us four others—100 at Port Pirie, 143 against Victoria, 124 against the Combined XI at Hobart and 163—part of a partnership of 282 with Hardstaff—against Tasmania at Launceston. There were in addition half a dozen scores of 75 or more.

To know Compton without ever having heard about his cricket you would never suppose he had made a run. There was no player with less "side" than Denis. At twenty-nine he remains utterly unspoilt, entirely friendly, even with the boys and girls who plague him with autograph books. In the outfield he has the Hendren gift of friendship with the crowd. If he had accepted the liquid refreshment offered him over the fence, his path towards the ball would have been a sort of road to Roundabout. As it was he ran hard and straight, and many was the four he turned into a two or three within a foot of the pickets.

Now and then during the tests he bowled an over or two of left-hand slows to relieve our hard-worked regular bowlers. His sixteen overs on these four occasions did not earn a wicket but cost only 78 runs. In other matches he now and then took wickets.

Compton tells me he intends to return to football next autumn— not only because his benefit for the Arsenal is due but because that club has treated him well and he likes football. I would like to suggest to him that he ought to abandon football soon. It would be a shame indeed if injury should deprive us of ten years' cricket from him. He can fill in the winters, if he so desires, with a cricket tour every year. I know that football appeals to him almost as much as cricket, but the risk of carrying on both games into the thirties is too great.

Test performances: First 17 and 15, with the ball, 6—0—20—0. Second 5 and 54, with the ball, 6—0—38—0. Third 11 and 14, did not bowl. Fourth 147 and 103 not out, with the ball, 3—0—12—0. Fifth 17 and 76, with the ball, 1.2—0—8—0.

Test averages: Batting (first): 10—1—147—459—51. Bowling: 16.2—0—78—0.

All first-class matches: Batting (second): 25—3—163—1,432—65.1. Bowling (ninth): 83.2—11—311—6—51.8.

W. J. (*Bill*) *Edrich* at thirty was the outstanding success of the tour as an all-rounder. What we should have done without him in the first three tests, in which he struck form denied to most of his comrades, it is difficult to imagine. In the past this player of in-and-out achievements in the highest class of cricket has sometimes been accused of not having the test match temperament; this time he certainly put the lie to that assumption. He was one of the last men whose choice was announced by the selectors; it is good that they repented.

Study of his performances shows that while his batting remained consistent to the end his bowling lost its fruitfulness in the later Australian innings. His nine wickets were all taken in his first three bowls; in the next five he did not add to the bag, and his analysis lengthened to nine for 483. But it can be said of him that he took his wickets when they were most needed. Six of them came during the long Australian innings of the first two tests.

As a batsman Edrich had probably more to do than any other with the reduction of McCool from a bowler to be dreaded to one still to be respected but no longer unplayable. McCool had Edrich out for 4 the first time they met, in the Australian XI match at

Melbourne. The second time—in the Queensland match—Edrich made 64 not out and 71, though the first of these efforts was during an M.C.C. innings in which the slow bowler took six for 105 Edrich fell to other bowlers in the first test. In the second his 71 and 119 were scored while McCool was again taking wickets freely. True, McCool had his wicket each time, but not before Edrich's nimble footwork and habit of watching the spinning ball right off the pitch had taken their toll. That 119, scored in a total of 371, almost saved us from the ignominy of an innings defeat.

In the third test—when his first innings of 89 was ended by the much-debated l.b.w. decision in Lindwall's favour—Edrich showed again how to play spin bowling, though McCool hit back in the second innings by getting his wicket cheaply. Altogether in the five tests McCool got Edrich out four times, but only after the Middlesex batsman had taken his whack of runs.

In the field Edrich was an unfailing support to his captain, whose place he took at first slip in the fifth test. His pluck was exemplified by his recovery from the knock on the knee he took at Melbourne when fielding silly short-leg to Barnes. That blow would have felled an ox, yet Edrich went on playing until he just had to leave the field for attention. Next morning he was back and took Tallon's wicket with his first ball.

Towards the end of the tour it was stated that Edrich was contemplating a change to amateur status. This has since happened and Edrich must come sooner or later into consideration for the captaincy of Middlesex, and maybe England. His wartime D.F.C. revealed him as a tough fighter, and his undaunted cricket in the recent tour bore out that reputation. An atom bomb of a cricketer, giving the impression when he is batting sweetly that he has 3,000 runs on the tip of his bat.

Test performances: First 16 and 7, with the ball, 25—2—107—3. Second 71 and 119, with the ball, 26—2—79—3. Third 89 and 13, with the ball, 10.3—2—50—3 and 18—1—86—0. Fourth 17 and 46, with the ball, 20—3—88—0 and 7—2—25—0. Fifth 60 and 24, with the ball, 7—0—34—0 and 2—0—14—0.

Test averages: Batting (third in the side): 10—0—119—462—46.2. Bowling (third): 115.3—12—483—9—53.6.

All first-class matches: Batting (fourth): 21—2—119—881—46.4. Bowling (seventh): 215—26—949—22—43.1.

If there is one member of the side able to look back on the tour with personal satisfaction he is *Godfrey Evans*, at twenty-five the "baby" of the party. He used to play for Kent second eleven in 1939, and army service prevented us from seeing much of him during the war. So he was sent to Australia with only one season of first-class cricket behind him. He showed, after being taken into the side from the second test match onwards, that he could bear comparison with Tallon himself.

Evans is a rather small, compactly built, dark, cheerful lad, whose skill is reinforced by his prodigious energy. At the end of the longest and hottest day in the field he seems as fresh as ever. Nor does he always leave the fetching and carrying to others. Occasionally he was seen hareing off to the deep leg boundary; his fleetest comrades had trouble in overhauling him, padded though he was. He flings himself across at anything wide on the leg side with a sort of joyful abandon—no soccer goal-keeper can achieve more agile saves than he. I would commend him to any football manager if I did not feel he ought to be kept for cricket alone.

Before he went out he had a reputation for being patchy in absorbing catches. But when he became a member of the England side he missed very little—certainly no more than his Australian opposite number. I do not remember, at any rate, his dropping an easy chance.

Twice during the series he came into special prominence. There was no bye during the Australian 659 in the second test, none in the first innings of the third, and none until 58 runs had been scored in the second innings of that match—1,082 runs before a bye passed him in test cricket.

The second occasion when he became big news was his stand with Compton during our second innings of the fourth test at Adelaide. One almost hoped then that he would achieve his century in minutes while his score was zero; indeed one's sense of artistic neatness almost induced the hope that he would not break that duck. Actually he began to compile his 10 not out after batting 95 minutes. All this must have gone sorely against the grain for Godfrey, who likes to make strokes. The trouble about his batting is that so often he makes one too many just after he has scored 20 or 30 quite charmingly. We had 80 from him in the minor match at Ballarat, and several nice twenties, thirties and forties. At Ballarat also, he achieved the ambition of every wicketkeeper condemned to watch other people bowling all his days. He took there a wicket for two runs, and, as a matter of pure arithmetic, heads the bowling averages for the tour.

One formed the impression that he will rapidly develop into a wicketkeeper batsman who, like his county comrade Leslie Ames, will be a most valuable aid midway down the England innings.

In matches against the States he distinguished himself once by stumping two Victorian batsmen, Meuleman and Miller, off our fast-medium bowlers Pollard and Bedser.

Test performances: First did not play. Second 5 and 9; caught 1. Third 17 and 0 not out; caught 4. Fourth 0 and 10 not out; caught 2. Fifth 29 and 20; caught 2.

Test average: Batting (tenth): 8—2—29—90—15.0.

All first-class matches (eleventh): 16—5—41 not out—224—20.3.

Laurie Fishlock was in Australia with Allen's side without playing in a test match. The only one he played during the tour now over was the last, in which he scored 14 in the first innings and was out first ball in the second. He has had two unlucky tours, for a broken finger in each put him out of action when the England side was being built. As he has never played for England against Australia at home this one match remains his only appearance of the sort. Injured in Adelaide in late October, he did not play in another match until the Gympie one in early December—too big a handicap for his test prospects. Here is an illustration of the ups and downs of cricket. At home in 1946 he could do nothing wrong in the Surrey side and forced his own selection.

Everyone was sorry for Fishlock, for no keener cricketer was in the party. Throughout the tour he played only twelve innings against first-class sides, chief of which was his 57 in the second match against South Australia. After that game Hardstaff was given a place in the fourth test in preference to him by what must have been a very short head.

Test performances: Batting (fifteenth): First four tests did not play. Fifth 14 and 0. Average 7.

All first-class matches: Batting (tenth): 12—1—57—299—27.1.

Paul Gibb did not have a successful tour, but he did at least realise an ambition denied to him before by ill-luck—that of playing for England against Australia. He was selected twice at home before the war. Once he was hit on the head during the Yorkshire match before the big event; the second time the match—that at Manchester—was abandoned through rain without a ball bowled.

This time his appearances in tests were limited to the first at Brisbane. It was obvious early in the tour that he was wicketkeeper designate, for he was played in seven of the first ten matches. The selectors relied apparently on his greater experience and his usefulness at home as a "sheet anchor" batsman when things were going wrong. But Gibb never thoroughly mastered the Australian wickets and some of his very modest scores were made scratchily and uncertainly. After he lost his place in the test side he was played in only three first-class matches—and this did not help him.

Certainly Gibb himself was not to blame for this inability to find the form he has shown in England and South Africa. No one could possibly have looked after his own fitness more assiduously than he. He played tennis, golf and squash regularly. He is, I believe, a teetotaller and non-smoker, and the only "vice" traceable to him is a prodigious love of ice-cream. I believe he could produce a ranking list showing the merits of all the big rival dealers in the commodity in England and Australia. This small weakness of Paul's was a frequent excuse for leg-pulling. When his comrades after a long day in the field would ask for a beer or two, Paul would go off in pursuit of one, or several, ices. I have found him a very good bridge player, more inclined in this game than in cricket to take a profitable gamble. At deck tennis aboard ship he is almost invulnerable; everything "comes back."

Test performances: Batting (eleventh): First 13 and 11; caught 1.
All first-class matches: Batting (thirteenth): 14—1—37 not out—199—15.3.

Most extraordinary of the tour's mysteries—even, probably to himself—was the inability of the captain, *W. R. Hammond*, to score more than 168 runs in eight test match innings. In 1936-7 he made 468 in nine innings, including 231 not out; in 1932-3 440 in nine; in 1928-9 905 in nine, including one score of 251.

The easy explanation that "Hammond is forty-three" does not cover the ground, for Hammond in first-class matches other than tests was second only to Hutton, with an average of over 77 for six innings.

When we arrived in Australia there was every sign that Hammond would continue the fine form he struck in England last summer. After a preliminary knock of 131—at which he retired—against the weak bowling of the Northam men he produced 208 against West Australia in the opening first-class match of the tour—his thirty-fifth double century. Nine against South Australia was followed by 51 against the strong Victorian attack. Up to that point we were saying that whoever might disappoint us the captain was in fine scoring trim.

His first test match figures—32 and 23—are illusory unless one emphasises how vile were the batting conditions. In the first innings of this match Hammond was top-scorer: in the second only Ikin got more runs than he. There was nothing here to indicate that Hammond would not be scoring centuries in the later tests. He had batted well.

Yet his six remaining test innings—illness prevented the number from being eight—yielded 1, 37, 9, 26, 18 and 22. Possibly the cumulative strain of captaincy—and it is a very real strain—left its effects. But I think the better explanation is that it was "just one of those things." Several times during those small innings the old touch seemed to be coming back, but just as we in the Press box were thinking that "it's all right now," Hammond was out.

This dire experience has befallen him before. Thirteen years ago in England, when Hammond was less than forty-three, his contributions to his country's totals in a test series against Australia were 25, 16, 2, 4, 37, 20, 15 and 43—162 runs in eight innings for an average of 20.25. This in a season when he was scoring hundreds for Gloucestershire. In the tour just over he did rather better than in that dolorous test season at home.

If the series now over were to be repeated I should back Hammond to make thrice the number of runs he did. I do not believe that as a batsman he was a spent force. His batting, up to the time he got out, often bore promise of centuries.

If the criticism is levelled against him that he would have run into form if he had played more, then records show that up to the time he was smitten by fibrositis near the end of the tour he had played in thirteen matches, large and small, out of the twenty-one then completed. A captain, especially over forty, is entitled to spare himself a little, and the only long holiday Hammond took was the one during the Tasmanian tour. It is more difficult to keep fit and in practice at forty-three than at thirty, but on the other hand the veteran player has to guard against burning himself out.

It used to be said that Bill O'Reilly, in the days when he and Hammond were test match antagonists, did more than anyone else to keep Hammond's scores within bounds. That was probably true, although O'Reilly took the Englishman's wicket no more than seven times in twenty-six innings. This time it cannot be said that any bowler in particular tied Hammond up. Toshack bagged him four times in the eight innings, but two of these occasions were at Brisbane on the sticky wicket. McCool had him twice, Dooland and Lindwall once each.

At first slip Hammond gave hardly anything away, although his catching opportunities were limited.

The failure of his team, and his own personal inability to make runs on the grand scale, must have been a deep disappointment to Hammond, although he talked little about it. He was keen on play-ing in the final test match, and Sydney would dearly have liked to see a farewell appearance from him on the ground where in former tours they had learned to dread his batting. Quite possibly that appearance would have been a triumph, for Hammond even at forty-three is too good a batsman to be denied centuries indefinitely. Not until two days before the match was it known that his back trouble had ruled him out. He could only watch from the dressing-room. Here was an anti-climax that Australians deplored as much as Englishmen.

Test performances: First 32 and 23. Second 1 and 37. Third 9 and 26. Fourth 18 and 22. Fifth did not play.

Test averages: Batting (seventh): 8—0—37—168—21.

All first-class matches: Fifth 14—0—208—633—45.2 Bowling: 3—0—8—0.

Ten years ago *J. Hardstaff*, on his first visit to Australia, played in all five test matches, and although not one of our most successful batsmen he scored 256 runs with an average of 28. The Kennington Oval match of 1938 produced 169 not out from him towards our gigantic 903 for seven. This time his test appearances were limited to one—the fourth test at Adelaide—in which he scored 67 and 9. Injury put him out of the running for the fifth test. In others he had long spells in the outfield as twelfth man.

I have already made the point that Hardstaff did not have enough first-class practice to play himself into form. The result was that too often, instead of the fearless forcing batsman we know in England, we saw him uncertain and hazy, especially against spin bowling. Yet when he did get going—as during his 155 against the Tasmanians—there was no better batsman in the side to watch.

His contribution to our first innings at Adelaide was invaluable. He and Compton came together when we had lost Hutton, Washbrook, Edrich and Hammond for 202 and carried the total to 320 in 156 minutes before Hardstaff was bowled by Miller. In the second innings of this match he stayed in for thirty-eight minutes, but never really settled down in face of Toshack.

So good does Hardstaff look when well set that one regretted not seeing much more of him. He did an occasional spell of medium-paced bowling, and by coming off against South Australia with three for 24, actually placed himself at the head of the first-class bowling averages for the tour! It was said that he had "bowled himself into the test," but was denied his opportunity there. Once, in a match against Victoria, he took the wicketkeeper's duties in an emergency and brought off an excellent catch.

Test performances: Played only in fourth match. Batting (fourth): 2—0—67—76—38.

All first-class matches: 13—1—155—471—39.2. Bowling: 13—1—50—3—16.6.

During the war the late Sir Stanley Jackson told me that he feared that *Len Hutton* would never play cricket again, so reluctant was that left arm of his, broken in an army gymnasium, to heal. The highest skill obtainable, plus the determination of the patient to make the arm strong, alone set things to rights.

"When the arm first came out of splints," Hutton told me, "I could not so much as lift a teacup with it. Months of graduated exercises were needed to strengthen it. I found specially useful the wringing out of wet clothes at home."

I doubt whether the arm, marked still by the scars of operations, is 100 per cent whole as the other even now. But, to judge from Hutton's batting against fast bowling, it must be 90 per cent or more.

Australia's climate did not seem to suit Hutton, for he had two or three minor indispositions before tonsilitis put him out of the last test when we had an excellent chance of winning it. Certainly he never seemed as robust as Compton and Edrich.

Yet he headed the batting averages for first-class matches of the tour, scoring 1,267 runs with an average of 66.6. Only Compton, 1,432, went into four figures with him. As I mentioned, in summing up the exploits of Compton, Hutton is first in the test batting averages as well if that 122 of his at Sydney is counted as a not-out. Otherwise he is second to Compton. His tour would have been completely triumphant but for the fact that his batting suffered a relative slump in the first three tests—7, 0, 39, 37, 2 and 40. Thereafter we had from him 94, 76, and his unfinished 122.

Early in the tour the Australians had the idea that Hutton was vulnerable to fast bowling—rather a serious defect in an opening bat. They were encouraged because Miller twice had his wicket in the first test match under abnormal conditions. Miller in particular seemed to believe that Hutton did not like bouncers and gave him plenty of them, but the only time he bagged the Yorkshireman in tests after that was the Sydney occasion when Hutton knocked down his own wicket. Before that happened Hutton had scored 37 in twenty-four minutes against Miller and Freer, including two fours off the one and four off the other—the best, if one of the briefest, innings of the series.

Thereafter Lindwall took Hutton's wicket once and the slower bowlers Johnson, Toshack and McCool the remaining four times. On the whole then Len survived the barrage pretty well. But we certainly ought to have a fast bowler on our side of the argument.

Not until the third test did the opening batsmen of either side give the innings a three-figure start. Then Hutton and Washbrook made 138 together and enabled later batsmen, with a struggle, to bring off a draw. They repeated the feat in both innings of the next test match.

In addition to his fifth test match century—an innings which

Crossing the Nullarbor Plain in style. At the piano in the saloon car of the Transcontinental train : Dick Pollard. Choir (left to right) : Jack Ikin, Rupert Howard, Len Hutton, James Langridge, Peter Smith, Bill Voce.

McCool, deadly among Australian bowlers, attacks Hammond in the
Australian XI match at Melbourne. Yardley is the other batsman.

looked as if, but for illness, it would have been going on still—
Hutton had two others in first-class cricket—151 not out against
Victoria and 136 against South Australia—plus two in minor
matches.

Hutton unquestionably will be our number one batsman when
the Australians come next season. At thirty he is at the very height
of his powers.

Test performances: First 7 and 0. Second 39 and 37. Third
2 and 40. Fourth 94 and 76. Fifth 122 (retired ill).

Test averages: Batting (second): 9—0—122—417—46.3. Bowling: 3—0—28—0.

All first-class matches: Batting (first): 21—2—151 not out—
1,267—66.6. Bowling (twelfth): 21—1—132—2—66.

There is in the cricket of *John Ikin* a flavour of the Yorkshire
versus Lancashire match. Ikin, with the bat or in the field, is above
all things a fighter. Except on one or two occasions he did not play
attractive innings; yet there were times when the Lancashire left-
hander, with all his apparent uncertainty, stayed there while more
showy batsmen were back in the pavilion. One always wanted
so resolute a last-ditcher to turn his useful scores into three-figure
ones, but it never happened.

He shone especially in the first three test matches, when he was
direly needed. In the second innings of the Brisbane match he made
a 32 which was the top score at a time when the ball was popping
all over the place—an innings which came when six wickets had
been lost for 65 and the chance of obtaining a three-figure total was
remote. True, by that time the chance of saving the match had
disappeared—we lost it by an innings and 332—but the effort
restored in some degree our English reputation for ability to bat
on rain-ruined wickets.

All too often in this series Ikin found himself trying to lay
the foundations of the innings rather than build freely on foundations
already laid. That 60—his best total of the series—in the first
innings of the second test was made in the manner of a man getting
Lancashire out of a jam on Whit-Monday. He and Yardley that
day had to face McCool and Johnson after our first five batsmen
had gone for 148. That the total was taken to 255 was due almost
entirely to these two.

Ikin similarly stiffened the later batting in the third test with
48 in the first innings. Only in the fourth was he able to go in with
the feeling that a reasonable number of runs were on the board and
that he could play a natural game. In the fifth he gained the distinction many a better bat has achieved—that of "spectacles,"
an unfortunate anti-climax to earlier performances.

D

He left home with the reputation of being a serviceable change bowler of slow right leg-breaks. In fact during the whole series he sent down only seven overs, costing 48 runs. His best piece of bowling throughout the tour was his four for 172 during the match against the Combined XI at Perth.

In the field Ikin, at gully or anywhere near the bat—and occasionally in the outfield as well—was a tireless trier and let very little pass him by. There never was a more whole-hearted cricketer. But if his place in the England side is to be confirmed there will have to be more big scores from him rather than the merely useful sort. They may come, for he is only twenty-eight.

Ikin is a "desert rat" and throughout the tour Australians of that courageous breed were shaking him by the hand.

Test performances: Batting (eighth): First 0 and 32. Second 60 and 17. Third 48 and 5. Fourth 21 and 1. Fifth 0 and 0. Bowling: 7—0—48—0.

All first-class matches: Batting (ninth): 24—3—71—590—28.1. Bowling (fifth): 107—8—481—13—37.

James Langridge, now in his forty-first year, takes his benefit from the Sussex Club in the August Bank Holiday match against Middlesex this summer. I hope it will be just as bumper an occasion for him as if he had played and succeeded in every test match, for no cricketer deserves it more than he. In Australia he was among the twelve chosen for the third test at Melbourne—the only one of his career against Australia. But in fielding practice a day or two before the event he felt a groin muscle go and that was that.

He might have played in the fourth at Adelaide, for he made a century in the preceding game against South Australia. But again his injury let him down and for the rest of the tour he was an involuntary passenger.

Langridge, like Hardstaff and others, had inadequate opportunity of showing what he could do. Throughout the tour his innings in first-class matches numbered only three, though he actually played in four such games. In addition, he made seven appearances in minor matches. We could have done with his left arm slows in tests when Bedser and Wright were so hard-worked. He could have been played with the knowledge that runs might be expected from him too.

That century of his at Adelaide was a plucky performance indeed, considering that he could never run full out between wickets. He was given the option of playing on that occasion, and, hoping against hope, decided to test himself. He and Hammond—scorer that innings of 188—took our total from 281 for five to 524, and made possible the compiling of the highest M.C.C. total of the tour, 577. But after bowling one over next day, Langridge had to leave the field and the match.

Langridge has won most of the honours of cricket outside tests against Australia. His was cruel luck indeed at forty.

Langridge's first-class averages on tour were: Batting (third): 3—1—100—130—65. Bowling (sixth): 99—15—288—7—41.1.

Richard (Dick) Pollard was the only one of our seventeen players not nominated in a test match twelve. Yet I never heard a "moan" from him, and he was unfailingly a cheerful member of the party. No one was more personally popular than the big Lancashire fast-medium bowler who put the same zest into bowling against Canberra as he would have thrown into a test.

The reason for his non-selection was that only one bowler of his type—unsuited to Australian wickets—could be given a place, and Bedser's form assured him of the preference. Pollard is thirty-four, Bedser twenty-eight, and in quick bowling years make a difference.

Pollard had the distinction of taking Bradman's wicket for 3 runs in our first match against South Australia, an occasion when his two for 23 put him in the running for the first test.

His tail-end position gave him only seven innings in first-class matches and his top score was 12 not out, made in the New South Wales game near the end of the tour.

On long railway journeys and in hotels Pollard cheered us many times by his ability as a pianist. He seemed to be able to play—and play well—any popular air that anyone wanted. One scarcely expected to find musical ability in this big, good-natured, ruddy-complexioned giant of a man, but it is there all right.

Performances in all first-class matches: Batting (sixteenth): 7—3—12 not out—45—11.2.

Bowling (tenth): 233—45—735—13—56.5.

In the minor match against New South Wales Northern districts at Canberra, Pollard took four wickets for 2 runs.

P. T. B. (Peter) Smith played in two test matches—the second and fifth—and might also have been chosen for the fourth if illness had not put him out of the running. His only wickets were those of Miller and McCool on the first of these occasions. They cost 172 runs, but it must be added that nearly all our bowlers had unflattering figures too.

In the last test he bowled, wicketless, for only ten overs in the two innings. In the second of these, when we were trying to prevent Australia from making 214 to win, Yardley, our acting captain, put him on for only two overs compared with 22 bowled by Wright, whom Smith had been chosen to support as a leg-spinner. Those two overs cost only 8 runs. Yardley no doubt was acting in the hope that Wright would be able to repeat his seven-wickets success of the previous day, and apparently feared that Smith would be expensive when runs were more than usually valuable. Anyhow, the result was that a man chosen as a bowler was hardly bowled at all.

The high spot in Smith's tour had come in the match on the Sydney ground immediately preceding this test. Against New South Wales he took nine for 121 in the first innings, including the wickets of Morris and Barnes. His next best was his five (including Bradman) for 93 against South Australia. In minor matches Peter was usually deadly, as in his five for 16 and three for 27 at Port Pirie.

His 24 in the second innings of the fifth test did much to keep the later batting going after Hutton's withdrawal from the game.

Smith, like Langridge, is due for his benefit this summer, and he deserves well of the Essex public.

Test performances: Second 4 and 2 and, with the ball, 37—1—172—2. Fifth 2 and 24 and, with the ball, 8—0—38—0 and 2—0—8—0.

Test averages: Batting (fourteenth): 4—0—24—32—8. Bowling (fifth): 47—1—218—2—109.

All first-class matches: Batting (twelfth): 8—0—46—154—19.2. Bowling (third): 259.6—16—1,073—35—30.6.

Rather than dwell unduly on *Bill Voce's* no wickets for 162 runs in the two test matches in which he played, I want to emphasise the signal service this great left-hander has done to his country's cricket in past tours. In 1932-3, when he and Larwood were the dread of Australian batsmen, he took fifteen wickets at 27 runs each; in 1936-7 he headed the averages with twenty-six at 22 each.

The unhappy change was due to several causes—easier wickets, Voce's injury early in the third test, lack of a season's hard bowling before he went out, and, one must assume, the fact that Voce is now thirty-seven and of a big heavy build which for fast bowling purposes does not carry the years well. He would have had Bradman's wicket in the first test if a certain umpiring decision had gone the other way.

At home last summer we were led to hope that Voce would still be a strong force in cricket against Australia, but it just did not happen. Voce told me that the groin injury which caused his absence from much of the third test was the first in his long career against Australia and other countries to make him leave the field.

In other first-class matches his most fruitful performances were his three for 48 in the first match against Victoria and his four for 125 in the second game against South Australia.

As a batsman Voce enjoyed himself, and pleased the crowd on several occasions, by his hearty hitting. His 21 against Victoria took him ten minutes. In the Brisbane test his 18 showed that attack succeeded as well as any other method on that dreadful wicket.

After the war our young bowlers had not matured last summer; they had had no chance to do so. That the experiment of sending out again an old hand like Bill did not succeed was not his fault.

Test performances: First 1 not out and 18, with the ball, 28—9—92—0. Third 0 and did not bat, with the ball, 10—2—40—0 and 6—1—29—0.

Test averages: Batting (twelfth): 3—1—18—19—9.5. Bowling: 44—12—161—0.

All first-class matches: Batting (fifteenth): 9—1—28—116—14.5. Bowling (eleventh): 174.4—33—660—11—60.

Australian bowlers had the company of *Cyril Washbrook* for just over eight hours in the third test—about half that time in each innings. On the first occasion he and Edrich made 147 together and Washbrook outlasted four partners; on the second he put on 138 with Hutton before the first wicket stand was broken, and scored his only century of the series.

That was Washbrook's best contribution to the English batting, but there were various other good ones. His 41 in the second innings of the second test was one. In the fourth test at Adelaide he and Hutton again achieved the century opening partnership.

In a season of disappointments Washbrook must be credited with a reasonably good tour. Which is not to say that he and Hutton are by any means a Sutcliffe and Hobbs. Washbrook has not the lissom grace of his partner, nor his strength on the off-side, but he is a stubborn, solid batsman with great power in the hook.

I hope that Washbrook will continue to hold his place in England's side indefinitely because of the pleasure he gives me in the field. He is about the best cover-point in cricket to-day, with a throw-in which, jet-propelled though it is, always comes to the wicket-keeper at a handy height. It is quite a relief from monotony when Cyril lets a ball past him.

Washbrook, now thirty-one, belongs to the age-group harder hit by the war perhaps than any other. Without that six-years gap he and Hutton might have been established together by now as a pair of great openers. Hutton had already "arrived" in 1938. Washbrook can console himself with the reflection that Jack Hobbs was nearly thirty-six when World War One was over. Yet after that age came the cream of his cricket career.

Apart from the test matches, Washbrook had centuries against South Australia and Queensland and in the minor match at Canberra. A four-square, determined, Lancastrian, reminding me more than a little of Maurice Leyland in temperament and mental attitude to the game.

Test performances: First 6 and 13. Second 1 and 41. Third 62 and 112. Fourth 65 and 39. Fifth 0 and 24.

Test averages: Batting (fifth): 10—0—112—363—36.3.

All first-class matches: Batting (seventh): 25—0—124—891—35.6.

Washbrook has the distinction of being the only member of the party of seventeen who did not try to bowl. Even the two wicket-keepers had the opportunity once or twice of showing the regular bowlers how to behave. Washbrook, no. But Washbrook and Compton played more innings in first-class cricket than any other English batsman—twenty-five. In innings of all descriptions Compton was ahead of the field with thirty-two to Washbrook's thirty.

But in matches played Ikin leads the field—twenty-two out of the twenty-five of the tour. Compton is second with twenty-one, Yardley and Washbrook bracketed third with nineteen.

Douglas Wright's twenty-three wickets in the five tests—seven more than Bedser, our next man, took—cost his side 43 runs each. I think that Douglas himself would admit that this is quite expensive, but he was the most unlucky bowler on either side. Time after time he had his man beaten—from Bradman downwards—without anything happening.

Yet, despite these figures, if Wright had been injured or ill the Australian totals, big as they were, would have become astronomical. There were times when he went off his length, but on most occasions batsmen had to treat him with the deference due to a bowler of pedigree. Now and then Wright rose to great heights. In the first Australian innings of the fifth test, when the wicket was assisting spin, he bagged Bradman, Miller, Hassett, McCool, Tallon, Lindwall and Tribe for 105 runs. We hoped he might do the same next day in the second innings and win the match for us, but it was not to be. Wright, having bowled twenty-nine overs in the first innings, could do no more in the second than take two for 93.

As with Bedser, so with Wright, he was over-bowled. In the five matches he produced 240 overs, more than anyone else except Bedser, as compared with 165 from his Australian opposite number, McCool—and Wright, much the faster of the two, takes more out of himself with his longer run than does McCool. I believe that, despite that 43 per wicket, Wright was the best spin bowler on either side. He took the wicket of Bradman only once, but he looked like taking it several times. That one for 169 of his during the long Australian innings at Sydney in the second test was a distorted reflection of his merits.

It has often been said of Wright that for one of his type he bowls so fast that he cannot use enough the subtleties of flight. That may be true, but at nearly thirty-three he is not likely to change his style now; and for what he may lack in "tossing 'em up," he often compensates in his nip off the pitch.

As a number eleven batsman Wright delayed making his first run of the tour—partly through lack of opportunity—right through October and November until the first test match, when he scored 4 and 10 not out. Thereafter he avoided the bottom place in the test averages, and in the second produced a 15 not out.

When not bowling Wright used to spend energetic hours in the deep third man and fine leg positions. I have sometimes heard his captain criticised for placing him in those regions. The explanation was that Wright liked to be there; he felt more at home in the country than in the in-field.

Off the field Wright is a quiet, shrewd, studious man with an engagingly humorous outlook on cricket and things in general. He seems to be slightly surprised, while by no means ungrateful, that 70,000 Australians can spare the time to watch him and others play cricket. He is always good company, even after he has taken nought for plenty. More than any of his companions Wright possesses the artistic temperament, which in his case has nothing to do with bad temper or irritability. I merely mean that he views slow bowling with the eye of an artist, for in a sense slow bowling, like cricket as a whole, is indeed one of the arts.

Test performances: First: Batting: 4 and 10 not out. Bowling: 43.6—4—167—5. Second: 15 not out and 0. Bowling: 46—9—169—1. Third: Batting: 10 and did not bat. Bowling: 26—3—124—2 and 32—3—131—3. Fourth: Batting: 0 and did not bat. Bowling: 32.4—1—152—3 and 9—0—49—0. Fifth: Batting: 7 and 1 not out. Bowling: 29—4—105—7 and 22—1—93—2.

Test averages: Batting (thirteenth): 8—3—15 not out—47—9.4. Bowling (second): 240.2—23—990—23—43.0.

All first-class matches: Batting (seventeenth): 16—5—20—76—6.9. Bowling (fourth): 395.4—40—1,699—51—33.3.

If you had told *Norman Yardley* before this tour that he would become one of England's stand-bys in test match bowling he would probably have replied, in that cheerful tone of his, "Don't be silly." One of his Yorkshire colleagues remarked to me that he only went on for the county "when we're in a jam."

Yet here are his test figures: 114 overs, 15 maidens, 372 runs, 10 wickets, average 37.2, top of the England list.

Nor were these relatively good figures obtained by running through the tail-enders, His wickets were those of Bradman (thrice), Barnes, Miller, Johnson, McCool, Lindwall, Harvey and Dooland. It is true that, each time before Yardley got him, Bradman had done heavy damage to our cause, but there the successes are.

In earlier tours Hammond used to give valuable service as a breaker of stubborn partnerships and a relief to the front line bowlers. Yardley succeeded him. He bowled less than half as many overs as Bedser and Wright, but he bowled them to good purpose, whether taking wickets or merely keeping down the runs while the others rested. Hardly ever were Australian batsmen able to make holiday at Yardley's expense.

At times his success was almost sensational. In the first Australian innings of the third test, for example, he took the wickets of Bradman and Johnson with successive balls. This was his best match as a bowler, for in the second innings he had the wickets of Bradman (for the third time running), Miller and Barnes for 67 runs.

Yardley bowls medium pace, with whip and lift off the pitch and great accuracy. He bowls, too, to his field. Perhaps after this he will be employed more by his county.

Bowling was only a quarter of Yardley's contribution. The other quarters were his batting, fielding and captaincy.

I do not believe in the tradition that captains of England should necessarily be amateurs. The Australians pay their captains, whatever their status may be called, and never seem to lack efficient leadership in the process. There are many professional players who would make better captains than certain of our amateur county skippers. To ignore them merely because they are paid is so much nonsense.

I take it that in sending Yardley to Australia the selectors had in mind the alleged need of having an amateur second in command to Hammond. Possibly, therefore, if Yardley had been a professional, he would not have been selected. Be that as it may, he certainly justified himself on playing grounds alone.

It is notable, by the way, that Yardley did not bowl a ball this tour for the first six matches in which he played. Then, in the Australian XI match at Melbourne, he was brought on for a modest four overs when Morris was well beyond his century and he and Bradman had put on nearly 200 together. In his first over Yardley had Morris caught at the wicket.

Someone that night in the hotel lounge shouted "Well bowled,

Norman!" He grinned. "No trouble at all," he replied cheerfully—which remark was purely by way of a joke. New vistas of usefulness for his vice-captain must have opened up before the eyes of Hammond. Thereafter there was hardly a match in which he did not bowl.

As a batsman his top score in the tests was 61 and in other matches 70. It was not the number of runs he scored as the fact that he scored them at the right time that made him so valuable. On that Flodden Field of a Brisbane wicket his 29 in our first innings came next to Hammond's 32 and but for him we should have been out for well under the 100. His partnership with his captain raised our total from a miserable 56 for five to a meagre 121 for six.

The third test at Melbourne was his best in batting as well as bowling. His 61 in the first innings made our total respectable. His 53 not out in the second was a rearguard action which alone enabled the match to be drawn instead of lost.

As a fieldsman Yardley was always reliable in slip and gully positions, or for that matter anywhere else.

Yardley took over the captaincy of the side in many matches, including the fifth test, in which our cause lost nothing in tactics or inspiration through the change. As a result he has been selected as captain against the South Africans at home this summer, no doubt with the Australian visit of 1948 in view. Yardley is thirty-two, and if he strengthens his batting to the point of scoring hundreds instead of sixties and seventies he must become a strong favourite for the leadership of our next touring side. He is personally very popular among our own cricketers and the Australians and—interesting if relatively unimportant—makes a very good speech. Once he dared to take the platform in one of Australia's major town halls in support of a Food for Britain appeal.

Old cricketers will remember that the late Frank Laver, when thirty-nine, came back to England in 1909 as manager of the Australian side, and headed the test bowling averages for his country in a team which included Cotter, Macartney, Armstrong and Noble. The parallel between him and Yardley hardly exists, but each performance had about it the element of the unexpected.

Yardley's "Y" is the last letter but one of the alphabet—and we had no cricketing "Z's" with us. The rest of this book will be devoted to stories of the matches, with sundry digressions when cricket becomes monotonous, as in a programme of twenty-five games it often does. How wonderful a relief it was, for example, to hop on to an aeroplane at Sydney on Boxing Day and go off to see the Davis Cup lawn tennis in Melbourne.

CHAPTER V

FOOD AND FROLIC

NEVER mind what the fly-everywhere advocates say—there is only one perfect way of sending a cricket side to Australia: the sea route. It takes nearly a month, but is worth it.

For this reason. The month gives time for rest and team-building, and enables the heavy baggage to go with its owners. And how heavy those cricketers - cum - golfers - cum - fishermen - cum - gramophonists can travel!

Players with a long season behind them, and about to begin another, ought not to be rushed from one to the other in a week. A month at sea is a perfect holiday. Seventeen men from nine counties can begin to think as a team. True, many of them had played together in England sides at home, but this temporary alliance is different from a seven months tour.

Strangest among the partnerships in the two-berth cabins aboard the *Stirling Castle*—which left Southampton on 31st August— was that of Len Hutton, the Yorkshireman, and Dick Pollard, the Lancastrian—the lion and the lamb. Which was which? Your guess is as good as mine. I believe the team began to find itself in hot games of deck tennis and quoits, in numerous rapid-action chess duels between Hammond and Hardstaff under the lounge ventilators; in concerts, dances and suchlike. Important to any Englishmen then, they all ate as well as played. By land standards our meals were enormous. Here was the menu for a complimentary dinner at which the liner's captain was our host:

Chilled grapefruit
Cream of Sussex tomatoes
Fillet of sole Gloucester
Kentish creamed sweet corn
Roast Surrey chicken
Braised Yorkshire ham
Essex green peas
Lancashire potatoes, rissoles

SWEETS
Bombe glacé, Hammond
Middlesex pastries

SAVOURY
Notts rarebit (note the spelling!)
Fruit   *Coffee*

Wines: None, the ship was "dry"!

"Gluttons!" say you, with home rations and queues your daily portion. Perhaps so. Yet all this food was of Australian origin; it had not been taken out of the home larder. And this was not a routine dinner, though even the routine ones were abundant compared with those at home. Whatever the ethics of the question, there the food was and we ate it. The etceteras of each meal were even more exciting than the meal itself. There were the sugar basins heaped with sugar; they brought forth butter in a lordly dish; the marmalade was always on parade at breakfast; oranges were available for the peeling.

Young athletes needed just such meals as this. It was said at home that the many sprains that cricketers had suffered during the summer were due to deficient diet. Now everyone put on weight. Most of the players were shy about revealing how much. Bill Voce and Alec Bedser, big men of the party, were weighed on the scales of the ship's butcher; the return for Bedser was 250 lb.—two pounds short of 18 stone; for Voce 230 lb., or 16 stone 6 lb. I fancy there must be something wrong here. They are outsize both, but hardly double outsize. In Australia Alec was 15 stone 10 lb.

Life aboard the *Stirling Castle* was not quite the same luxurious business of previous tours. She was still a Government transport. After carrying troops all the war all over the world she had been turned over to carrying brides and fiancées of Australian service men. Cricketers and cricket writers were merely an extra. Yet in the circumstances we had little to complain about. Our food by home standards was luxurious; our quarters were good enough, better in fact than those of some of the women who had to sleep ten in a dormitory. But one missed the old leisurely calls at Gibraltar, Toulon, Naples, Port Said, Aden and Colombo, at each of which we once had a long run ashore. The aim of the Government was to take all this femininity—about three women and children to every man—to Australia in the quickest time. From Southampton we were only twenty-four days out to Fremantle. Never once could we set foot ashore. Our one port of call was Port Said, and that by night. One unfortunate result was that Ceylon was deprived of its time-honoured one-day fixture at Colombo, where they were even more disappointed than we. From Suez to Fremantle we saw no land for a fortnight; not even a ship. The Red Sea had been at its hottest and stickiest; thereafter we had cooler breezes, quite a lot of equatorial rain and dull days like an English summer.

Those brides and betrothed girls were facing test matches of their own as obscure in their outcome as ours. No doubt most of them have settled down happily enough, even though some had seen all too little of the men they were about to marry, or had married. Later in the tour I chanced to meet one of them who had been acquainted with her prospective husband for only about a week before he went overseas and was made prisoner of war. Now, meeting him again, she had decided against the match and was looking for a job.

We arrived at Perth more than a fortnight before the first important match. Apart from practice it was holiday for the players.

If ever you want to settle in Australia, think hard about Perth before you trouble to go farther east. Twice before I had landed there, or rather at Fremantle twelve miles away, for cricket tours. The first two visits were brief. This time we had nearly a month in the lovely capital of Western Australia, and it broke my heart to leave it.

Perth is roughly the size of Newcastle-on-Tyne, but there the resemblance ends. A distinction all its own is given to Perth by the Swan river, a fine meandering stream, half a mile or more wide in places, which wraps itself about the city in fascinating creeks and bays. Wherever you go you seem to run into water, which makes a paradise for yachtsmen, oarsmen and fishermen. The streets, shops, cathedral and Government buildings are nobly planned. Overlooking the city is King's Park, whence at night can be seen a panorama of twinkling lights over land and water. Directly we arrived we were told by the Mayor in a public reception that "if you don't enjoy yourselves it'll be your own fault." Everyone did enjoy himself. People asked us into their golf, lawn tennis and social clubs and their homes. They motored us incredible distances. They took us to the Royal Show, where farmer-writer George Duckworth cast an expert eye over the bulls and sows. They showed us that strange combination of rugby and soccer known as Australian Rules football. On the cards inviting us to this and that I could almost bid three no trumps.

At once everyone plunged into the business of sending parcels home. Every food store had its organisation for making this easy. One of the stores presented its customers with a pamphlet detailing various standard parcels and their make-up. By way of illustration an Australian chef was seen handing a steaming Christmas pudding across the sea to an English maiden whose right foot obliterated the county of Somerset while her left pinned down the city of Birmingham.

Australians took very seriously this business of helping our sparsely-fed people at home—not only in Perth, but in every city I visited. They wanted to help, and were annoyed at any regulation or any restriction of transport which made help difficult. When, rather later in our tour, the Federal Cabinet revoked the order controlling the making and selling of cream in Australia, the *Sun News-Pictorial* of Melbourne attacked the decision as "a truly monstrous betrayal of our under-nourished British kinsfolk." Without any intention of entering into Australian politics, I quote this criticism as showing how concerned Australians were, and probably still are, at our food difficulties.

Time after time I was asked about the state of the English domestic larder. Sometimes I felt that the questioners had too grim a picture in their own minds; I kept on assuring them that we were not starving at home, although, to be sure, diet was monotonous and housewifery a perplexity.

The Christmas ship from Fremantle must have carried home tons of parcels. The official cricket party had nineteen members; there were then about a dozen English journalists. At the very modest estimate of twenty parcels each—I knew someone who sent sixty—here were more than 600, in addition to thousands sent by the people of Perth themselves. Our only regret was that about a quarter of the cost went in packing and postage.

Australia is a land of plentiful food; yet we had to have our ration books—very much, to the masculine eye, the same unintelligible collections of letters and numbers as in England.

Food rationing in Australia was simple compared with ours, for it covered only four items—butter, sugar, tea and meat. All except tea are grown in abundance in Australia and the only reason for rationing at all was the commendable one that more was left for export to Great Britain. Rations were fairly liberal; only tea, at two ounces a head every week, was on the meagre side. The Australians are incomparably better off than we, not only because their rations are more liberal but because "off-the-ration" foods are more abundant. Fruit, sweets and cakes for instance. Bananas, oranges, apples, pineapples, passion fruit, pears were heaped up in the shops; almost every sort of sub-tropical and temperate zone produce was available without stint in season. We kept constantly replenished plates of bananas in our rooms. Nor did meat appear to be scarce; steak and chops, with a couple of eggs thrown in, were available even at breakfast.

Australians were not so fortunate in clothing, but they were better off than we because boots and shoes and knitted woollen garments like socks and pullovers were off the ration. Cotton materials and suits seemed to be as dear in coupon values, and dearer in money, than at home.

The only commodity which seemed to be scarcer than in London was tobacco. Perhaps it was that I "didn't know my way about" in the shops, but I found "no cigarettes" notices more frequent than in London, and queues formed when word went round that new consignments were available. Drink was easier to buy and cheaper than at home. Scotch whisky cost less 12,000 miles away, and was obtained more readily, than in London. And there were the excellent beers and wines of Australia in abundance.

CHAPTER VI

GOLF, TENNIS—AND CRICKET

AT Perth there were born among the cricket tourists various "clubs" for various purposes but with one common requirement—the wearing of a particular tie on certain days. The team itself devised a startling atrocity in the form of a bow tie of the M.C.C. touring colours, red, gold and blue, which had to be worn at breakfast on the first day of each month. That was first let loose on an undeserving world at the desert railway depot of Cook, where the Trans-Australian train happened to stop on the morning of the due date.

Then the English newspaper and radio men, not to be outdone, formed a "Fourteen Club," so called from the number to which later we were swollen. Victor Lewis, one of our number, searched the haberdasheries of Perth for an appropriate tie. The best he could do was one dotted all over with the death's head and cross-bones. He bought up the entire stock for our use. The fourteenth of the month was the compulsory date of display. Happily this monstrosity was replaced later by a blue tie with a XIV worked into the middle of a map of Australia. The death's head became side-tracked as a "founder's tie," whatever that meant.

More serious in its purpose was, and is, the Empire Cricket Writers' Club, formed at Perth "to play cricket and assist its development generally." As several of our members had played test cricket, and many others were more than useful performers, we were able to turn out a very powerful side, and on the journey east we gathered reinforcements like Clarrie Grimmett, Vic Richardson, Brian Sellers and others. Even in the west the schools, like Guildford Grammar School, Aquinas and others, found this very senior opposition formidable, with Jack Fingleton and Dick Whitington opening the batting, George Duckworth keeping wicket, Bill Bowes and Arthur Mailey bowling. The Club, with Mr. R. G. Menzies, former Prime Minister of Australia, as first President, E. W. Swanton as chairman, Mailey and myself as secretaries, and with a committee of Whitington and Tom Goodman representing Australia and Duckworth and E. M. Wellings, England, set about the business of expansion in both countries, and other parts of the Empire too. The many matches played in Australia will be followed, we hope, by others in England. The schools are perhaps our chief interest, but the Club is not afraid of taking on senior sides when newspaper duties allow.

At Perth the cricketers who also play golf—and most of them do—had many a blood match, with side stakes (a phrase more appropriate to boxing). Len Hutton was the side's best golfer; the captain played too; so did Denis Compton, who must have learned the game while football training with the Arsenal, Laurie Fishlock, Godfrey Evans, Bill Edrich, Joe Hardstaff and Peter Smith.

I was more interested in lawn tennis, in which two cricketers were useful performers—Norman Yardley and Paul Gibb. We had some strenuous afternoons at Perth on Dr. D. R. Gawler's perfect grass court—they play on turf there all the year round. Clarrie Grimmett and Vic Richardson are fond of tennis; Clarrie plays as he bowls—with deep cunning. At Kitchener Park, the tennis school run by Herbert Edwards, once at Queen's Club in London, I saw in action such a crowd of enthusiastic boys and girls learning the game as any London club or coach would be proud to instruct.

From Perth, too, I was taken, at my own request, sixty miles out to the Kingsley Fairbridge Farm School at Pinjarra—the great institution formed by the Oxford Rhodes Scholar of that name to bring boys and girls from the home country out to Australia's vast unsettled lands. I found that the war had tragically interrupted the work. Mr. A. F. Stowe, the secretary, and Mr. C. P. Grant, the acting principal, told me that after Christmas only two of the children brought out before the war would still be of school age; they and a few rather older trainees would alone be left until there were reinforcements from home. Yet essential work such as the maintenance of the farm had to go on. Fairbridge is a lovely place, beautifully equipped, and one can only hope that by now 300 new boy and girl emigrants will have replenished the numbers.

But this book is—or ought to be—mainly about cricket. The trouble in a tour of this sort is that cricket matches keep intruding. They ought to be abolished, or at least rearranged, with the test matches over and done with in the first month and the rest of the tour for some real cricket and real fun.

But since no tour arranged that way would be a financial success—either for cricketers or, more important, for cricket writers—we have to tread gradually the long, long trail that winds into the land of our nightmares. That trail, ending in the fifth test match at Sydney in February-March, began obscurely at Northam, West Australia, whose cricketers, gathered in from a radius of fifty miles or more, took on for two October days the cricketing might of England. That they lost heavily—by an innings and 215 runs—mattered less than the fact that they had their fill of cricket by day and killed the fatted lamb for us by night.

Northam, about sixty miles by road or rail from Perth, looks rather as if it had stepped from a Wild West film, an impression heightened because its main street had been torn up entirely for repairs. The town stands on the wide Avon river, but no one would confuse it with Stratford; its ancient buildings are of wood and iron—fully fifty years old they looked; its modern ones were smart-looking shops, banks and hotels. A curious mixture they are. My hotel was the "Transcontinental," adequate enough indeed but hardly as magnificent as its name.

There is no one better than a "tweaker" for getting out rural sides cheaply. Peter Smith's leg breaks took ten wickets in the match, and Edrich, Voce and Ikin claimed the others. Hammond, after making 131 in our only innings, decided he had had enough of it and retired. Hutton, Washbrook, Compton, Ikin and Edrich all helped themselves liberally by day to runs and by night to the finger-eaten mutton chops which were the main dish at a barbecue at a farm five miles out—an occasion more interesting than the cricket. The whole hilly countryside that night was eddystoned by car lights converging on the farm of one Bob Smith, who did us really proud. So did Major Hammond—unrelated to "Wally"— and bank manager Bott.

I had expected to find an entire ox messily roasting over the bonfire; instead, two or three sheep had been dissected off-stage and their chops were grilled for us handily, which meant more nutriment and less trouble. In case we still felt hungry there was cold turkey as well. Of thirst there was never any danger at all. Nor of boredom either, for in a decorated barn a dance band played "hot" music. Which shows how very modern even the semi-out-back can be. All the invited girls of the countryside came along as dance partners.

This all happened during our one night at Northam. Next morning cricket was due again at noon. But before that time we had looked round an agricultural college sixteen miles away, had gone the rounds of a military hospital and had watched a squad of sheep-shearers at work. One bantam-weight shearer, who looked about five feet two, and eight stone, seized and subdued a big fat ewe, gripped it, belly outwards, between his knees and in two minutes and a few seconds by my watch had stripped the entire fleece away as easily as peeling the skin from a tangerine orange.

He told that the pay was £2 a hundred, that his daily average "crop" was 150 and that he had sheared as many as 270 in eight hours in favourable conditions. He used an apparatus like a giant barber's mechanical hair-cutter; it buzzed in our ears with unhappy memories of moments with the dentist. When I took hold of it, it throbbed uncomfortably in the grasp. Denis Compton tried his hand on a sheep, and found the gadget more difficult to handle than a cricket bat. Afraid of turning the sheep into mutton by skinning it too close, he left as much wool behind as he removed.

E

CHAPTER VII

208 FROM HAMMOND

BACK—rather reluctantly—to cricket. Match number two, though still not labelled first-class, was by no means inferior second. Our opponents in a one-day game at Fremantle, twelve miles from Perth, were described as "colts." Some of them showed every sign of maturity. Scores: M.C.C. 197 for 4; Colts 138 for 6, including a nice innings from W. Langdon, which gave him his place in the State side against us. Gibb, Fishlock and Ikin had useful batting practice and Douglas Wright showed signs of running into form with the ball.

Near the end of our month in Perth came the first two matches that mattered, both unwisely limited to three days, although there was time and to spare for four-day fixtures. In neither did we look an invincible side. West Australians had "political" reasons for doing well against us. In cricket, as in other matters, they feel remotely cut off from the rest of the Commonwealth. Now they wanted admission to the Sheffield Shield competition, Australian counterpart of our County Championship. What better way of showing themselves worthy of it than giving M.C.C. a beating? True, the Australian selectors had not sent one of their number across the Continent to take stock of Westralian strength, but results must count even as far away as Melbourne and Sydney. Since then they have been taken into the competition.

In the first match on the Perth ground the unaided State team batted into the second day in scoring 366 against Voce, Edrich, Smith, Wright and Ikin. Their top scorer, 85, was a Scotsman, David Watt, educated at Edinburgh High School, and one of eight brothers who migrated to West Australia with their parents. He and a bright hitter, M. Herbert, collected 118 in an hour for the fifth wicket. Herbert even had the effrontery to hit the new ball, bowled by Voce, over the long-off boundary for six, part of his score of 53.

That we were able to beat by 111 runs this score—a record for the State against English visitors—was due to Hammond, and in a lesser degree Ikin, Hardstaff, Yardley and Smith. Coming in with our total a meagre 146 for 3, Hammond remained until the end of the innings, when, with Wright his last partner, he took a slam at a ball from the best of the opposition bowlers, Charles Puckett, and was last out for 208.

This was Hammond's thirty-fifth double century in first-class cricket. It took him nearly five and a quarter hours, a strong indication that, forty-three though he was, his stamina remained. Indeed, just after the completion of his 200 he raced a sharp single like a two-and-twenty year old. How unlike Hammond the early part of the innings was may be judged by this fact: his first boundary hit did not come until he had scored 57. But once he had assured himself that the Westralian total would be passed he opened out and the whole innings contained sixteen fours.

Despite some rough treatment from Hammond, Puckett, an inter-state baseball pitcher, took five of our wickets for 126—and great was the local outcry for his recognition by the test match selectors. The Perth evening paper, forgetting for the moment high international politics, devoted its leader to urging his claims. Certainly he looked good; all that could be said against him was that he was thirty-five. Later he had the distinction of selection for an Australian eleven against us at Melbourne.

On our side Wright was the best of the bowlers. He and Smith had four wickets each in the long Westralian innings and Voce two.

For our second match at Perth a week later we had to meet a combined team, with four Australians from the Eastern States as reinforcements for the Westerners. It didn't look at all hopeful for the future when we finished the three days 160 behind on the first innings—a draw with all the honours on the other side. Australia's Board of Control sent over Sid Barnes, hailed in his own country as "Australia's answer to Denis Compton." He was with the Commonwealth side which visited England in 1938, but then was almost a boy and played in only one test match. With him in Perth were little Ken Meuleman, Victorian opening batsman with test possibilities, Ian Johnson, batsman and off-break bowler, another Victorian, and a leg-spinner from South Australia, Bruce Dooland.

There is long term strategy in Imperial cricket. So we heard with no surprise that Wright would not be playing for M.C.C. Similarly the Board had forgotten to send certain of their bowlers from the East. A three-day match was a pretty certain draw anyway, so why worry?

Hammond left himself out of the English side, which was in Yardley's captaincy; but the batting looked enormously strong with Hutton, Washbrook, Edrich and Compton leading an eleven every member of which down to number nine had scored a century in first-class cricket at home.

The Combined Team, winning the toss—we had lost it in the previous match as well—did only moderately well up to 177 for five. Ikin achieved an athletic caught and bowled which put Barnes out for a well-made 45. It was left to a West Australian,

David Watt again, to pull the innings round by scoring the first century against us during the tour. He was twice missed in the slips very early, and this and other blunders in the field cost us dear. He and Johnson (87) took the total from 177 to 394 before Hutton, in the long field, caught Johnson off Langridge. Watt was run out— his wicket thrown down by Compton as he attempted a single. His 157, added to the previous 85, meant an average of 121 against the cream of English bowling by a batsman apparently not even remotely in the running for test matches against us. Which didn't sound good.

Our batting reply had its good and bad features. Washbrook, whose previous performances had been rather scratchy, played again like an England opener for his 80, and Compton was only two short of a splendid century when he was stumped in running out to drive Dooland. But of the others only Yardley and Langridge iustified themselves. In a mesmeric period in the middle of the innings Dooland, with his leg-spinners bowled into a high wind, and Johnson, breaking the opposite way at the other end, tied our batsmen up in the painful way seen during the previous tour. From the time Washbrook was out five batsmen left for a mere 55 on a nice easy wicket. Dooland is a good bowler, but no Clarrie Grimmett, and his four for 88 were flattering figures.

Yardley came to the rescue and found in Langridge a partner able to stay with him. Candidly, I thought at home that Jack Robertson of Middlesex was unlucky to be excluded from a party which included the Yorkshire amateur, but on this occasion Yardley showed not only that he could bat but that he had a cool head and the "guts" required of a captain. He raised the siege which the slow bowlers had imposed on our batting. Dooland had him in the end—a simple catch at short slip—but his 56, and his 63 partnership with Langridge for the eighth wicket, made our score at least respectable. Langridge tried to shield Bedser from the bowling, but in vain, and when Pollard went after surviving only one ball Langridge was left high and dry with 30. We were all out 302 on the verge of time against their 462.

When we left Perth there were misgivings about the bowling more than the batting. In neither match had our fast-medium bowlers been able to break the early partnerships in their first spell—except for one success to Edrich in the brief Westralian second innings at the fag end of the match. That apart, our seam bowlers had taken no wicket higher in the batting list than number six—which, of course, threw a strain on the spin bowlers who took over.

In the first match Voce had two for 75 and none for 5; Edrich none for 78 and one for 14. In the second Bedser (specially unlucky through fielding lapses) took one for 86, Pollard one for 68, Edrich one for 20. The result was that Ikin, not our front rank spin bowler, had to send down thirty-five overs for his four for 172 and Langridge thirty-two overs for his one for 85. With sterner opposition ahead one had qualms.

Not a man among us who did not deplore the need for leaving Perth, that companionable small city of plenty, that Saturday night in late October. Its citizens saw us and our swollen belongings stowed away in the Kalgoorlie train and gave us a tremendous send-off. So many men and women had made our month there memorable that I can hardly mention names, but that of Geoff. Burgoyne, who had made contact with us in the ship on his way back from the Empire Press Conference, stands out. He had done everything for us, from introducing us to the Perth Club to arranging outings and parties on our behalf. There was no limit to his friendliness and that of others.

CHAPTER VIII

WIDE OPEN SPACES INDEED

THREE times have I travelled across Australia in the "Trans" train; this journey, beginning at Perth on Saturday night and ending, for the time being, at Port Pirie, 1,488 miles away, the following Tuesday morning, was neither more nor less comfortable than the other two. Every visitor to Australia ought to undertake it at least once, for the very desolation of the Nullarbor Plain (nulla, no; arbor, tree) is worth seeing.

The Commonwealth Government, I was told, has great schemes in hand for placing all the railways of Australia on the same gauge, but it has not happened yet—which is bad in peacetime and might be disastrous in war. Consequently our journey had again to be done in two trains—the first for the 380 miles to the gold town of Kalgoorlie, the second—the "Trans" train proper—for the remaining 1,108 miles of our journey. I almost slept in the rather shaky first sleeper; I never failed to sleep in the luxurious second car. Here were dining and lounge cars, shower baths, a piano, easy chairs—everything that could be done to beguile us on the way. There were beguilements outside too, as when we watched four emus run a very even race with the train over a mile.

Kalgoorlie, I should imagine, scarcely looks its brightest on Sunday morning. We killed time there by strolling through its wide, half-deserted streets in the warm sunshine. It is no bad-looking town, except that it suffers from the curse of treelessness. Its water has to be brought all those 380 miles from near the coast in pipelines which run alongside the railway. Only by constant watering can even a small patch of lawn be kept green. I had met aboard the *Stirling Castle* a young bride, married to an Australian Air Force officer and travelling with him, whose future home was to be Kalgoorlie. She came from Hereford, greenest and fairest of English cities. Hereford to Kalgoorlie! Well, the advantage is not entirely in favour of England; Kalgoorlie at least is assured of sunshine.

East of Kalgoorlie the vegetation thinned and grew more stunted until, in the Nullarbor Plain proper, only small tough bushes remained on the reddish-yellow soil. A. B. Paterson has idealised the Plain thus:

> ". . . . . And I crossed again
> Over the miles of the saltbush plain—
> The shining plain that is said to be
> The dried-up bed of an inland sea,

Where the air, so dry and so clear and bright,
Refracts the sun with a wondrous light,
And out in the dim horizon makes
The deep blue gleam of the phantom lakes.
For those that love it, and understand,
The saltbush plain is a wonderland."

Well, we who rumbled across the Plain that day did not "love it and understand." But we were interested, very. I was reminded again that in the 1,108 miles between Kalgoorlie junction and Port Pirie there is not one permanent stream of fresh water. Supplies are drawn from wells, bores and dams; often water has to be treated by special plant to make it fit for use in locomotive boilers.

The journey over the actual Nullarbor is about 400 miles; three-quarters of the distance is without a curve—the longest stretch of straight track in the world, the Commonwealth Railway Commissioner states.

Scattered along the distance between Kalgoorlie and Port Pirie are various small places with picturesque names like Karonie, Zanthus, Loongana, Tarcoola and Bookaloo. Most of them are depots where live and work the railway maintenance staff. The workers and their families are supplied with food, clothing and other needs at their own stores; employees at the smaller places are served from the "tea and sugar" train which passes along the line weekly and contains refrigerated vans.

At Cook—918 miles east of Perth, and right in the heart of the desert—I fell into conversation with an Englishwoman, married to an Australian railway worker, who has lived there eight years. Her home used to be at Southfields, near Wimbledon. I assumed rashly that she was longing to be back in dear old London. Not a bit of it. She preferred Cook.

"I think," she said, "that the children would prefer the wide open spaces, where they can make as much noise as they like. No, I don't think I'd like to go back. There's no housing problem here; we have our store; we have our social life. I don't regret coming to Cook or staying in it."

It is good to see the desert ending; first some tough wiry grass instead of the eternal saltbush, then small trees of the eternal "gum" variety with their dark foliage, then larger trees, with an occasional glimpse of a grazing sheep. For some hundreds of miles before Port Pirie is reached there are large sheep stations, supporting a million sheep. But whereas in England we count sheep to the acre, there they count acres to the sheep.

No, there is no "scenery" on the Nullarbor Plain as there is in the C.P.R. trip across the Canadian Rockies. But there is a certain fascination about seeing nothing at all. One could at least feel

assured that we were not "missing something" through not eternally
looking out of the window. We could give our undivided attention
that Sunday night to the sing-song of which the mainspring was
Dick Pollard, Lancastrian fast bowler of ruddy complexion. Dick
could play pretty nearly every song of to-day, and many of yesterday,
from memory, without hesitation.

Port Pirie, where we sleepily disembarked from the "Trans"
train that Tuesday morning, is a small, unlovely industrial town
whose expanding industries include a great lead-smelting plant
and some shipping, for the place stands on an arm of the Spencer
Gulf, about 130 miles from Adelaide. One characteristic is that the
railway to Adelaide runs down the wide main street and passengers
board the trains as they would a tramcar.

The match there, against a country eleven, was a two-day
one, won by an innings and 308 runs. The only reason for matches
against weak country sides like this is the "missionary" one, and
if the populace arrive in sufficient numbers the one-sided nature
of the cricket can be overlooked. The Port Pirians, to judge from
the attendance on the only day I attended the match, did not seem
very enthusiastic.

Hutton (164), Compton (100), Fishlock (98), and Hardstaff
(67 not out) all enjoyed themselves in a day's batting which began
three hours after we had left the train. Compton in his lighter
moments could give an exhibition of trick shots on the same lines
as Joe Davis, the billiards player. Once he swung round to a ball
and, pursuing it with his bat, hit it for four over the wicket-keeper's
head.

In the two Pirie innings Peter Smith and Douglas Wright had
eight wickets each and Jim Langridge four at trifling cost.

By the way, the scoreboard here labelled the match in-
congruously:

"ENGLAND v. PORT PIRIE"

Other grounds, including Melbourne, made the same error.
The only time "England" is in the field is at the test matches;
all other games are "M.C.C.", for the tests are the only fixtures
at which the full strength of the side is necessarily in action.
Similarly in England matches against the counties are played,
not by "Australia" but by "the Australians." There is a real difference in the distinction.

Skipping the second day of the Port Pirie match, I went down
early to Adelaide, and wonderful it was to be there again. The
Adelaide Oval is certainly the most lovely ground of test match
status that I have ever visited, with the side opposite the big stand
covered with grassy banks and open enough to allow a clear view
of the fine neo-Gothic cathedral and the Mount Lofty range of
uplands. Its amenities are second to none, except that, as often

in Australian grounds, the big stand allows only a midwicket view of the game. That, I believe, is due to football, which almost invariably is played on the same turf as cricket—a wonderful tribute to the power of recovery of the Australian grass. A month after football has been played right across the "table" cricket takes its place on a perfect wicket.

The dressing-room accommodation at Adelaide is wonderful and the players have cushioned tip-up seats, with a full view of the game for the batting side. If they tire of watching cricket they can see lawn tennis or bowls at the back. Spectators are well looked after and we newspapermen work under ideal conditions, with Bill Ferguson the scorer and the giant scoreboard to give us our hard facts and a cable and telegraph office at our very elbow. Indeed it is easier for an English journalist to report a test match from Adelaide—or elsewhere in Australia, for that matter—than from any of our home grounds. The constant anxiety at home is the telephone line. A reporter may write like an angel (though I doubt if he would) but all is lost if it doesn't "get through." Evil communications corrupt good manners. Abroad that ever-obliging institution Cable and Wireless carries the burden.

In charge at Adelaide is Mr. "Bill" Jeanes, secretary to the South Australian Cricket Association and to the Board of Control, who managed the last Australian tour in England. Never have I found him anything but helpful. For example he spent lots of time seeking hotel accommodation in Australia for the English newspapermen, who increase in numbers every tour. This time there were fourteen of us; next time, I expect, the writers will outnumber the players, and indeed, why not? Certainly without the newspapers and radio there would be no fine tours on the present scale for cricketers.

CHAPTER IX

RE-ENTER—DON BRADMAN

ADELAIDE is the home of Don Bradman, about whom the eternal query was being asked, "Will he play in the tests?" Not this time because of any difference with the Board of Control about his writing, for he had ceased to write and become a member of the Board and selection committee. Doubts arose because his health had been indifferent and because he has now a stockbroking business in Adelaide on his shoulders. I had been told in the West that Bradman had gone into his shell so completely that he would talk to no newspaperman. Yet I found him cheerful and conversational. The point he made to me was that there was no need for him to declare his intentions weeks ahead of the event, which indeed was reasonable enough. He had said all that could be said at the moment and that was that. I don't often decry my own profession, but at times a member of it here and there can be, let us say, a little trying.

Bradman, like you and me, had aged during the war. Even in his prime as a cricketer he never looked as robust as, let us say, Stan McCabe or Vic Richardson. Now he appeared to have lost some weight. He took some quiet practice in the nets that evening and two days later captained South Australia against us.

Various people, English and Australian, said as they watched him in the field during our long innings that he wasn't the Bradman of old. They shook their heads at the supposed fading of his powers. Batsmen, they said, were stealing runs when he stood at cover—they never would have dared ten years before. Well, no man is as spry in a cricket field at thirty-eight as at twenty-eight, and Australians probably "fade" earlier than Englishmen for reasons of climate. Yet in this match, short of practice, he scored 76 and 3—the former at faster rate than any Englishman except Compton, even though when he came in two wickets were down for 26; he fielded competently if with less vim than of old; and he captained his side with great astuteness. Why then the lamentations? There was in all this no indication that the Don's place ought to be a bath chair; every indication that he would be a powerful adversary in the matches to come. He might not get his double centuries, but single ones are not to be ignored.

This match against South Australia was our first against a Sheffield Shield state, albeit on the previous season's showing the weakest in the competition. There were special reasons why we should do well, if only for the sake of the team's fighting spirit. Hammond won the toss on a wicket so easy that our 506 for five declared might almost have been expected. Hutton and Washbrook batted together all the first day for 237 runs; early in the second, Washbrook was out for 113. The first wicket yielded 240. Hutton (136) did not long survive his partner, but Edrich and Compton, with 71 each, Yardley, with 54 not out, and Ikin, 35 not out, built solidly on strong foundations. Hammond, 9, was the only batsman without double figures, but he would probably never have attempted the stroke which led to his being stumped off Bruce Dooland if he had not been anxious to push along the score.

Of the eight bowlers whom Bradman tried Dooland—three for 142 in forty overs—was the best, but J. L. Mann, a left-hander, did fine service in keeping batsmen quiet.

The South Australians, with two whole days left after Hammond's declaration, were all out, despite Bradman's effort, for 262 early on the last day of the match. They followed on, and when after tea the Australians had seven wickets down for 142 with an hour and forty minutes to go victory looked certain. But R. J. Craig, with a four-hour century, Mann 62 not out, and the fast bowler J. Noblet 25 not out united in passing our score— a plucky effort by them all. At the end South Australia, with two wickets left, were 36 ahead of our first innings total.

Wright and Voce had been kept out of sight of Bradman for that match and Smith, Pollard, Langridge, Compton and Edrich shared the wickets; Bradman fell to Smith in the first innings and Pollard in the second.

Hammond, who had bowled only three overs in the previous home season, now permitted himself to bowl three more. He took a "wizard" catch at short mid-off to Compton's bowling to break a stubborn partnership in the second innings. Our speed bowlers in this match achieved better results than at Perth, but it was again the spinners who took most of the wickets.

In that first visit to Adelaide there was little time for anything but cricket. And Adelaide is a place where everyone wants lots of time for this and that. Our only official functions were receptions at the town hall from the city fathers and the State cricketers and at Government House, where the Governor of South Australia, Sir Willoughby Norrie, was our host. Adelaide believes in a certain dignity in its welcome; no mere glass or two of beer and "They are jolly good fellows" there. Instead the whole side passed up the main aisle to the platform of the town hall to organ music, headed by the mace bearer and the red-robed Lord Mayor and Walter Hammond, with a "crocodile" following after. Then speeches, which had the great merit of brevity. The captain of the side did just what former captains had done: he called on each man to stand up and identify himself. A very presentable, if self-conscious, lot they looked. I had heard it suggested before we left England that Hammond's speech-making would not equal his batting. Certainly his innings on the platform were short, but they had neatness and wit. Many worse speeches are made by politicians paid to make them. Everywhere he went Hammond insisted that Bradman's presence on the cricket field would be good for the game. Now he said it to Don himself on that platform. No one doubted the truth of the compliment, but when two days later the Don's runs were mounting into the seventies we were fearing too much of a good thing. Then Peter Smith took his wicket and all was well—for the time being. So long as Bradman keeps within the century his opponents are very satisfied.

All the while we were at Adelaide newspaper headlines about a train strike in Victoria competed with those about the cricket. As the side were to play Victoria at Melbourne only two days after the end of the Adelaide match an urgent problem in transportation arose. Hitherto M.C.C. had set their faces against air travel. Who should blame them? I know that air risks these days are very tiny, but if our seventeen cricketers were to crash not only would there be seventeen personal tragedies but the tour would end there and then. This time there was nothing else for it but air travel if the side were to keep faith with the welcome arrangements at Melbourne next day. So off they went by air in the early morning, with the expected safe arrival. But since there was a rush on aeroplanes some of us were crowded out, and willy-nilly had to travel the 500 miles by motor coach—from 9 p.m. that night until 11 next day.

I swear that now and then we almost slept. Clarrie Grimmett, on the adjoining seat, seemed to achieve that miracle completely. So did Bill Bowes, Brian Sellers and George Duckworth; at least they were caught napping, which never happened to them on a cricket field. We missed the Lord Mayoral reception at Melbourne; no doorkeeper up to his job would have let us in.

This first Melbourne visit of a fortnight was filled with cricket—first a match against Victoria State and then another against "an Australian Eleven" captained by Bradman, rather similar to the try-out Australian sides are given in England against strong M.C.C. elevens.

CHAPTER X

VICTORY OVER VICTORIA

VICTORIA seemed formidable. Her team had won the Sheffield Shield the previous season without defeat, and the match promised to be as tough as those Australians on tour have to play against Yorkshire. Almost like a test match, in short.

To our tremendous satisfaction M.C.C. won by 244 runs. For the sixth time running, in England and Australia, Hammond beat Hassett in the toss, and this proved a powerful influence on the result. After the first day the wicket behaved in un-Melbournelike fashion by crumbling badly. Remember, this was the first match played upon it for five years, for during the war the Melbourne Cricket Club ground was given over to American troops. Three individual feats contributed to the triumph—a memorable 143 by Compton in the first innings; a splendid 151 not out by Hutton in the second on a turning wicket, and the bowling of Wright in both.

Voce, with three wickets in the Victorian first innings, bowled better than all the tour thus far, but it was Wright, with six for 48 in the first and four for 73 in the second innings, who made the Australians feel that he was destined to trouble them in the tests more than any other bowler. The Kentishman, a bowler with the temperament of the artist he is, needed just that stimulus to give him confidence.

I thought that the Compton innings, 143 in 190 minutes, was about the best I had ever seen from him in stroke variety and attractiveness, an innings quite memorable. Compton himself preferred his 76 not out at Lord's against the Australians in the 1938 series, when he was only twenty.

That match was arranged a day early. The Melbourne Cup race—the Derby of Australia—followed immediately afterwards. Mad as Australians are on big cricket, many of them are madder about racing. We had been warned about this back at Perth, where one day a big race was broadcast in the stand while cricket was on and outfielders in between overs bent an attentive ear to the fast-speaking loudspeaker. Can you imagine his at Lord's?

At Melbourne on Cup Day morning, the morning tea tray at ny hotel bore a race programme "with the compliments of the hotel management and best wishes for an enjoyable and successful day." You see the point: I was in Melbourne, where else would I be going but to Flemington? A Londoner on Derby day might go about his lawful occasions and hardly be aware of the Derby. No one in Melbourne not blind and deaf could be unaware of the Cup. Proportionately the attendance at big sporting events in Melbourne, with a million and a quarter people, is enormously bigger than in London, with seven or eight millions. If we had similar crowds per thousand of population in England no stadiums would hold our football and cricket throngs.

Flemington is much more easy to reach than Epsom. It is only about three miles from the centre of the city. Electric trains every three minutes from Flinders Street—which lays claim to the heaviest suburban traffic of any station in the world—take race-goers right to the entrances to the course. Prices by English standards are cheap. A first-class return railway and grand-stand entrance ticket can be had by a man for 17s. 6d. and by a woman for 10s. Flemington itself is beautiful, with a perfect view of the racing all the way round, and has two parallel courses, one for flat and the other for steeplechase races. Indeed the Melbourne Cup was followed by the Cup Steeplechase. Long rows of totalisators attracted almost the only queues I ever saw in Australia, although, to be sure, here and there one did see a tobacco shop crocodile. I went out to Flemington at the time of peak traffic and out and home had no delay whatever. Within about a quarter of an hour of leaving the course I was back in Melbourne. Racing is no favourite amuse-ment of mine, but if I liked it I would as soon go to Flemington as anywhere.

This time the Cup was won by Russia, a horse of which to this day I know nothing beyond the fact that it did not carry the few shillings which, in order to be in the swim, I ventured at the Tote. I gathered that of the cricketers only Joe Hardstaff was a sound prophet, but what he won on the swings he probably lost on the roundabouts. I believe Len Hutton and several others were up on the whole day's racing. Eighty thousand jolly bank-holiday people saw the race, which was 20,000 fewer than expected. We had that afternoon a perfect example of the changeability of the Melbourne climate. It was sultry hot for the early races; then, as if at the pressing of a switch, the cool breeze blew and the tempera-ture dropped 20 degrees in a minute. Our English climate is taxed with changeability, but never did I know the likes of Melbourne. Our weather by comparison is stability itself.

Three days later we were supposed to be playing the biggest match thus far of the tour—against an Australian eleven—a real prelude to the tests. I say "supposed" because that Friday in November (corresponding to the English May) was one of the wettest in memory. Major Rupert Howard, manager and treasurer to the tour, is secretary of Lancashire at home. Now he knew again that rain can kill cricket in other places besides Manchester, and in other countries besides England. All hope of play that day was abandoned. As there was a spare day the following week it was agreed to extend the match accordingly. Even so the fixture was ruined by rain, for the third day of the rearranged period was washed out as well. Thus far we had not lost a match. We might well have lost this one if it had been completed, for in answer to our first innings total of 314, Bradman and his team scored 327 for five. We rediscovered Bradman, and discovered two other menaces to our cricketing health—Colin McCool, the twenty-seven-year-old Queensland leg-break bowler, and Arthur Morris, twenty-four, the left-hand N.S.W. opening batsman.

To take the bowler first. This wrecker of our first innings with his seven for 106 had come down from Brisbane, though in origin he is a New South Wales man. By the time he had done with us everyone was wondering whether a new Clarrie Grimmett had arrived. This feat of his was divided between two days. On the first Hutton and Washbrook had opened confidently enough against the faster bowlers, Puckett from West Australia and Ellis from Queensland, and had scored 122 for the first wicket. We were expecting a 500-600 total when the damage began. Hutton, who tried time after time to punch McCool's flighted slows through the ring of cover fieldsmen, tried once too often, although he was playing the right attacking game. When 71, he struck a blow at full strength and the tall Freer used his reach and agility by throwing out his left hand to capture a ball speeding past his head. It was one of the best half dozen catches of the tour. Edrich stayed twenty uncomfortable minutes, tried to hook McCool and was leg-before. Washbrook, after completing his 50, was bowled round his legs and McCool had taken three for 16, which expanded to three for 38 while Compton and Hammond held the fort for the rest of the day.

So back to McCool on the Monday, after a Sunday in which he may have entered our thoughts. Before play began Australian colleagues told me that McCool is by no means invincible against his own countrymen; indeed, they said, he can bowl very badly. He certainly did not bowl badly that Monday. He had Compton's wicket straight away—stumped by Saggers as he leaned forward. From the stand it certainly did not look as though he lifted his foot, but I was told afterwards that the toe did come up an inch—and that was enough. Yardley stayed three-quarters of an hour with his captain while they added 26, mainly from the other end. Then he was beaten and bowled playing back. In his first spell that day McCool bowled ten overs for four maidens, 12 runs and two wickets. Bradman, rather mysteriously, raised the siege himself by taking the new ball immediately the 200 came up and putting on the fast bowlers again.

After lunch more McCool, though the first wicket to be taken—
that of Ikin—belonged to Puckett. Hammond, whose long duel
with McCool was the most fascinating feature of the day's play,
completed his 50 with Evans in. Then he attacked the tormentor
heavily. Twice he drove him for four past mid-off, but in running
out for a third such drive was caught by Miller. Of the late batsmen
Smith played McCool as well as anyone and Voce hit him for
three mighty fours before giving the inevitable catch in the deep.
"It was good while it lasted," said he later with the air of a man who
would have liked to hit harder and longer.

Pollard, whose only batting thus far had been two balls at
Perth, scored his first runs of the tour and hit McCool for a four
and a two. But despite this rough treatment McCool's figures
read 38-6-106-7, and the seven included Hutton, Washbrook,
Edrich, Compton, Hammond and Yardley. A new force in test
cricket had obviously come among us, his bowling reinforced by
quite a reputation as a half-way-down batsman and a slipfieldsman.

So to the Australian reply. Bradman, coming in at a score 39
for one, stayed with Morris uneventfully until close of play. As
next day was a washout we had long to wait for the completion of
that partnership, which added 196 to the total—Bradman first
to go for 106 and Morris 115. The two century-makers were not
quite hale, for Bradman during his innings developed a leg strain
and Morris had a strained stomach muscle. These injuries did not
seem to help our bowlers materially, though they may have slowed
the scoring rate down and Bradman was no dasher between wickets.
Again this was a more restrained Bradman than of old, although
until he went lame there seemed every likelihood of full revival.
He started the day with 28 runs against his partner's 39, but he
was first to his fifty, only to be overtaken again in the nineties in
the slow-time race for the century.

Morris was no flier—his hundred took him four and a quarter
hours—but he can make strokes—in particular his hook and drive—
when he likes, and he is dishearteningly solid in defence. Bradman's
century was spread over three and a half hours and as there was no
chance of a result and he was injured he presented his wicket to
Compton, the bowler who had faced him better than anyone
else. Morris was caught at the wicket off Yardley, who had a four-
over spell after Voce, Pollard, Smith and Compton had all tried
in vain. Yardley, who seldom bowls at home, was to prove himself
a useful breaker of stubborn partnerships.

The later Australian batsmen, chiefly Hassett, Pettiford and
McCool, ensured that their total passed ours with the loss of half
their wickets. Keith Miller, whose batting was admired so greatly
in the Australian Services side which toured England in 1945,
again failed to make headway. He had been in America and was

A Hammond-Gibb-McCool incident in the first Test. The captain runs to the wicket while the wicketkeeper retrieves a ball.

The sort of board we need at Lord's—but not the sort of score. Photograph taken during the Bradman

Photo: *Telegraph, Sydney.*

out of practice, so that his three innings against us for his state and the Australia XI match yielded only 32, 8 and 5. It was his century for Victoria against South Australia just afterwards that ensured his place in the first test match.

We finished our first Melbourne programme not entirely satisfied. Truly the side had not yet been defeated, but twice—in the Combined XI match in Perth and the Australia XI match at Melbourne—we had been behind on first innings.

CHAPTER XI

ALL AGAINST THE RULES

AUSTRALIA has "a bullock-wagon constitution in a jet-propelled age." No, I wouldn't dare to say this, but the Lord Mayor of Melbourne did so during a long talk I had with him one morning between cricket matches. I had called because I had heard that the Lord Mayor, Councillor Raymond Connelly, had enlightened views on a subject which has often puzzled me—the hotel and liquor laws of the land. There are as many of them as there are gauges to the country's railways, and I wanted his ideas for reform. His answer was both simple and flattering—adopt English hours of opening; run hotels on the lines of the English public houses. His views have drawn heavy fire upon himself. He does not mind in the least.

In Perth we found that people out for the evening in hotels dined and went home dutifully to bed at nine o'clock. Early-ish, you will agree, but reasonable compared with what we found happening in the big cities of the east. At Adelaide when a friend drove me back to my hotel after the cricket at the blameless hour of 6.15—p.m., of course—I invited her into the lounge for a sherry. "You don't know our rules here," said she. "You'll soon learn that non-residents cannot be served after 6 except during a meal." At that hour all public bars close; the hotel resident must take any drink he wants either at the dining-table or in his room.

Much the same restriction applies to Melbourne and Sydney, both of which have six o'clock closing. It is only when one reaches the thirsty land of Queensland that an oasis is available to the traveller in the evenings; he may sip his beer, if he wishes, until ten at night, if there is beer to be sipped. This makes that state, along with Tasmania, the most common-sense in Australia in matters of drink.

In Melbourne, and, if I remember aright, the other cities public houses are entirely closed on Sundays, but with an evening meal a guest may have drinks until eight.

Yet, astonishing to the English visitor, the public houses are opened at nine o'clock every weekday morning, when few have the need, and fewer the inclination, to drink.

"Have you ever noticed," asked the Lord Mayor, "what happen here between five and six at night? Men crowd into the bars and take three or four hurried drinks on an empty stomach after rushing

80

away from unfinished work. As with every such restriction a black market results in the form of sly grog shops. You may see the outcome in the streets at night.

"Which is better—the little local inn in England where dad and mum and their boy and his girl friend can go together on a Sunday evening, or a different procedure, where the boy fills up the car with booze and takes the girl with him to the beach?"

I asked the Lord Mayor why local authorities did not vary the hours. He replied that the State Parliaments alone control licensing hours, and well organised minorities are clamorous against reform. It was then that, mentioning that Australia has thirteen different Houses of Parliament, he talked about the bullock wagon constitution. In Western Australia, a case which he cited, the same hours, under the same control, prevail in the far north, where the temperature may be 120 in the shade, to the extreme south, where a man may need an overcoat.

The Lord Mayor wants Sunday opening not only of public houses but of picture houses, golf courses and tennis courts—after people have been to church.

"Melbourne on Sundays," said he, "is a perfect rehearsal for the grave. You cannot go on indefinitely carrying on a city of one and a quarter million people with this parochial outlook. We are living six days a week in 1946 and the seventh in the fifteenth century."

Hotel life gives one a different impression of a city than home life in it. Yet allowing for this I should say that the average Australian man and woman drinks at least as much as his opposite number in England—despite all the restrictive laws. The restrictionist holds that greater liberty and longer hours would bring more insobriety—which doesn't seem borne out by experience here at home. However, it hardly becomes an English visitor, travelling about part of the country for a few brief months, to enter into Australian politics. He can merely record his own personal bewilderment, which after all would be no greater than that of an Australian I once took out to lunch in a celebrated London snack bar, now unhappily lying among the bomb ruins. Part of this building, when it was a building, used to lie in the City of London and part in the Borough of Holborn, and there was half an hour's difference in the opening hours. So a red cord, rigged up along the City boundary within the house, used to be as a great gulf fixed until the half hour had elapsed, then the handles could be pulled all along the counter. Australia may be slightly mad in some of her drink regulations, but not quite as mad as that. Perhaps here the Lord Mayor would agree with me.

An Alice-in-Wonderland story, this one from London. What

about this cutting from a local newspaper in South Australia, with only names deleted:

> Two cyclists were convicted without a penalty by a magistrate for having drunk liquor within 300 yards of a dance.
>
> A detective gave evidence that about 9 p.m. he saw the cyclists sitting on a doorstep of an hotel. They admitted having drunk from a bottle of beer and told him that they had that day competed in a cycle race.
>
> "We have been to a dinner for the cyclists," one of them told the detective. "We are strangers here, and just sat down to have a drink. We had had only one drink before you came along."
>
> Replying to the magistrate, the detective said that the cyclists had been drinking, but were not drunk. He did not believe that they had attended the dance in the town hall that night.
>
> The magistrate said that defendants had offended the letter rather than the spirit of the legislation, and although there had been a breach of the law it was not of the type aimed at by legislation.
>
> "It is possible for persons to commit a breach of this section without knowing that a dance is in progress. These men apparently were not drinking while going to and from the dance," he added.

It all leaves one slightly bemused.

If I cannot admire the licensing tangle in Australia, I can compare, very much in her favour, her traffic regulations with ours. In Adelaide one day I was absent-mindedly about to cross a road when I heard a voice at my elbow exclaim, "Hey, take a spell!" A policeman was watching me about to move across against the lights. I explained to him that in London a pedestrian is allowed to commit suicide on crossings without let or hindrance. He replied good-naturedly with the Australian equivalent of "You can't do that there here." The jay-walker, if he misses the hospital, finds himself in the police court. The driver is as closely watched as the walker. Used as I am to driving about London, I wouldn't dare take a car about an Australian city without a long course of instruction. The method of turning to the right, for example, is entirely different. When approaching his turn the motorist must pull in to the left instead of the right, and after passing the green light must stop on the crossing and await the green light in the crosswise direction. He must never drive against the red.

Very many right turns in busy streets are forbidden altogether and long detours result; indeed, it seemed to me that this restriction is overdone. But despite all precautions people slay and are slain in the streets there as here. In Perth I saw on the roads frequent white crosses. They marked the spots where fatal accidents had happened and were a rather grim feature of a safety-first drive.

There is one suggestion I should like to make to traffic police in all Australian cities. They ought to make contact with visitors in hotels and elsewhere and let them know what is expected of them. Big-type notices explaining what is liable to happen to the jay-walker would prevent the ignoramus from England from wandering about breaking the law. As it is, we found out by trial and error, and it is not easy because every state seems to have a set of rules of its own.

One of my colleagues while crossing Queen Street—the Oxford Street of Brisbane—was pulled up by a policeman who was not as polite as my friend in Adelaide. He wanted to know adjectively what my friend thought he was doing; the answer back came with equal force and before we knew where we were names and addresses were demanded. With the gates of prison opening in front of him my friend mentioned his—entirely unofficial—connection with the cricket side. Result—an immediate lowering of the temperature and a warning to be more careful in future. What would have happened if he had been there on some less weighty matter—politics or trigonometry for example—I shudder to think.

Such misunderstandings could be avoided if the police would let strangers know that they are no longer in a village like London but have come among real traffic.

The reliance on trams as the chief means of public transport in Australian cities is another perpetual problem for the motorist. Streets are marked out in "safety zones," enclosed in yellow-painted lines, within which people may wait in the middle of the road for their tram. As passing a stationary tram is forbidden and it is frequently impossible to pass a moving one, motoring is a job needing extreme patience. In London we are ridding ourselves of these lumbering, middle-of-the-road vehicles as quickly as possible. In Australian cities, I hear, they are on the increase all the time, and one seldom sees a petrol or trolley bus. They are in a tiny minority.

There is another form of public transport wholly admirable— the ferry boats plying up and down Sydney harbour between one delightful suburb and the other. For a few coppers one can run down to some delightful beach, take the ocean air and return in an hour or so. Why cannot we have lots of water buses dodging about the Thames and taking people to business and pleasure? There are pleasure boats, I know, but the Sydney ones are nearly as frequent as a bus service. There they beat us hollow.

A hint for the L.P.T.B.: number the London bus and tram stops, as they do in Brisbane. The stranger can so easily be directed.

CHAPTER XII

SMART, SOPHISTICATED SYDNEY

AND now on to Sydney, least beautiful of Australian cities in its centre, most beautiful of them all in its suburbs and close-at-hand beaches. Sydney—jostling, sophisticated, femininely smart, Americanised, strident-voiced, hospitable as big cities go but not in the Perth and Adelaide fashion. Sydney, whose main streets compare no better with Melbourne's than London's Strand with the Champs Elysées in Paris. Sydney, sprawled so widely along all the ramifications of "our Harbour" that one wonders how the rest of Australia, with its far-flung few millions, can afford to support it. For this biggest of Australian cities, more populous with its million and a half than any white city in the Empire save London, has within its boundaries about one-fifth or one-sixth of the people of the whole continent.

Think also of Melbourne, with a million and a quarter, and Brisbane, Adelaide, Perth and Newcastle, each with a substantial slice of a million, and you realise how over-urbanised Australia is. To pioneer out in the bush needs not only skill, pluck and endurance, but capital—and all these are of small account in long seasons of drought. To seek city jobs is so much safer; it is also pleasanter for most men and women, whether Australians or migrants from home. There is the problem—the opening up of reserves of wealth. It is one that the mere short-term visitor for cricket is unqualified to discuss; that is a job for an economist or politician.

The man of sporting tastes has everything he can want in Sydney —racing, cricket, football, water sports, boxing and so on. The "movie" lover can choose between scores of cinemas. There is good music, including that of the sacred sort at the cathedral, whose choir is up to the best standards of our home cathedrals. But of one amenity it is as sadly short as the rest of Australia—the legitimate theatre. Theatres there are, of course. On our first visit there we had two widely advertised shows—Tommy Trinder in the flesh at one and *Follow the Girls* at the other. Trinder was and is excellent of his kind; we had all enjoyed him immensely by invitation at Melbourne. I did not follow the girls, though I dare say they would have repaid it. But when I thought of the score or more of West End theatres in London, giving a nightly choice of everything from Shakespeare to Noel Coward, I felt homesick.

I know there are good "straight plays" in Sydney at times,

84

but the choice is sadly restricted in a city with about a fifth the population of London. Remoteness from the stage life of England and America is no doubt a tremendous handicap. I did long to find more theatres where I could see serious plays; perhaps such cultural oases did exist in Sydney while I was there; if so, they did not obtrude themselves on my attention. In London the serious stage holds its own against the pictures; in Sydney I found no signs of dramatic revival.

We reached Sydney in mid-November, the spring of the year in those parts. They showed a commendable example there in giving us one official welcome—in Usher's Hotel, the side's headquarters. Here everyone entitled to make a speech made it, and one response from the team's leaders sufficed. An admirable arrangement, saving words and energy, and enabling the players to concentrate on their practice. The only other official function at this first visit was an evening one—a dinner at the Cricketers' Club, presided over by Mr. Sidney Smith, president of the New South Wales Cricket Association. This Cricketers' Club, of which we journalists became honorary members, has no counterpart in England. I wish it had. It is on one floor of the offices, in the centre of Sydney, of the N.S.W. Cricket Association. This building also has nothing like it in English cricket. Again I wish it had. The administration, with that ever helpful official Harold Heydon as secretary, is carried on in rooms that would do credit to a city council. Above is the Cricketers' Club, whose amenities are open to all cricketers of recognised club or state standing. On the roof is a practice wicket. The aim is to make the club residential, so that members of visiting sides can be accommodated. Until that day comes opponents of the day can mingle in a drink or game of billiards in the evenings; an ideal arrangement which would be a godsend to county sides staying in London if such a centre existed.

Everywhere we went this December we ran into rain. We ran into lots of it during the New South Wales match, drawn after the second and third days had been left entirely blank and the first and fourth half spoilt. Hammond won the toss and to the general surprise put the home side in. There may have been reasons outside the match itself for this decision—a desire, for instance, to give our under-bowled fast bowlers, Bedser and Pollard, plenty of play.

Anyhow, when the first four Australians were out for 84 criticism was disarmed. Bedser, bowling very well indeed, had the wickets of Carmody—whom we know in England—and Saggers; Edrich that of Barnes for only a single; and Wright that of Pettiford, another of our service visitors. At 97 for four in two and a half hours under leaden skies the rain came. Next day was Saturday and much of Sydney wanted to see the play. There was not a hope; indeed play was called off for the day at noon. So a 40,000 gate and about

£3,000 in takings were lost. A reasonable calculation at this stage in the tour was that £5,000 had been lost to English cricket.

As on Saturday so on Monday—the rain never allowed any hope of cricket. A cartoonist in one of the newspapers portrayed a sheep station owner, in some part of Australia where even then sheep were dying of thirst, exclaiming, "We must send for those English cricketers!"

But on the fourth day there was some cricket, though only of the exhibition sort. New South Wales did not lose another wicket. Those two left-handers Morris and Alley took the total to 165, when Barnes declared. This meant that our batsmen would have a chance of taking a look at Ronald Lindwall, hailed in Australia as a really fast bowler as distinct from the common or garden host of fast mediums. He certainly lived up to that reputation. Conditions were bad both for batsmen and bowlers, for the light was bad, the pitch damaged and the run-up slippery. He bowled only four overs for the wicket of Washbrook and 20 runs. Quite obviously he was an awkward customer, for he made the ball lift even though he was not very accurate.

Hutton had scored centuries in Adelaide and Melbourne. One would have been his at Sydney too, if he had not been run out in the last over of the match. At 97 to him, his partner, Paul Gibb, blocked the first ball of the over and the pair of them tried for an impossible run, for each was eager to see that century. Hutton was run out by several feet—and there was still time for Compton to come in and score a single. The chances are that that hundred would have been landed all right but for over-eagerness. We were 156 for two at the close of an entirely uninformative drawn game.

CHAPTER XIII

KOALAS AND CONTROVERSY

Now northwards to Brisbane for two matches—against Queensland State and the first test. True to established procedure the players went by train; mindful of an extremely hot and sticky eighteen hours' journey ten years before, I flew the 500 miles in about two hours. A lovely panorama this flight gives of the magnificent rocky indented New South Wales coast north of Sydney, with its islands, capes, lighthouses and creeks.

A complicated country and a beautiful one. At Brisbane, for the first time in the tour, we struck really hot weather—a humid heat which does not show itself on the thermometer so much as in the feel of the air. Think of the sultriest day with which London is blessed once a summer, with the petrol fumes oozing up between the lines of shops in Oxford Street, and you have Brisbane almost every day from November to March. It is a city of shirt-sleeves, flowering shrubs and mosquito nets which make the nights seem hotter. It has quite a noble river meandering through it puzzlingly, imposing main streets with shops equal to our best in London and, in the suburbs, thousands of verandahed bungalows on stilts. They live exalted lives in Brisbane because this lay-out is supposed to be cooler and the ground-floor level can be used for cars, prams, store and wash rooms and the like. Every house encourages the draught in its design as much as possible. To live in London in a Brisbane bungalow would be to die.

My hotel—the Bellevue—stands opposite the Botanical Gardens, where most of Queensland's wild animals and birds are on show. A remarkable if noisy collection they are—kangaroos, deer, emus, budgerigars, parrots of gorgeous hues. And the most wonderful show of flowering trees, including the best of them all, the red, widespreading poinsiana which beautifies the whole city.

All sorts of interesting expeditions may be made from Brisbane. I had time only for one—the up-river trip by steamer to Lone Pine, the koala bear sanctuary kept by Mr. C. M. A. Reid, who knows all that a human being can know about the marsupial animals of Australia. The koala is surely the most lovable animal in nature. I believe it true that the "teddy" bear of our nurseries was designed in imitation of him, and a very good imitation it is. The larger nursery specimens are about the size of the koala, a huggable creature which seems to like to have human arms around it. Any one of our party could pick one up under supervision and be photographed hugging it. Though the koala still exists wild—it is strictly protected—Mr. Reid breeds his own specimens, of which he had about sixty when I was there. The trouble about the koala is its faddiness about food. Of more than 300 varieties of eucalyptus in Australia the koala will feed only on the leaves of about eighteen. Leaves of these trees are his sole diet.

I do not remember seeing a koala in the London Zoo, though I believe specimens have been there. Mr. Reid told me that they are adaptable to colder climates and that the proper sort of "gum tree" on which they feed has been grown in this country. He hopes to bring koalas to England, and if this happens they will become "the rage." Our public would kill them with kindness if they had the chance.

When hurt the koala cries like a child, but no one but a brute would hurt it. Mr. Reid revealed to me the astonishing fact that this little fluffy, grey, prick-eared, black-nosed animal, weighing several pounds in adult life, is only three-quarters of an inch long at birth. It finds its way by the light of nature into its mother's pouch, where for some weeks it hangs on to a teat which by its pulsations pumps nutriment into it. As digestion is 100 per cent the mother's pouch remains clean right to the time when the baby koala climbs out and faces the world.

Wooloongabba—meaning in the aboriginal tongue "scented wattle"—is the district of Brisbane where the test cricket ground of Queensland is situated. Never did I discern the scent of the wattle, for the ground is in rather a congested part of the city, with none of the pleasant surroundings of Adelaide. In everything except the playing surface, which is excellent when it does not rain, the 'Gabba ground, as it is popularly called, suffers in comparison with Sydney, Melbourne or Adelaide. Thirty thousand there is a big crowd, two-thirds of whom must sit in the sun—and I would not do this in Brisbane to see a cricket match between a reincarnated W. G. Grace's eleven and a world eleven of to-day. The ground had been smartened since my previous visit, but the stands, of wood, corrugated iron and asbestos, are not up to the standards of the southern cities.

Fourteen English and treble that number of Australian newspapermen went the rounds of the tests. I regret that in Brisbane— alone among the first-class grounds—was there soreness against authority. Everywhere else—Sydney, Adelaide, Melbourne— journalists were made honorary members of the clubs, with the run of the pavilion. They were invited with the players to official functions. In Brisbane they were railed off in their own quarters with an oblique view of the wicket, and were left very much to themselves. Some of the writers were distinguished old players who had fought their countries' cricket battles in the past; it made no difference.

This surely is an unnecessary as well as a short-sighted policy, for the fullest and friendliest co-operation between cricket executives and the newspapers is desirable. We left Brisbane cricket ground without regret; we left Sydney, Melbourne and Adelaide with very real regret.

The match between M.C.C. and Queensland which preceded the test was drawn: Queensland 400 and 230 for six declared, M.C.C. 310 and 238 for six. Our batsmen were able to take another look at Colin McCool, who in the Australian Eleven match at Melbourne had taken seven for 106 against us. Here in the Queensland match he had the wickets of Hutton, Washbrook, Hammond, Yardley and Bedser for 105 runs in the first innings, and of Washbrook, Ikin and Compton for 78 in the second. Evidently the more looks we had at him the better.

Queensland began impressively with a 111 partnership for the first wicket between R. Rogers, one of the hardest hitters in Australia, and G. Cook. Rogers, missed at the wicket off Bedser from the first ball of the match, made his 66 in good time, but Cook batted all the first day and more than two hours of the next for his 169 and was still there at the end of the innings. Gibb made up in part for missing that catch by taking four others. Bedser had bowled much better than his figures, two for 83, implied. Yardley, put on with his medium-paced stuff late in the innings, had the best figures with three for 19. Which often happens to third or fourth change bowlers. Our batting included a nice 55 from Compton in the first innings and 124 from Washbrook. He and Edrich (71) raised our score from 10 for one to 172 for two. We had been left with 222 minutes to make 321 to win and at the close were 82 behind with four wickets left. A flutter of excitement was caused by the rapid fall of wickets in the last half hour, and Washbrook was given out, caught by Tallon off McCool, from the last ball of the match.

CHAPTER XIV

THE FIRST BATTLE LOST

Now the first test match, with its freak weather and disastrous result. We lost it by an innings and 332 runs after the storms of Brisbane, including the most frightening hurricane with thunder and lightning I have ever seen, had provided our batsmen with a Brisbane "sticky" on two successive days.

Brisbane had always been a happy city for our teams. A. P. F. Chapman's men had won there in 1928 by 675 runs; D. R. Jardine's in 1933 by six wickets—the match that clinched the famous "body-line" series—and G. O. Allen's in 1936 by 322 runs. In this last match Voce and Allen ran through the Australian side for 58 runs on a wicket similar to those which afflicted us this time. We had never been beaten in a Brisbane test, for these had been the only three played there.

The sides were as follows: England—W. R. Hammond (captain), L. Hutton, C. Washbrook, W. Edrich, D. Compton, J. Ikin, N. W. D. Yardley, P. A. Gibb, W. Voce, A. V. Bedser, D. V. P. Wright. Omitted—G. Evans, J. Hardstaff, J. Langridge, P. Smith, R. Pollard, L. Fishlock (injured).

Australia: D. G. Bradman (captain), S. G. Barnes, A. Morris, A. L. Hassett, K. Miller, C. McCool, I. Johnson, D. Tallon, R. Lindwall, G. Tribe, E. Toshack.

FIRST DAY—BRADMAN AGAIN

I suppose that Bradman deserved to win the toss this time, seeing the last seven tosses between him and Hammond in Australia and in England had gone in Hammond's favour. Win it he did and in winning it won the match for his side. The weather saw to that; so also did Australia's batsmen, to give them their due. The temperature was a humid 85 in the shade and as a result only 17,000, paying £3,370, saw this opening day's play. The grassy banks were only half filled and occupants used every device, from broad hats to handkerchiefs, to protect their heads.

We began really well—Morris, the New South Wales opening batsman who had scored 115 against us at Melbourne, was out for 2 with the total at 9; and Sid Barnes for 31 out of 46. After Voce had bowled a maiden, Morris took a single off Bedser for the first run of the match. Barnes, facing Voce, let loose his favourite hook —later to cause his downfall—for four runs. Morris had shown a desire to nibble at the going-away ball and after a quarter of an hour he gave Hammond a catch at first slip off Bedser. Which brought us unexpectedly early to the problem of Bradman, accustoming his eyes to the sun as he crawled out to the wicket to join Barnes.

It was a very unhappy Bradman we saw at first. He snicked the second ball he received from Bedser; it fell just short of Hammond. Just afterwards he popped a ball up close to Ikin at short leg, but the fieldsman could not reach it. When he had scored 6 he sent one off the edge from Bedser near Yardley in the gully, but again the ball fell in front of the fieldsman. None of these miscues was a chance but this was due more to good luck than good management.

All this was in the first half hour of his innings. Barnes meanwhile had been making some productive strokes, mainly hooks, but he was out soon after Wright had come on for Voce. Barnes put all he knew into a hook and sped the ball over the head of Bedser, standing at short square leg about fifteen yards from the bat. Bedser, with astonishing agility for a sixteen stoner, sprang aloft and stopped, then captured, the ball, it seemed about fifteen feet in the air. So far so very good, but then we ran into trouble. Not another wicket could we get all day, at the close Bradman was 162 not out and Hassett 81 not out, and the total 292 for two.

Before lunch there was an incident that had an enormous bearing on the match. Ikin, standing second slip to Voce, took a ball touched by Bradman, then 28, and stood still, evidently thinking he had made the catch that mattered. Bradman did not move and the umpire disallowed the appeal. I must say that from my distant seat I thought the ball came "off the deck." So apparently did the umpire. But our fieldsmen had no doubt in their minds that the catch was good. Bradman told me afterwards that if he had thought he was out he certainly would not have remained there.

There are, legitimately, two diverse opinions about the incident and no one will ever know which is correct. But everyone knows that if Bradman had been out for 28 the whole history of the match would have been different. Not only would the massive Australian total have been halved, but the Australian batsmen would have had their share of the sticky wickets.

After lunch—77 for two—Bradman was a different batsman. Though Hassett, who loves sporting cricket, held himself back against his inclinations, runs now came with fair freedom. When Bradman faced Voce he took three fours in two overs, including a leg hit and two really sweet Bradmanesque off-drives. By three o'clock Bradman had reached 50 in just under two hours. Hassett hit Bedser one huge on-drive for four which was almost a six. Yardley bowled thus early in the match.

All day long the energetic Compton was haring along the fence in his best Arsenal touch-line manner. He might, if he had cared to accept them—which he didn't—have had enough glasses of beer from the hospitably-minded crowd to make him steer a less direct course. Once he turned an apparently certain four, Bradman off Edrich, into a two by running twenty-five very direct yards, stopping the ball with his foot and taking a purler before bouncing up and returning the ball. Hassett was past his 50 in 132 minutes and soon the partnership had established a test record for this ground. At tea-time Bradman and Hassett had taken the total to 185 for two.

Bedser was away unwell after tea. In a quarter of an hour Bradman had reached his 100—his sixteenth in tests against England, his ninety-sixth in first-class cricket and his third that season. That after-tea period during a long innings is always specially irksome in the heat to a fielding side. Now Bradman, with a drive for four off a tired and unlucky Voce, brought up the 200 partnership after he and Hassett had been together for rather less than that number of minutes. Bradman, who had been quiet and uncertain earlier, now took on youth again in dealing with the bowling, especially with his hooks and off-drives. When he was 138 he gave what that fine cover-point Washbrook strove his hardest to convert into a chance. It was off Yardley that he hit the ball into the air. Washbrook flung himself down for a catch which only just eluded him. He barked his elbows for his pains. Bradman reached his 150 in four and a half hours, during an over from Wright in which he took two fours and a three. Close of play—or, in the Australian vernacular "stumps"—score 292 for two, Bradman 162, Hassett 81.

SECOND DAY—ALL AGAINST US

At the end of the second day—Saturday—it was obvious that the match could not be won. By that time Australia were 595 for five. "Super-collosical," as the Yankee pugilist said. Bradman gave us only half an hour more of his company—of which in all we had five and a quarter hours for his 187 runs. His partnership with Hassett added 276, an Australian third wicket record.

Edrich was the successful bowler. Coming on at twelve-thirty, this whole-hearted cricketer launched his small but sturdy self into the effort and with his fourth ball of superb length and top speed, and seemingly coming in from the off, he got past a defensive stroke. That morning Bradman had already hit four of his nineteen boundaries, and 25 of the 30 runs added then were from his bat.

Bedser, though still not well, was playing again. Miller, the next man in, treated him rather roughly while Hassett was crawling towards his century. By lunchtime the total was 371 for three. Hassett was still two short of the 100, having scored only 17 all morning. Miller was then 35.

That Saturday afternoon 23,650 people, festooning the ground with shirts and dresses of every summery hue, watched the cricket. By comparison with Sydney or Melbourne it was a tiny crowd, but in the restricted 'Gabba ground it looked a million. There was still a place in the sun for any latecomer who cared to come along, but not one in the shade.

Soon came Hassett's first test century, with a square cut for three against Wright. There is no more likeable cricketer in either country than Lindsay Hassett, and even though the 100 did take him 342 minutes, with no more than seven fours, it was a popular one. I imagine that Hassett's go slow policy was adopted under orders, for he is not that sort of delayed-action scorer as a rule. He likes to score his runs cheerily. But in that horrible institution known as test match cricket long-term decisions are taken; matches are no mere battles, but campaigns. There will be no remedy until wickets are made better for bowlers and a time limit of no more than four days is fixed. Then sides holding an advantage will have to go out for the runs.

Hammond usually absorbs all that comes to him at first slip, but when Hassett's score was 109 he appeared to miss a catch off Wright to which he got his hands without holding the ball. Soon afterwards Bedser, standing where he had caught Barnes so brilliantly, failed to catch Hassett off Compton. Hassett's comment on the escape was six off a no-ball from Wright, not merely clearing the fence, but bounding off the high roof of the members' stand back on to the field.

Miller passed his 50, Hassett was scoring faster and the 400 total and 100 partnership came up. Wright, like Bedser, reached his century in runs against for one wicket. Voce had had no wicket at all, though he had bowled without luck twenty-two overs for no more than 70 runs.

But everyone must be out, or go out, sometime. Hassett's innings of six and a half hours and 128 runs was finished by Bedser. Hassett tried to drive him and gave Yardley a simple catch, chest-high. Miller and McCool put on 37 in three-quarters of an hour before tea. McCool, after scoring only a single, was missed on the off-side at the wicket. Gibb threw himself to the hard catch, but let the ball slip from his grasp.

Miller was out with the last ball before tea and was 21 short of a century in his first test. Wright puzzled him for several balls and had him l.b.w.—465 for five.

In the evening McCool and Johnson, both excellent batsmen though played as bowlers, piled on 50 in forty minutes; one over from Voce yielded 12. McCool's 50, 32 of which had been scored in boundaries, came along. Ikin became the seventh bowler tried that day, but Hammond could find no one to dam this spate of runs. In the hour and three-quarters between tea and the close these two had added 130 and were undefeated. Bedser. at the end of the day was bowling his twentieth eight-ball over.

THIRD DAY—RAIN TAKES A HAND

Play was limited by rain and bad light to an eventful hour and forty-two minutes and was divided into six spasms, in one of which one ball was bowled and in another no ball at all.

First an uninterrupted hour in which the Australian innings was finished by Wright—three wickets—and Edrich—two—for the addition of 50 runs, mainly from the hard-hitting fast bowler Lindwall. Wright, bowling on a wicket that had been damped by overnight rain, had Johnson all at sea for three balls of his first over before having him l.b.w. with a tossed-up delivery, probably a top-spinner. In his next over he had McCool out in the same fashion. McCool, though a Sydneyite, now plays for Queensland and up went a lament because he had missed his century by only five runs. He had batted for two and a half hours. Tallon and Lindwall—two sixes off Wright—put on a quick 30, but then Edrich, taking the wickets of these two and of Tribe, ended the innings—not before time.

The Australians had batted about eleven hours for 645, which until the Sydney test later, was the highest test total ever scored in Australia. Our bowlers had been guilty of twenty-one no-balls, chiefly from Bedser, Voce and Wright. As ten of them had produced runs from the bat here was quite a nice twelfth innings for Australia.

Wright had come out best among our bowlers. That day he had taken three for 32 despite the rough stuff from Lindwall. Bowling 350 balls, he had only 167 runs scored from them and he had the wickets of Barnes, Miller, McCool, Johnson and Lindwall, all of whom had scored centuries in first-class cricket. Edrich—with Bradman his chief prize—and Bedser had shared the other five wickets.

Hutton and Washbrook had an uncomfortable quarter of an hour in a dull light before lunch against the two fast bowlers, Lindwall and Miller. Lindwall, Australia's new discovery in such

Photo: Telegraph, Sydney

No bye was allowed by Evans during the Australian innings of 659 for 8 in the second Test. Evans seen in action, with Barnes (234) batting.

___, who scored 60 in the second Test Match, hits McCool hard to leg.

bowling, is undeniably "quick" by any standards. He is not specially accurate, but can make the length ball lift despite his low-arm delivery. Twice Hutton had to duck him; once he was hit on the thigh; but 8 runs came without reverse.

There was a mutter of thunder as Hutton took strike again after lunch—and was promptly out to Miller. The ball came in very fast and the batsman was late with his stroke. Edrich came in and drove the first ball past mid-on for 2. There was an unaccepted appeal against the light, but after Edrich had driven a no-ball from Lindwall in front of the wicket over mid-on's head for four, rain drove everyone to shelter. This delay lasted only twenty minutes. Then in another twelve our total was raised from 17 to 21. Rain again, for half an hour.

Now came another playing period of only one ball—blocked by Edrich off Lindwall. Bad light, followed by more rain.

In three-quarters of an hour the players appeared again after tea, but it was a mere formality. An immediate appeal against the light was allowed. This was at four-fifteen and there was no more play that day. Our total: 21 for one, Washbrook 5, Edrich 8.

That night nearly two inches of rain descended on the ground and our fate was sealed.

FOURTH DAY—THE HURRICANE

Next day play was possible to time, for the light soil and the morning sun dried the wicket so well that the captains did not refer the question of fitness to the umpires. Yet we all knew that evil lurked in that seemingly innocent turf. Hammond had the wicket cut and applied the heavy roller to squeeze water to the surface.

The very first ball—from Toshack—showed that mischief was afoot. It reared like a cobra striking. Miller bowled with him, at only about half speed. Even thus, so eccentric was the pitch that facing him was a distinctly unpleasant activity. His first ball grazed Washbrook's head and removed his cap, though he was not hurt badly enough to prevent his running rather dazedly the misnamed leg-bye. Four times during the rest of that over was Edrich hit—on the arm, hand, ribs and hip. Another ball soared past his face as he drew back.

At home in England, Miller's bowling that day was described by someone as "bodyline," which it certainly was not, if by "bodyline" is meant what happened during the Jardine-Larwood tour fourteen years earlier. I am not going to discuss the ethics of that bygone bowling again; suffice it to say that there was not the faintest resemblance between the bowling and setting of the field

G

on the two occasions. Moreover at Brisbane in the 1936 test
match the Australians had had to face Allen and Voce in exactly
similar conditions. No, there was not an unfair ball bowled during
this match. But we could have done without the laughter with which
a small minority favoured us as Edrich took his knocks.

Washbrook was out after twenty minutes. Off Miller he put
up a soft catch to Barnes at silly mid-off. Compton ran out to the
first ball he received from Miller and smothered it. The next he
played for a single. Then he had to watch Edrich taking more body
blows. When at last Edrich really hit Miller hard for 3 it was his first
scoring stroke of the morning. Compton hit a 2 in the same over.
He and Edrich added 24, 17 of which were to him, when he was
l.b.w. to a ball which squatted instead of lifting.

Hammond had twenty-three minutes' batting before lunch.
His only scoring stroke during that time was an off-drive for 3
off Miller. Thirty-five runs had been scored during the morning.
In the process Edrich had been hit nine times—eight by Miller,
once by Toshack; Washbrook once by Miller; Compton four times
by Toshack; and Hammond once by Miller. Batsmen stood their
ground against the unpredictable behaviour of the ball and took
the consequences.

The lunch score of 56 for three soon degenerated to 56 for five,
for Miller took wickets with his second and third balls. Edrich
was caught at first slip after a stay of 105 minutes for 16—not very
grand, stated thus baldly, but really an innings without price, more
deserving than most centuries. That day he had made 8 runs in
eighty-three minutes, which shows how hard was the going. Ikin,
who followed him in, was caught first ball by the wicketkeeper,
Tallon, stretching across as the batsman tried to turn the ball to
fine leg. Yardley took his first ball on his pads and there was no
hat-trick.

The wicket, which had dried materially, was still very awkward
but not quite so difficult as before lunch. Hammond and Yardley
survived the fast attack of Lindwall and Miller, and against Toshack
and Tribe developed quite a partnership. Then the rain returned
The players did their best to stay in action, and took a wetting fo
their pains. They had to stop for twenty minutes and when the
returned Yardley hit the first boundary for hours—a hook from
a long hop sent him by Tribe. Even Miller was driven to the bound
ary by the same batsman off two successive balls. Just before te
the 100 came up in 193 minutes, and never was any 100 mor
deserved.

Just after the break the day's play was over. The light wa
atrocious and at the third time of asking the umpires assented to
stoppage. Hammond and Yardley had added 60 in seventy-eigl

minutes—a fine feat in the conditions. Miller had taken all five wickets for 44. Toshack, though bowling twelve overs for nine maidens and 10 runs, had failed. He had wasted the wicket by bowling too much outside the leg stump—too many balls that could be left alone. Miller on the other hand bowled straight and kept his length well up to the batsmen, who had to play at him.

CHAPTER XV

GREATEST STORM EVER

AFTER that the deluge—the greatest I have ever seen on a cricket ground, or for that matter anywhere else. There was first a salvo or two of thunder, with lightning zig-zagging across the gloom. Then a fanfare as hail struck the roof of the stand. Up came the wind—at seventy-nine miles an hour, we were afterwards told. It blew hail and rain in on us horizontally in the press stand, reducing paper to pulp, soaking our typewriters, drenching us. I felt like a fisherman on the deck of a smack in a wild North Sea.

One of the end covers of the wicket was torn up. A stump left lying out there floated down wicket. The middle vanished from view in a waste of water. The big scoreboard was blotted out. The whole ground was awash. So deafening was the row that we could not discuss the size of those millions of hailstones; legend will say that they were the size of the cricket ball itself!

"And," in the language of Genesis, "the waters prevailed, and were increased greatly upon the earth; and the ark went upon the face of the waters." Our stand served indeed such a purpose.

When after an hour the rain became "ordinary" two boys waded out to the wicket and tried to replace the cover.

We learned later that two and a half inches of rain had fallen in half an hour.

FIFTH DAY—ANOTHER "STICKY"

You would not have thought, that Tuesday night of the storm, that Brisbane ground would have been fit for anything but aquatic sports next day. Yet, lo and behold, our innings was on again only a few minutes after the normal noontide. With one sticky wicket we might have coped to the extent of making a draw of the match. A second, specially manufactured for us by the hurricane, was beyond the powers of our side, or indeed any other. Soon after tea we had been beaten by an innings and 332 runs.

Right from the first over again the ball whipped about in a manner peculiar to Australian wickets drying after rain. Before lunch our first innings was completed and Hutton and Edrich had gone in our second.

Twenty minutes from the noontide resumption Hammond was out, with 2 runs added to his own score and 4 to the total. He had resisted two hours and with Yardley had added 67 runs. Miller and Toshack were bowling again and the batsmen's tactics were the same as the previous day—to leave alone very nearly everything that could be left alone; in that act of discretion they time after time had to stop the ball with their bodies. The ball from Toshack which bowled Hammond kept rather low and the batsman did not play at it, thinking apparently that it would not hit the stumps. It hit his pads and he was given out l.b.w. One hundred and twenty-one for six.

Three minutes later, Yardley, whose innings had lasted nearly as long as Hammond's, was caught at the wicket by Tallon off Toshack. One hundred and thirty-four for seven, most of the 13 added having been scored by Gibb. The little Yorkshireman, with his reputation for pawky play, attracted round him eight fieldsmen almost within handshaking range. You could hardly see him for them. He snicked one four through the slips but stoutly off-drove Miller past the besetting sentries for four. His new partner, Voce, played doggo, but the position became hopeless when, after staying seventeen minutes, Gibb was bowled by Miller. Bedser was l.b.w. next ball, making nine for 136.

Thus far Wright, the last man, had not scored a run all the tour. His batting had consisted of o not out, o and o. And here he was with a hat-trick to stop in a test match. He turned the first ball to leg for four, but in the next over from Toshack was caught at the wicket. Total 141, or 504 behind. I do not think the opposition would have reached treble figures on this wicket. Miller that day had had two for 16, or seven for 60 in all. Toshack, three for 7 that day or three for 17 in all, was reported to have had some sage advice from Bradman over-night about sticky wicket bowling. Anyhow, he was a different bowler.

We might have saved the match even then if the first innings had lasted until lunchtime, giving the wicket time to dry further during the break. But we had to bat again for twenty minutes before the interval—for naturally Bradman invited us to follow on. This time, Hutton, like Stan Worthington ten years earlier on the same ground, was out to the first ball of the innings. He played a forward defensive stroke to Miller; the ball popped a little and Barnes, fielding in his favourite close-in position on the leg side, had a good left-handed catch.

Edrich this time had a short innings. A four fell to him and another to Washbrook and then, in Toshack's second over, Edrich was out l.b.w. Thirteen for two. At lunchtime two wickets had gone for 18, Washbrook 8, Compton 2.

Ten minutes after lunch Compton had a slice of luck which, as it proved, was not of much avail. As with Herbert Sutcliffe on a famous Sydney occasion, he played a ball on to the stumps without displacing the bails. The difference was that Sutcliffe afterwards made a century and Compton did not, nor could it be expected of him.

Soon Washbrook shared the fate of Hutton after staying three-quarters of an hour for 13. Now, with the re-entry of Hammond, we were returning to the first innings morning batsmen—a sort of "second house." Compton was far from happy to both bowlers. This sort of dabbing defence, this belated scotching of a skipping ball, is foreign to his temperament. Hammond immediately hunched his great shoulders and hit Toshack for two sixes and one four in the same over, in direction varying between sight screen and mid-off. In thirteen minutes Hammond had scored 18. The wicket was now drying, even as it had the previous afternoon.

Compton's stay of sixty-eight minutes for 15 was ended when Barnes, with a combination of somersaulting and juggling worthy of vaudeville, caught him off Toshack in the leg trap. Of the 29 added for this wicket Hammond had 22. Ikin came in and Hammond was bowled immediately by a ball from Toshack at which he groped forward. Yardley was out at once, caught by Hassett while trying to hook Toshack. Gibb, hitting a four, prevented this two-wicket over from being a maiden.

Ikin and Gibb gave us the most prolific partnership of the match, adding 47 in thirty-two minutes, including four fours from Ikin, mainly to leg. The last ball before tea gave Tribe, the slow left-hander, his first wicket—a ball that beat Ikin. Immediately after tea Gibb was l.b.w. to Toshack after a thirty-seven minutes' stay. Voce hit 18 in as many minutes, including a six off a no-ball from Toshack, but was caught in the deep by Hassett. After this the hitting of Bedser and Wright served but as entertainment before an end which was not long delayed.

Toshack that day had taken in the two innings nine wickets, including Hammond's twice, for 89 runs. We were beaten by "circumstances outside our control," although self-pity ought not to blind us to the fact that the Australians had scored 645 runs against us. That takes more explaining away than a mere hard luck story.

On the last day of the match Lindwall was absent. He had got chicken-pox, which had attacked him at a not very inconvenient moment, seeing that the other bowlers hardly needed his help.

Better chicken-pox with the match more than half-won than on an opening day with a fast bowler really wanted.

So was the Brisbane England-must-win tradition broken.

FIRST TEST MATCH SCORES

AUSTRALIA

FIRST INNINGS

S. G. Barnes c Bedser b Wright	31
A. Morris c Hammond b Bedser	2
D. G. Bradman b Edrich	187
A. L. Hassett c Yardley b Bedser	128
K. Miller lbw b Wright	79
C. McCool lbw b Wright	95
I. Johnson lbw b Wright	47
D. Tallon lbw b Edrich	14
R. Lindwall c Voce b Wright	31
G. Tribe c Gibb b Edrich	1
E. Toshack not out	1
Extras	29
Total	645

BOWLING

	O.	M.	R.	W.
Voce	28	9	92	0
Wright	43.6	4	167	5
Bedser	41	4	159	2
Edrich	25	2	107	3
Compton	6	0	20	0
Ikin	2	0	24	0
Yardley	13	1	47	0

Fall of wickets: 9, 46, 324, 428, 465, 596, 599, 629, 643, 645.

ENGLAND

FIRST INNINGS		SECOND INNINGS	
L. Hutton b Miller	7	c Barnes b Miller ..	0
C. Washbrook c Barnes b Miller ..	6	c Barnes b Miller ..	13
W. J. Edrich c McCool b Miller ..	16	lbw b Toshack ..	7
D. Compton lbw b Miller ..	17	c Barnes b Toshack ..	15
W. R. Hammond lbw b Toshack	32	b Toshack	23
J. T. Ikin c Tallon b Miller ..	0	b Tribe	32
N. W. D. Yardley c Tallon b Toshack	29	c Hassett b Toshack ..	0
P. A. Gibb b Miller	13	lbw b Toshack ..	11
W. Voce not out	1	c Hassett b Tribe ..	18
A. V. Bedser lbw b Miller ..	0	c and b Toshack ..	18
D. V. P. Wright c Tallon b Toshack	4	not out	10
Extras	16	Extras	25
Total	141	Total	172

BOWLING					BOWLING			
	O.	M.	R.	W.		O.	M.	R.	W.
Lindwall	12	4	23	0	Miller	11	3	17	2
Miller	22	4	60	7	Toshack	20.7	2	82	6
Toshack	15.5	11	17	3	Tribe	12	2	48	2
Tribe	9	2	19	0					
McCool	1	0	5	0					
Barnes	1	0	1	0					

Fall of wickets: 10, 25, 49, 56, 56, 121, 134, 136, 136, 141.

Fall of wickets: 0, 13, 33, 62, 65, 65, 112, 114, 143, 172.

CHAPTER XVI

BANANALAND

Ever heard of Gympie? To my shame, I had not until I saw it mentioned in the M.C.C. itinerary for 1946-7. We were to go there for a country match immediately after the first test. We came; we saw; we conquered—at least morally. I had forgotten the result, which in any event did not matter, until my notes reminded me that in answer to the Gympieite total of 208 we scored 282 and the local boys in their second innings mustered 311 for nine. It doesn't sound exactly like a moral victory for us, but not even the most ardent Queensland countryman would argue that the proceedings on that last day, with our bowling down to the Hardstaff-Gibb level towards the end, were exactly serious. Our men could have won that match out of hand if time had allowed.

Gympie is about 130 miles nearer the Equator than Brisbane, which means that even as early in the Northern summer as December it is—well, rather warm. Most of my English colleagues decided that a quick return to Sydney from Brisbane, with whatever attractions Sydney held for them, was preferable to a long bus journey farther north. They were mistaken. They knew not their Gympie, where hospitality reached heights never attained elsewhere in that most hospitable of continents, Australia.

The way to Gympie was long, hot and dusty, even though the rewards were adequate after arrival. The players went before, we camp followers followed after, in two buses normally used, I believe, in the more urban surroundings of Brisbane. And here for the first time I heard that slightly disreputable chorus introduced to me, the only Englishman in the bus, by my Australian confederates:

> *I wish I were a fascinating lady,*
> *With a future that is bright and a past that is shady.* . . .

No, perhaps I had better not go on.

As it happened, we followed far after the players, for phut went one of our front tyres on a mountain road of unspeakable surface. It took the united efforts of our driver, a sturdy helper from a passing lorry (the comradeship of the road here) and Percy Taylor of the *Melbourne Argus* to get us going again.

103

Gympie, I was told, had started many years ago as a gold-mining town, but the gold had given out and now agriculture is a very staple industry there. It is a neat, smart, picturesque town with good shops and fine bungalow homes—Australian one-floor houses out-number those in England by ten to one.

Our allotment holders at home will hear with interest that round Gympie beans are a winter crop, alternating with tropical products that flourish all over the district. Nearly 57,000 cases of them have been sent out of Queensland from the Gympie neigh-bourhood in a recent year. There were 13,000 cases of bananas, 20,000 of pineapples, 12,000 of pawpaws (to me the most delectable fruit ever grown) and lots of tomatoes, cucumbers, marrows and other things besides, such as mangoes, passion fruit and custard apples.

Hotel accommodation in Gympie was rather strained, so Clarrie Grimmett and I were seized immediately after arrival and borne off to the home of Mr. and Mrs. Frank Russell for the week-end. It speaks well for our hosts as good mixers when I say that within an hour of arrival we were allowed to help in the "washing-up." Their home—verandahed and overlooking a lovely garden—interested me as a cold-temperate-climate Englishman. Here in England we do all we can to prevent draughts. In Gympie they do all they can to encourage them. In this bungalow all the rooms opened one into the other to achieve a free air current, and there was not a fireplace in the house. I was told that sometimes in winter a little warmth is comforting, but an electric radiator is enough. Meals can be taken on the shady verandah all the year round. Winter does bring its night frosts, but the days are unfailingly warm.

That week-end—Friday to Monday—included a reception, a cocktail party, two dances, a meal every hour or so, a slightly bewild-ering car round of the district and—for me anyhow—a church service. And there was some cricket.

A neighbour of mine in London, writing to me about this time, confessed that she "did not buy at Christmas many pineapples at 35s. to 40s. each." I thought of the folk at home as we were driven up to a pineapple farm where we could pick up and take away the fruit for the asking—like turnips from an English field—and where men with big knives sheared off thick slices and handed them out to us for munching. Why the gap between the £2-a-time fruit in England and the free fruit on this farm, or the trifle of sixpence or a shilling one pays for a pineapple in a Brisbane or Sydney shop? "Transport difficulties" is no doubt one of the answers; certainly it is the stock one. But surely something more could be done, two years after the war, to bring the cheap, delicious Australian pineapple and other fruits to us at a price that is not sheer madness.

Now I am back in England, no longer able to be a glutton in fruit, the memory of what happened near Gympie is all the more acute.

I remember years ago a *Punch* cartoon showing two urchins at a Sunday-school treat. Says one, "Let's go and gavver mushrooms." "Yes," answers the other, "I'm a beggar to climb." Before the visit to Gympie my ignorance about pineapple culture was nearly as dense as that. The cactus-like plant, with sword-shaped leaves, grows only a foot or two off the ground, sending out "suckers" which bear the fruit. Like every other form of fruit, the pineapple is most exquisite when fresh. Sweet juice poured out of the fruit in a cascade as the knife went through it.

That Sunday afternoon we were taken up several hundreds of feet into the sub-tropical forests of this southern part of Queensland. The State Government is planting and re-planting hundreds of acres of hard- and soft-wood timber, including the Southern fir tree. It experiments with trees of promise from all over the world, in particular California. We were taken into a forest, but not encouraged to stay there because of the "ticks" which abound and are not very comfortable companions under one's socks. Burnham Beeches, after all, have their advantages.

That evening, utterly exhausted, we found that our hosts' verandah, with certain cool essential fluids close at hand, need be the furthest limit of our wanderings. Never in my life had I spent a more informative, energetic Sunday.

One must congratulate the local—in a wide sense of the word—cricketers on the good show they made against the pick of our English players. Theoretically a country side, with its very limited opportunities of practice in the best company, ought to stand no chance against a visiting side many of whose members make cricket their livelihood. Yet it is very seldom, even in the smaller Australian centres, that someone or other does not play cricket that would not disgrace any side.

Take the case of Tom Ball, fast medium bowler, who had travelled from far north, about 800 miles, for this match. In our innings he took the wickets of Hardstaff, Compton, Smith, Evans and Pollard for 69 runs. Yet normally he has only district club cricket as practice. And H. Zischke, who played two nice innings of 32 and 31. He is known as the "Bush Bradman" and would have appeared in inter-state cricket if he had not turned his back on it because of the farm. Australia produces cricketers as easily as she produces pineapples; they seem to grow in hundreds.

On our side in this match there was a welcome reappearance by Laurie Fishlock, whose broken finger had kept him out of the game since Adelaide weeks before. Now he made a nice 62 and Hardstaff, one of the other temporarily out-of-the-tests, 64.

Even when the return bus was ready immediately after close of play it was difficult to get away for the long night drive. We newspapermen found ourselves mixed up in an informal farewell party—"They are jolly good fellows," speeches and the rest of it. I firmly believe that every Australian concludes the family Sunday dinner with a speech or two. As the "hat-trick in tours" journalist from England I usually found myself responding on behalf of someone or other at these functions. It isn't difficult. The same speech will serve in Gympie as in Perth, and any journalist used to keeping an eye on cable costs knows how to be economical in words.

CHAPTER XVII

DEFEAT NUMBER TWO

W E lost the second test match at Sydney—13th, 14th, 16th, 17th,
18th, 19th December—by an innings and 33 runs, which I suppose
is a degree better than the innings and 332 of Brisbane. But this
time we won the toss and we could not claim to have had the worst
of the wicket.

Totals: England 255 and 371; Australia 659 for eight declared.

FIRST DAY—BOWLERS ON TOP

Our selectors made two changes—Evans for Gibb as wicketkeeper and Smith for Voce—more spin and less fast medium
bowling. The Australians were without Lindwall, who had
developed chicken-pox during the Brisbane test and was still unfit.
In his stead Fred Freer, the Victorian fast medium bowler, was
introduced. Meuleman was again twelfth man for Australia;
Hardstaff for us.

We in that eagles' nest of a press box—with ninety-nine steps
leading up to it—saw signalled the glad fact that Bradman had
been let down in the toss by the English four-shilling piece which he
used. There was at the beginning quite a small crowd compared
with the multitude which flowed in later. The famous hill, by
repute a forbidding eminence, but really when untenanted more
like the bank where the wild thyme blows, still showed patches
of green uncovered by humanity.

Keith Miller opened with an erratic first over which yielded
8 runs and an acrobatic display behind the wicket by Tallon on
the leg side. The first ball went for four byes, the second brought a
3 to Hutton and then came a single to Washbrook. Then our
troubles began. The fifth ball from Freer brought to that bowler the
distinction of a wicket in his first over in a test match. He gave
Washbrook a good length ball; he groped forward and missed.
Ten for one after only eight minutes' play.

Edrich, coming in, found with Hutton a contrast in seam
bowling—Miller at one end inaccurate but making the ball lift,
Freer at the other swinging awkwardly and accuracy itself. Once
Hutton, ducking to one of Miller's risers, fell and the ball apparently
glanced off the batsman's left arm—the one he broke during the war.

107

These two settled down to a useful partnership of 78 in face of the two fast bowlers, replaced presently by the swarthy big Toshack, bowling his medium-paced left-hand attack on the leg stump, and the small fair Tribe, slow left-hander, who is a better bowler than his test figures showed. That leg-side attack of Toshack's, with five men supporting it, slowed the scoring and the 10 runs taking the total from 40 to 50 took twenty-three minutes, including the drinks pause. The batsmen found him difficult to get away without undue risks. Toshack had bowled seven overs for 6 runs when Bradman took him off and tried Miller again. Once there went up clamorous appeal against Hutton for a catch at the wicket and 2 runs later the same batsman snicked a ball close to third slip. Certainly Hutton did not look happy against Miller's pace. The pair kept the flag flying until lunchtime, when the total was 66 for one, Hutton 34, Edrich 21. It had been a rather grim morning's play.

After the interval there was a certain liveliness as Edrich, the more confident batsman of the two, slammed a four off Tribe over his partner's ducking head and then turned the same bowler for 3. But twenty-five minutes after the re-start Ian Johnson, the off-break bowler, shared the distinction already won by Freer of taking a wicket in his first test over; he had played in the Brisbane match, but did not bowl. Now he had Hutton caught at the wicket—88-2-39. Hutton had been in for nearly two hours. It cannot be said that even towards the end of that time he looked like really mastering the bowling.

In came Compton, hit Tribe for a quick four and was promptly faced by McCool, who struck decisive blows at once. He got the wickets of Compton and Hammond, so that these two and Hutton had been dismissed with only 11 runs added to the score.

Compton, having scored 5, was caught at the wicket—97 for three; 2 runs later Hammond, after scoring a single, shared the same fate.

All these three last wickets had gone within twenty-four minutes' play and the back of our innings was broken.

What of the wicket? Before the match certain experts detected what they termed "spots." Certainly both McCool and Johnson were making the ball turn in an un-Sydneylike manner for the first day, but, as I cabled home at the time, it was imprudent to attribute our failures to anything but bad batting and good bowling until we saw what use Australia made of this same wicket. They scored 659 for eight on it.

Edrich's new partner, Jack Ikin, had his advantage as a left-hander against McCool's leg-breaks destroyed at the other end by Johnson's off-spinners. This partnership set dourly about the task of saving something from the wreck. How slowly they went about it may be judged from Johnson's performance in bowling eleven overs, eight of them maidens, for 3 runs. At the other end remained McCool, giving a little more away but more dangerous. He was driven by Ikin for 3 and by Edrich for 4. So we scrambled past the 100 total and Edrich reached his 50, for which he had batted with fine resoluteness for more than two and a half hours with four fours.

Ikin was dropped by Tallon off Johnson when only 4, but the pair were still together at tea—133 for four, Edrich 63, Ikin 11. They had been together nearly an hour for 34.

After tea came two quick gifts—a full toss by McCool, dusted by Ikin for four, and another from Johnson—rare event indeed—similarly treated by Edrich. But twenty minutes after the break Edrich's stay of three hours and twenty minutes was ended by an l.b.w. decision against him in McCool's favour, 138-5-71, the partnership having added 49 uphill runs. Seventy-one, by the way, had become a sort of bogy score to Edrich; this was the third time in the tour that he had fallen for that tally.

Yardley came in, the last of our front line batsmen. He took a quick four off a slow long hop far out on the off-side. When the dogged Ikin had scored 21 Tallon invited the umpires to take a look at the stumps. Ikin apparently had played a ball from McCool on to them, but the umpires decided that the bails were unmoved.

The score crawled along and when the last drinks of the day were brought out Johnson had bowled nineteen overs for 16 runs and one wicket. At last Yardley raised the siege by hitting McCool for two fours in one over. But when he and Ikin had added 29 in fifty minutes Tallon took his fourth catch of the day at Yardley's expense. The batsman leaned wide out on the off-side to drive Johnson and edged the ball—187-6-25. Smith stayed insecurely for a few minutes and was then l.b.w. to Johnson—197-7-4. Evans came in for his first test match innings in time to see Ikin's 50 come up with a stroke off which he was missed by Barnes at forward short leg. Evans was soon out trying to hook Johnson—205-8-5—and Bedser stayed the quarter hour until the drawing of stumps at 219 for eight.

A thoroughly bad day. Early losses had deprived our later batsmen of the enterprise to attack this spin bowling and hit it off its length. All day long the bowling was all too obviously on the attack; the batting attempted by subdued methods to keep wickets standing, with no one really having a go. Easier said than done, no doubt, but there it is—the soul of the defence against Australian spin bowlers lies in counter-attack.

SECOND DAY—AN HOUR AND A HALF

Rain, which had followed us everywhere, overtook us again in Sydney, so the second day was limited to about an hour and a half's cricket. Just over half an hour completed the English innings for 255; then, after a blank afternoon, the Australians had fifty minutes' batting in which Morris's wicket was lost for a total of 27.

Thunder was in the air when play began. But the Australians had unjustified faith in their weather, for the whole ring was lined with light shirts and blouses. The half hour during which the tail raised our score by 36 runs was more entertaining than anything seen the day before. Bradman, who had strained his leg while fielding, left Hassett temporarily in command. Both Ikin and Bedser made scoring strokes against McCool and Johnson. They had their luck, for Bedser might have been caught by McCool if he had made ground quickly enough at mid-on to Johnson's bowling, and Ikin was let off by Tallon twice—a catch and a stump—but this rally was too good to last. Ikin was caught by Hassett at mid-off in trying to hit Johnson after batting nearly three hours for his 60. His had scarcely been an attractive innings, except to admirers of pluck, but its value no one could doubt. Without him our score would not have been even respectable.

Wright, a good number eleven, showed straight away that a full toss from McCool should go the same way as any other full toss from any other slow bowler. When McCool was replaced by Tribe he hit the new bowler for another four. The last pair added 21 before Bedser was bowled by Johnson.

Johnson's figures—30.1-12-42-6—and McCool's—23-2-73-3—were astonishing, but they had been helped by weak batting. Tallon had given them strong support behind the wicket. Always our batsmen in playing forward to the slow bowling realised that they had him behind them.

As the umpires came out for the Australian innings inky clouds, and the roll and flash of a thunderstorm, threatened trouble. Immediately there were appeals by Barnes against the light, at first refused and then allowed, and the players came off after only nine minutes' batting—6 runs to Barnes and a single to Morris.

Ten minutes later came the rain, and though this storm was only a pale imitation of the Brisbane one it was a better one than we often see in England. The crowd in the open dashed for the shelter of the covered stands and a swirl of newspapers, released as their owners rose and fled, passed over the ground in the gale. Some of the crowd forced their way into the members' enclosure. A film formed over the wicket and half the outfield became invisible. The ground indeed soon looked like a Pacific archipelago.

There was talk as we took lunch about the batsmanship of
Wright earlier in the day. He had not scored a run all the tour
except in the Brisbane test, and now, with 29 scored for once out,
his average was higher than anyone else's except Edrich and Ikin.

Two hours of rain, and then a long period of waiting with the
crowd getting fidgetty. Patrols pushed out from the hill visited
the wicket and were repulsed by the police. At last play was re-
started at four o'clock; there had been none since one. Even now
the cricket was of the stop-start order, as showers drove the players
off. Twenty-four runs had been scored—18 since the resumption—
when Morris was out. He stepped across his wicket to avoid a ball
from Edrich which he thought would miss the stumps; the ball
hit his body and bounced into the wicket.

Bradman sent Johnson in as a stop-gap in an exalted position
in the batting order and there followed a series of bad light appeals.
Four of them were rejected, but a fifth succeeded and play ceased
with the total 27 for one—Barnes 21 and Johnson none. I wondered
why the fifth appeal was successful, for the light did not seem to
have grown worse than at the first.

There was no more play that night. The only entertainment
was supplied by a brave who sneaked over the fence, ran to the
middle and tried to souvenir the middle stump at which Edrich had
been bowling. Two policemen started in chase and were close to
him when he reached the fence and threw the stump over. A fellow
spectator collared him and two policemen walked him off.

Be it noted that all this rain fell on a Saturday. Sunday saved
Australia, for the blank day gave the wicket time to dry nicely
before Monday's play. There, all day Sunday, was the sticky wicket
of our dreams—or nightmares—and no one was able to get to work
upon it.

THIRD DAY—BAD FOR ENGLAND

Barnes and Bradman were twin rocks on which our ship found-
ered. They were expanding their great stand, to reach 405 on the
morrow, when stumps were drawn with the Australian total only
behind ours and six wickets left standing.

No rain had fallen during Sunday and the hot sun had dried
all the vice out of the pitch. I drove to the ground that day
with Major R. J. Macleod, Suffolk Regt., whom duty had brought
8,000 miles from Japan—duty now mixed with pleasure. He told
me that he listened to the first day's play in the air and flew over
the ground just as stumps were being drawn.

The day's beginning was encouraging. After a quarter of an
hour and 10 more runs Johnson was caught easily by Washbrook

at cover to Edrich's bowling. Two for 37, a worse beginning tha
ours had been.

No Bradman yet. His injured leg had caused him to hold him
self back until number six. Barnes and Hassett added 59 for th
next wicket. They were attacked by Edrich, Bedser, who bowle
seven overs for 12 runs that morning, Wright and Smith. It canno
be said that the Australians looked as indecisive against our slo
bowlers as our batsmen did against theirs, but the struggle was ver
even.

Ten minutes after lunch a hubbub arose on the hill, with me
throwing things about in sheer playfulness. It was followed by th
fall of Hassett's wicket. Hassett tried to hook a short-pitched bounce
from Edrich and gave Compton a standing catch near the squar
leg railings. Ninety-six for three, all of which had been taken b
Edrich for 26 runs.

When Miller arrived Barnes completed a sure but very slo
50 in two and three-quarter hours. Miller, who to me is about th
most attractive batsman playing, now scored 40 in a partne
ship of 63. He had his luck. Once Wright deserved his wick
when he tickled a ball between the wicket-keeper and slip for 4 run
Wright, indeed, was bowling well but without luck. Indeed, i
these early tests it was always astonishing that he could bowl s
admirably for so few wickets.

After Barnes and Miller had been together three-quarters
an hour and we were beginning to fear the worst Smith broke th
partnership just before tea. He pitched a leg-break just wide of th
off-stump and Miller pursued it as it turned away, giving Eva
a catch. One hundred and fifty-nine for four.

That was our last success of the day. At "stumps" Barne
109, and Bradman, 52, had taken the total from 159 to 25
Bradman limped in. He looked from his gait and the early un
certainties of his innings as though he would give no trouble
all. In the first hour he scored just 14—a two and twelve single
But by the end of the day's play fifty minutes later his score w
52 and he had hit six fours, almost entirely hooks and strokes th
did not entail running out of his crease.

In the first twenty minutes of this partnership 4 runs we
scored. Smith bowled one over, in particular, full of teasers
Barnes, and Wright at the other end was difficult too. Barnes
last got 4 past cover from a ball bowled by Smith and the scori
rate increased a little.

When Bedser returned we saw at last a real stroke from t
champion—a hook for four off a short ball. Barnes meanwh
had mis-steered a ball from Smith very close to Hammond
slip. Bradman followed with another four and a two off Beds

using the new ball, and the 50 partnership was reached in seventy minutes. It was followed by Barnes's 100, reached in five hours twenty minutes. He had been the Edrich of the Australian innings.

In the last hour of the day, as usually happens, scoring became more free. Both Barnes and Bradman apparently liked our fast bowling better than our slow. In the last half hour it became possible that our total would be passed that evening. This did not quite happen.

The takings, £7,264, were a record for any one day on this ground, because prices are increased nowadays. The crowd, 51,427, was a record for the Monday of a test match there.

FOURTH DAY—BARNES AND BRADMAN

If day number three was bad for us, day number four was worse. Barnes and his captain kept company until a quarter to six in completing their 405 partnership, the highest for the fifth wicket in England and Australia tests and second only as a partnership to the 451 which Bradman and Ponsford amassed for the second wicket at Kennington Oval in 1934. Barnes and Bradman each made 234.

They were out within two minutes of each other with the total of 564 unaltered—Bradman to Yardley and Barnes to Bedser.

In this gruelling stand our bowlers were triers throughout. It was not that they bowled badly, but they did not bowl well enough. Not until after tea did the attack become ragged. Bradman at times limped, but his injury did not prevent him from playing his shots.

In Australia the health of Bradman is as much a national concern as that of a racehorse like Bernborough, whose unconquerable career on the Turf was ended by a breakdown while we were there. That morning one of the Sydney papers told us that Bradman had gastric trouble. Yet there he was at eight-thirty in our hotel breakfasting cheerfully with his wife. I feel that if Bradman were reported to be dying he would still confound the news-gatherers by turning out and scoring centuries.

Half an hour's play and 20 runs were scored, 17 of them by Barnes, for Bradman at that time was having to struggle for survival against Wright, who bowled two successive maidens to him. Once Bradman turned a ball which fell only a foot or so from Bedser near the square-leg umpire.

Wright gave away no more than 10 runs in five overs during this first spell of the day. Edrich and Smith bowled, too, but runs came steadily—48 in the first hour, 28 to Barnes, 20 to Bradman.

I will not follow that great stand change by change of bowling. Enough to say that in the hour and a half before lunch 73 were scored; in an hour and three-quarters between lunch and tea

116—both average rates; but in the hour and a half after tea before the partnership was broken 130 were added against tired bowling. Seven bowlers were tried during the day—Bedser, Edrich, Wright, Smith, Ikin, Compton and Yardley. The Australian record fifth wicket partnership—between Bradman and Alan Kippax, 183—was passed soon after lunch; the English record, broken later, was 206 by Compton and Eddie Paynter at Nottingham in 1938.

Remarkably, Bradman's century—which became a double one—was his first against England on the Sydney ground.

Both batsmen passed the highest individual score by any Australian against England at Sydney—S. E. Gregory's 201 in 1894. But the highest by an Englishman in tests there—R. E. Foster's 287 nine years later—was unassailed.

Bradman shook his partner warmly by the hand in the middle of the pitch after Barnes had broken that Gregory record.

Bradman, hitting 16 off one over from Compton, had just overtaken his partner when he was out. He tried to slash a half volley from Yardley, missed and was leg-before to a ball which would not normally have taken his wicket. Two minutes later Barnes was out too, without a run added to the 564 already there. Barnes, trying to drive Bedser, sent a high catch to Ikin at mid-on.

See the difference in times for just the same score: Bradman 391 minutes, Barnes 642 minutes, a difference of more than four hours. Barnes's innings was not the longest in test cricket. I believe that record is Hutton's thirteen hours twenty minutes for his 364 at the Oval in 1938.

McCool and Tallon stopped the rot! They were together about ten minutes that evening for 7 runs.

FIFTH DAY—FIGHTING BACK

Too late in the match, alas, our batsmen played like real batsmen. Faced at one o'clock with the apparently hopeless deficit of 404 they cut it down at close of play to 157 for the loss of the wickets of Hutton, Washbrook and Compton. There even seemed a chance, in the event unrealised, of saving the innings defeat.

Three hundred and sixteen runs ahead though he was when play was begun, Bradman decided to bat on. That overworked pair, Bedser and Wright, thus far with one wicket between them for 268 runs, bowled again to Tallon and McCool. After a quarter of an hour Peter Smith replaced Bedser and there was an immediate wicket—that of McCool, who chopped at a leg-break and gave Hammond a simple catch at short slip. Five hundred and ninety-five for seven, 24 having been scored quickly that morning.

Freer hit Wright into the pavilion seats for six, but soon afterwards the Kent bowler got a wicket at last by catching Tallon off his own bowling. One hundred and fifty runs had been scored off Wright before this success. I have never seen anyone bowl so well for so many runs and so few wickets. Freer and the little left-hander Tribe hit at everything and one over by Wright yielded 18. Soon the record score, 645 at Brisbane, which had been the highest ever in a test match in Australia, was passed, and Bradman declared at 659 for eight. There have been four higher totals in England—903 for seven by England at the Oval in 1938, 729 for six by Australia at Lord's in 1930, 701 by Australia at the Oval in 1934, and 695 by Australia at the Oval in 1930.

It is a record I never wish to see beaten by either side. These eternal innings on perfect wickets spoil test cricket. Let's give the bowlers a chance.

Bradman, who had not fielded during the close of the England first innings, now limped ahead of his men on to the field.

Hutton and Washbrook began the England second innings as though they had not a care in the world. In ten minutes they had scored 23 to the bowling of Freer and Miller, Hutton 20, Washbrook 3.

Hutton gave an unaccepted chance—a very hot one—to Miller—in the gully off Freer in the first over, and then proceeded to lay about him with all manner of delightful strokes as though he were knocking off the few runs needed for victory. In twenty-four minutes' batting Hutton had 37 runs, including six fours, and his partner 11.

Then a cruel piece of ill-luck befell Hutton. Playing a stroke to Miller he broke his own wicket. He told me later that the thumb of his batting glove slipped off and became entangled with the bat, which, out of control, passed over the batsman's shoulder on to the stumps. This was on the stroke of lunchtime. Here was a new Hutton to Australian eyes, a hitter right from the start of the innings. They appreciated him, would have liked another hour or so of him.

Washbrook and Edrich, to whom the slow bowlers Johnson and McCool were brought on after lunch, made 69 together in about an hour when Washbrook was caught by the agile McCool, who threw himself along the ground at silly short-leg to Johnson's bowling.

Compton had some rather unhappy opening minutes but survived them. After Johnson had bowled twelve overs for 32 runs and Washbrook's wicket, Bradman gave Toshack his first turn. He set a close leg-trap and the Middlesex pair could only parry his opening overs. Just before tea Edrich completed a faultless 50 in double the number of minutes, which emphasised that of all our batsmen he was most in form at that period. Tea came at 133 for two—Edrich 51 and a rather inactive Compton 18. Compton had just been missed by Tallon off Toshack's bowling.

Compton was happier after tea and the partnership stuck

so firmly that seven bowlers in all were employed against it—Miller, Freer, Johnson, McCool, Toshack, Tribe and Barnes. This time Edrich passed the 71 total which was his hoodoo. Compton's more assured march towards his 50 was stayed while Tallon, who had dislocated a finger, went into the pavilion to have it put back— a delay lasting five minutes. When Compton did reach the half-century it was his first of the series, his earlier efforts having been 17, 15 and 5.

We had hoped that this partnership would outlast the day, and indeed the crowd was thinning in the belief that nothing in particular would happen. Then Compton was out, for he edged a ball from Freer to Bradman at second slip. Two hundred and twenty for three.

With twenty minutes left for batting Hammond came in, straight drove Freer for four, hit a six off a no-ball from Johnson and stayed with Edrich to the end of the day.

SIXTH DAY—ANOTHER INNINGS DEFEAT

There was rain in the early morning of the last day, but the wicket rapidly absorbed it, and the conditions seemed unaltered for Edrich and Hammond except that the noontide was sunless. Hammond took two twos and a single from Miller's opening over and then there was a long period without scoring—two maidens each by McCool and Miller. It was twenty-five minutes before Edrich scored his first run.

Bradman replaced Miller with Johnson but retained McCool, in the not unfounded belief that Hammond did not like him. After three-quarters of an hour, during which the partnership carried the over-night score of 27 on to 60, McCool broke the back of his side's job by capturing Hammond's wicket. Hammond hit a four so hard past this bowler that he prudently pulled back his hand. Trying to repeat the stroke two balls later Hammond lifted the ball over McCool's head to Toshack running from mid-on. Hammond had been batting an hour for 37. Two hundred and eighty for four— still 124 behind, with four and a quarter hours left for play.

With Ikin in, Edrich reached his 100—his own first of the tour and the first scored by any Englishman in these tests. It had taken him four hours and twenty minutes, with only six fours, but he had had to bear the brunt of the side's innings. He had dealt with those troublesome Australian spinners satisfyingly.

His partnership with Ikin lasted thirty-five minutes for 29 runs, then was ended by Freer, who bowled Ikin with a ball of perfect length at which Ikin tried to play back. Three hundred and nine for five. Yardley stayed with Edrich until lunch, when the position was the hopeless one of 316 for five—Edrich 113, Yardley 1.

For twenty minutes after the interval these two added an occasional single and then Edrich, whom we had come to regard as a permanent feature of the landscape, vanished from view. After five hours and a quarter of resistance from him McCool bowled him with a leg-break which he appeared to touch on to his wicket. Bradman walked up to the bowler with a handshake, but it was equally Edrich who deserved it. Three hundred and twenty-seven for six.

Smith stayed ten minutes, during which he saw Yardley hit 12 off one over from Johnson and himself dealt one blow at McCool. Then he tried to hook Johnson and Hassett caught him. Three hundred and forty-six for seven. Yardley and Evans collected 20 by summary methods before Yardley was yorked by McCool. Five minutes later Evans was stumped off the same bowler. Wright was caught at the wicket and how many runs Bedser would have made will never be known. The crowd gathered round the wicket like mourners round a grave. It was all over at five minutes past three, so that a draw had never really been in prospect. Our defeat was by an innings and 33. Until Hammond was out before lunch there had seemed some possibility of saving the match, but when McCool, whose analysis at that stage was nought for 85, took the captain's wicket there was no real prospect of anything but defeat. McCool finished with five for 109.

It is a sad thought that if Hutton's batting glove had not slipped the result of this test match might have been different. Cricket is a funny game—a remark I seem to have heard before.

ENGLAND

First Innings		Second Innings	
L. Hutton c Tallon b Johnson	39	hit wkt b Miller	37
C. Washbrook b Freer	1	c McCool b Johnson	41
W. J. Edrich lbw b McCool	71	b McCool	119
D. Compton c Tallon b McCool	5	c Bradman b Freer	54
W. R. Hammond c Tallon b McCool	1	c Toshack b McCool	37
J. T. Ikin c Hassett b Johnson	60	b Freer	17
N. W. D. Yardley c Tallon b Johnson	25	b McCool	35
T. P. B. Smith lbw b Johnson	4	c Hassett b Johnson	2
T. G. Evans b Johnson	5	st Tallon b McCool	9
A. V. Bedser b Johnson	14	not out	3
D. V. P. Wright not out	15	c Tallon b McCool	0
Extras	15	Extras	17
Total	255	Total	371

Fall of wickets: 10, 88, 97, 99, 148, 187, 197, 205, 234, 255.

Fall of wickets: 49, 118, 220, 280, 309, 327, 346, 366, 371.

Bowling	O.	M.	R.	W.
Miller	9	2	24	0
Freer	7	1	25	1
Toshack	7	2	6	0
Tribe	20	3	70	0
Johnson	30.1	12	42	6
McCool	23	2	73	3

Bowling	O.	M.	R.	W.
Barnes	3	0	11	0
Tribe	12	0	40	0
Johnson	29	7	92	2
McCool	33.4	4	109	5
Toshack	6	1	16	0
Freer	13	2	49	2
Miller	11	3	37	1

Miller wide, Toshack two no-balls.

AUSTRALIA

First Innings

S. G. Barnes c Ikin b Bedser	234
A. Morris b Edrich	5
I. Johnson c Washbrook b Edrich	7
A. L. Hassett c Compton b Edrich	34
K. R. Miller c Evans b Smith	40
D. G. Bradman lbw b Yardley	234
C. McCool c Hammond b Smith	12
D. Tallon c and b Wright	30
F. Freer not out	28
G. Tribe not out	25
Extras ..	10

Eight for (innings declared) 659
Fall of wickets: 24, 37, 96, 159, 564, 564, 595, 617.

Bowling	O.	M.	R.	W.
Bedser	46	7	153	1
Edrich	26	2	79	3
Wright	46	8	169	1
Smith	36	1	172	2
Ikin	3	0	15	0
Compton	6	0	38	0
Yardley	9	0	23	1

So we were two test matches down already. Broadly speaking we had lost them because our batting and bowling were not up to the Australian standard. Ill-luck there had been of course, and umpiring decisions not at all to our men's liking, including the l.b.w. decision against Edrich when he claimed he had hit the ball. But there the fact remained—that our bowling had not been up to its task and our batting, on which we had counted, had not lived up to ex-pectations. That reputedly tottering old man Bradman, whom

Australians at Perth had considered out of the tests, had managed to score 187 and 234 against us, although a Methuselah of thirty-eight. We had had atrocious luck with the wicket at Brisbane with its twin "stickies," but let it not be forgotten that the Australians had scored 645 against us before the rain.

Their bowling superiority arose because the Australians had been quicker off the mark after the war, which had not left the same tragic imprint on their country as on ours. When we landed in September we were told that over in the east there was a fast bowler called Lindwall who looked good for the tests. But apart from him, the selectors did not know where to turn for bowling. Yet Bradman now had bowlers to burn. McCool, a product of parks cricket in Sydney, Freer, Johnson, Tribe, Toshack, Dooland had never been heard of before the war; all our bowlers except Bedser were established long before 1939. The average age of the Australians in the match was just over twenty-nine; ours was two years older.

On the way from the ground I met Mr. George Garnsey, whom I had known ten years earlier as a coach there—a real zealot of cricket. Now he is school-teaching, but his interest in the game remains. He told me that in and near Sydney they have 15,000 registered junior cricketers playing in competitions under expert eyes. Garnsey discovered McCool, then a timid little chap, among them. No wonder Australia holds her own at cricket.

Only six days remained before Christmas when the second test ended. In the meantime there was a two-day match, which I shirked, at Newcastle. This enormous centre of the coal and iron industries is the sixth city of Australia, ranking only after the five state capitals. I was told that from the players' hotel one could run straight across the road and gambol in the surf with the sharks of the Pacific. Actually I have never seen a shark, or heard a shark alarm, in all the visits I have made to Australian beaches. A whole season may go by, with its millions of bathers ("surfers" in the vernacular), without a single swimmer being "taken." Yet the prospect of being snapped up is such a shady one that I always had sharks in the back of my mind when puffing about in four feet of water. I remained, like braver men and women than I, at about minnow depth.

However, about Newcastle. The match was embellished by centuries from Hammond and Fishlock in the first innings—Hammond's third and Fishlock's first of the tour—and the bowling figures of four for 46 by Voce. Scores.—M.C.C.: first innings 395, second innings 146 for six. Northern Districts N.S.W.: 202. Our second innings was no credit to us. Six wickets were down for 40 and Hammond had to go in at number eight and help Compton to make the total respectable. Even our minor matches had their crises.

So to Christmas, a very brief one spent in Sydney. Mass celebrations are not popular with touring sides, so after dinner the men went off with their friends and followed their own devices. In Sydney the beaches are the chief attraction. People do go in for our English Christmas dinners, with all the trimmings—indeed, many more trimmings than we have in England now. They like to do so for sentiment's sake, even though plum pudding and mincepies are an ordeal in an Australian midsummer. For the rest, our Christmas and theirs differ completely.

I spent the holiday with Gilbert and Molly Mant and their family. Gilbert—now of the *Sunday Sun* in Sydney—is my old "cobber" and sharer of many a sleeping berth with me in two previous tours in which he represented Reuter's Agency. Now he has settled, for the time being anyhow, in the enviable city of his birth. We attended Christmas morning children's service at St. Mark's, Darling Point, where half the children of the district and their parents more than filled the church. Then after dinner we took a long train journey to Gordon, a far northern suburb, to the fine home of Mr. Neville Cayley, whose paintings of the bird life of Australia have won him a national, indeed an international, reputation. Here we found ourselves at a children's party at which the star attraction was a Christmas tree growing in the middle of the lawn and duly illuminated, decorated and bearing a wonderful crop of presents. A stuffed pony became my heritage, before mosquitoes drove us back to the house.

Sydney, unlike London, does not often rise to fog at Christmas time. But as we were coming home we noticed down harbour a curious thickening of the atmosphere. In the papers next morning we read that one of the ferry boats running between the city and Manly beach had grounded during her return trip with some hundreds of passengers. Happily there was nothing worse than a delayed journey and anxiety on their account at their homes. The sixpennyworth down to Manly after dinner on hot nights is a trip I have often enjoyed. There is nothing comparable to it in London life.

On Boxing Day we had to leave Sydney—the side to go to Canberra by rail for a country match, some of us newspapermen to fly to Melbourne direct for the Challenge Round of the Davis Cup between the lawn tennis sides of Australia and America. The Canberra match, like various others of the tour, was rain-ruined. On the first day Hutton and Washbrook made 254 together. Hutton 133, Washbrook 115 and Compton 76 were chief contributors to our 465 for eight declared. On the second day Dick Pollard, making the ball move as he can in his beloved Lancashire, was just enjoying himself to the tune of four wickets for 2 runs when the heavens opened with the countrymen's total 11 for four. Judging from the look of the parched country as I flew over it on the way to Melbourne the rain was more important than the cricket. Canberra, which I had visited ten years earlier, did not look from above to be any more densely populated now than then. It is a bush capital, with here and there a fine building but an air of incompleteness destined some time to be remedied.

CHAPTER XVIII

DAVIS CUP INTERLUDE

LAWN tennis quite displaced cricket for the time being as the Thing that Mattered in Australia. My aeroplane did not arrive at Melbourne in time for the first day's Davis Cup play, but all the way down the pilot handed back radio messages about the opening battle between Schroeder and Bromwich—duly absorbed by passengers who maybe did not know the difference between a tennis ball and a tomato. Every Australian apparently expected this match at least to be "in the bag" for Bromwich, although the Australian number one had not played outside his own country since before the war. When word came that Schroeder was leading two sets to one there was astonishment. When Bromwich won a love fourth set there was relief and a feeling that "It's all right now." But it was not all right. Schroeder pulled off the final set 6-3 and the very match Australia had counted on winning was lost. The next single, between Dinny Pails of Australia and Jack Kramer, went to America without the loss of a set.

Next day I went down to Kooyong to see the double—Bromwich and Quist against Kramer and Schroeder. Never have I seen temporary stands towering so near to heaven. They looked as though a scaffolding were being run up for a new Empire State Building. And every seat was filled, for this was the match that must be won by Australia if the Cup itself was not to be lost. It was a disappointing display. The Cup defenders could not win a set, though they took the second of the three they lost to vantage games. All through the Americans were attacking and their opponents scrambling about in defence. Kramer and Schroeder were nearly always first to the net—with all the advantage that means in a first-class double. Their killing of lobs, many of them short, was deadly—indeed I have never seen finer smashing since Borotra's day than that of Schroeder. Bromwich seemed tired and stale, and Quist was not the same all-alive-oh player I saw win the Wimbledon doubles twelve years earlier with Jack Crawford.

So the Cup was lost. I must say the Australian crowd took their licking very sportingly. After a rain-spoilt Saturday the last two singles were played on the Monday; they further emphasised American supremacy, for Kramer, playing well within himself, beat Bromwich and the reserve Mulloy defeated Pails, in each case without the loss of a set. Here was a five matches to love defeat, with only two sets—taken by Bromwich from Schroeder—in the Australian bag.

When a month or more before the Challenge Round I had made some small wagers with Australian friends that America would win I was regarded as a financial benefactor. I had seen Kramer play at Wimbledon last June; they had not. I realised the tremendous pep and power, not only of the front line Americans, but of the reserves. And I knew that their game had been tempered in the fire of international competition.

One immediate reason for the defeat of Australia stands out a mile. This was ill-advised preparation. Except for Pails and Brown, who came over semi-independently of the Australian Lawn Tennis Association, the Cup "squad" were denied the advantages of playing in the British, French and American championships during the northern summer by way of re-introduction to world lawn tennis. This lack of top-class practice was followed at home by too intensive and nerve-racking training in the weeks immediately before the big event. The players passed from one state championship to another, and in the intervals between kept at it in practice, during which the long delay in learning who was to partner Bromwich in the doubles did not help. Last moment decisions of this sort are no more likely to be right than those of weeks in advance, and the nerves of the players—a nervous breed of men—are kept on the stretch. Moreover the stories of some of the livelier Australian newspapers were not conducive to quiet and strainless preparation. At times one wondered what sort of Donnybrook the minority scare writers were trying to make of the training camp. Was this a boxing fight, one almost wondered, or amateur lawn tennis? The nervous energy of a tennis player is not inexhaustible and too heavy drafts ought not to be taken on it just before a Challenge Round, which in itself is about the "nerviest" occasion in sport. Tennis has a man against man duelling aspect which team games like cricket escape.

But the fundamental reason for Australia's defeat lay deeper. Bromwich, number one defender of the trophy, played mainly from the baseline, and a good all-court player will beat a good base-liner most times. Now and then there arises a genius of tennis, a Lacoste or a Crawford, who can win the biggest matches with little or no volleying, but Bromwich, great player as he is, is not quite in this class. Australia's future Cup players, if they are to succeed, will have to volley hard and often—like Kramer and Schroeder. Someone remarked to me after the matches that the sort of game which Sir Norman Brookes, now president of the Australian Lawn Tennis Association, defeated and proved out of date at Wimbledon thirty years ago had now been revived by the young Australians.

It was good to see top-class tennis again after watching so much championship and Davis Cup play long ago in Europe. The Cup itself, which had spent the war in the vaults of a Melbourne bank, was there for all to see. To me, though I had not seen it since Great Britain lost it to America at Wimbledon in 1936, it was still a familiar sight—a great bowl, rather than cup, about big enough to bath a baby, standing on an enormous pedestal on which are engraved the names of the winning nations. Though the Cup has been in competition since 1900, only four nations have won it among the thirty and more who have competed—Great Britain, America, France and Australia (in earlier days Australasia). One cannot help the prophecy that America will go on holding it for some years, so abundant are their keen young players, so well organised their ladder training from the junior "Davis Cup squads" dotted about the States right up to the senior squad itself. We certainly have nothing like it in England. If we have the talent, which I doubt, we do not develop it with anything like the same systematic fervour as in the States.

Weeks later I saw in Sydney the film of the Challenge Round which the firm of Slazenger enterprisingly had "shot" for display all over Australia, and in New Zealand, South Africa and probably America and England too. It gave us not mere snatches of the tennis but long slabs of it, so that one could form an intelligent impression. Some hundreds of thousands of tennis people have seen it by now—in clubs, business houses, public halls and so on. Many copies have been made, and several operators sent out on tour with it. I was told that in future young Australian players will be taught that speed of the American pattern must be cultivated as the first essential in the game. On the concrete courts of California the Americans learn, from boyhood upwards, to *hit* the ball rather than pat it, and the Australians will take a leaf out of their book.

Enthusiasm for tennis in Australia is tremendous. I was told that there are about 600,000 players, more probably than the number of cricketers, and about one-eleventh of the total population. Wherever one goes in the cities there are rows of courts, many of them with artificial lighting. One owner of eleven public courts in Sydney has all of them booked for every hour of every day for a year. Obviously they are hard courts, for no grass would stand up to it. It is curious that although Australia officially is a grass nation and has turf courts, playable all the year round in many cases and second to none in the world for quality, yet 95 per cent of the nation's tennis is played on hard. When a young player becomes promising he goes on to grass, but nearly all the rank and file club tennis, with a competitive network unknown in England, is played on antheap, rubble or asphalt surfaces. They are not equal to the best lawns but are much better than the piebald, patchy grass of which so much is seen in the minor clubs at home. When grass is good it is very, very good; when it is bad it is horrid. The hard courts of Australia are in tennis what the park concrete wickets are in cricket: they teach boys and girls to make their shots with confidence, in the knowledge that the pitch of the ball won't let them down.

I played several games at the White City, headquarters in Sydney of the New South Wales Lawn Tennis Association. A fine sight it was to see forty fine grass courts all in action. Six guineas is the membership fee here, and most of the best young players of the State belong. The whole atmosphere was so much more democratic than that of our All England Club, headquarters of lawn tennis. If we are ever to stand a remote chance of winning the Cup again we must organise from top to bottom, with more competitive play in the clubs, better and cheaper facilities for rising players and a total disregard of class distinctions. In Australia tennis is a game for all classes; in this country relatively few of what are called the "working classes" have ever seen the game, much less played it. In the elementary and in most of the secondary schools it is unknown.

Here is an immediate and practical suggestion: let the Middlesex and Surrey Associations, and the provincial ones too, start graded league competitions on the each-play-all instead of the knock-out principle, so that every club shall have a needle match every week. Let singles, instead of doubles only, be given their place. Then we shall begin to discover promising young material. Let the county championship be entirely remodelled, so that it is a real live event instead of a pleasant week's holiday at the seaside. The ladder of promotion in tennis, as in cricket, should be club, county, country. Open tournaments, good as they are for some players, are entirely out of the reach of nine out of ten who have to work for a living.

I have wandered far from the Challenge Round of the Davis Cup, about which one point remains to be made. The press facilities were far inferior to those on the great cricket grounds, where unlimited encouragement is given to writers on the game. At Kooyong we overseas visitors had seats in the "gods" which needed an athletic feat to reach, and no one came along to say how d'ye do or offer us a cup of tea. Which is very uncharacteristic of Australian hospitality.

Here are the results of the Cup matches:

F. R. Schroeder (U.S.A.) beat J. Bromwich (Australia) 3-6, 6-1, 6-2, 0-6, 6-3. J. Kramer (U.S.A.) beat D. Pails (Australia) 8-6, 6-2, 9-7. Kramer-Schroeder beat Bromwich-A. Quist 6-2, 7-5, 6-4. Kramer beat Bromwich 8-6, 6-4, 6-4. G. Mulloy (U.S.A.) beat Pails 6-3, 6-3, 6-4.

After the matches Kramer told me he intended to make a bid for the 1947 Wimbledon Championship "if I have to strip my bank roll to nothing to do so." He would probably have won the title last year if he had not developed the worst blisters I have ever seen on any tennis player's racket hand. Next to seeing an English man win at Wimbledon—an inconceivable event this year—I would as soon see Kramer succeed as anyone. Not only is he a great player in the Cochet-Perry-Vines-Budge line, but he is one of the most likeable young champions I have ever met. Sometimes Americans are accused of "side." There is no trace of it in Kramer; nor indeed was there trace of it in Vines or Budge.

Australia, profiting by her sad experience, also is to let us see her Cup side at Wimbledon. The policy of isolation does not pay.

Everywhere I went in Australia I saw boys and girls imitating the two-handed game made popular there—but nowhere else— by Bromwich, Brown and, earlier, McGrath. Here is a silly fad which ought to disappear in the interests of Australian tennis. I am convinced that these three became great players not because they hit the ball with two hands but in spite of it. For this reason— that no man can stretch as far with two hands on the racket as with one, and changing from one wing to the other, especially in the quick cut and thrust of a double, is difficult and complicated. Sir Norman Brookes, who needed no more than his good left hand to beat all-comers in his day, told the conference of interstate delegates at Melbourne last January that he was not in favour of double-handed players, for they had definite limitations. He is right.

I must not leave lawn tennis without telling of the Million Club—a score of veterans forming a group within the White City Club at Sydney. I became a rather junior and unfortunately very temporary "Millionaire," so named for reasons of age rather than affluence.

It is no exaggeration to say that their average tennis four totals about 250 years. They vary from mere youngsters in their fifties to keen lads of eighty. Most of them are retired business men, or company directors who at least have no need to seek anyone's permission to play on the Tuesdays and Thursdays when the Millions meet. I did hear, however, of one eighty-year-old who handed over the running of his business to his son and who now says he cannot come to midweek tennis because the lad (of fifty or more) won't let him off duty!

Many of these veterans—secretaried by Jim Conway—are old tournament or inter-state players and the standard they set to-day is hot enough for the general run of junior sides. One of the visitors with me was F. M. B. Fisher, now living in New Zealand, who in his day was high up the Wimbledon ladder. To-day he remains formidable in any double.

Photo: *Daily Mirror, Sydney*

Over to you! Compton in the second Test at Sydney sent a catch to Johnson at first slip, off whom the ball bounced back to the wicketkeeper, Tallon, who held it.

Ambition has not left the members of this unique club. One of them, excluded from a four in which he was not quite capable of holding up a corner, complained—as millions of others have complained in thousands of tennis clubs—that if he was not allowed to play with stronger men than himself he could not possibly improve his own game. He was seventy-five!

"Father" of the Millions Club is Mr. T. P. Carr, now eighty-three, and still enjoying his tennis game. It was as an inter-state footballer that he formerly shone. He is father of another member, Captain Leo Carr, inter-state tennis player, and father also of another athlete of distinction, "Slip" Carr, the runner. Member of a third generation is E. W., now eighteen, who may run for his country in the Olympic Games in London next year. Another "Millionaire" is Mr. Ted Wolfenden, accountant, financial adviser to the Commonwealth Government and chairman of the Australian Board of Slazengers.

Age is cheek by jowl with youth at White City. While I was there, for example, more than 900 boys and girls were competing in the age and school championships, in which there were various events varying from the under-thirteens to the under-nineteens. I cannot think of any English junior competition comparable in numbers to this one.

Another enterprise of the State Association at White City is Country Week, to which rural players flock with the double purpose of playing tennis and holiday-making and shopping in Sydney. Still another event is the Great Public Schools tournament run by Mr. E. J. Clinch. This team championship has unearthed several internationals, including Vivian McGrath and Norman Peach.

White City has this advantage over any English ground—that its grass courts can be used hard all the year round and still remain in first-class condition. I was told that courts on which I played had been out of action only for about a month in the last year, when they were raked and top-dressed back in the southern spring. Since then they had stood up to the N.S.W. Championships and any amount of club play; yet they were true as a billiards table and hardly had a bare patch even on their baselines. In some seasons they are rested only for a fortnight. Their grass is couch, with its creeping roots under the soil. It is not as fine as our Cumberland turf, possibly does not give a surface quite as agreeable as our courts at Wimbledon, but it wears as no English grass ever can.

Australia ought to produce Davis Cup winners, because Nature and organisation do everything possible for their young players. To compete with her in the Cup competition our lawn tennis players and administrators in England will have to develop a ginger sadly lacking at the moment.

I

CHAPTER XIX

NEW YEAR TEST

CHRISTMAS to New Year week in Melbourne—the biggest sporting seven days known even in this sports-mad city. After the Davis Cup pill had been swallowed attention was switched from Kooyong to the Melbourne Cricket Ground, where the third test was begun on New Year's Day. Australia lost the Davis Cup; she did not win this test match, but hers was certainly a moral victory.

Look at the scores: Australia 365 and 536; England 351 and 310 for seven. Rain deprived the Australians of forty-six minutes' play on the last day, which ended with England 240 runs behind the Australian aggregate. This, I suppose, was better than defeat, but not much. The draw at least kept the result of the rubber open a little longer.

FIRST DAY—EDRICH HURT

Again on the first day we had atrocious luck. It was our turn to lose the toss, so we could not grumble there. But we could moan at losing Edrich injured before he had bowled and Voce injured just after lunch. Yet in limiting the Australian score for the day to 255 for six our men did not do at all badly. Voce, back again in the side in place of Smith, was the only English change. Australia left out Freer, now that Lindwall had parted company with his chicken-pox, and Bruce Dooland, the young leg-spinner bowler from Adelaide, was given preference to Tribe.

This Melbourne test match crowd is always an answer to the notion that the game is dying. Picture Wembley Stadium, with its green rectangle enlarged into an oval big enough for cricket, and you have an idea of the Melbourne Cricket Ground. No one can say that the new concrete stands—incomplete when we were there last—are pretty, but they do hold the people. On this New Year's Day the official figures were 66,274, which was 12,328 fewer than for the opening day ten years earlier. But the takings—because of increased prices—were a record for one day of a test match. They reached £8,557, of which £1,974 had to be paid away in amusement tax.

Summery feminine dresses and masculine shirt sleeves festooned the ground in the sunshine, though the day was no hotter than a good English summer specimen.

Hammond, patting himself on the chest after losing the toss to Bradman, deceived even his own team in the dressing-room into the notion they would be batting. Instead Voce and Bedser were bowling soon to Barnes and Morris. After only a single to each batsman Morris snicked Bedser fine on the leg side and Evans, standing back, was given a very difficult chance wide on his right side. He juggled with the ball, while Ikin at fine leg stood ready to assist, but could not quite get his fingers round it. A pity, for it would have been nice to attack Bradman with the ball still new, the bowlers fresh and the morning liveliness in the wicket.

Morris, relieved, hit Bedser for the first four of the match. After 17 laborious runs Voce came off for Wright—a change which indirectly brought about Edrich's injury. He was standing close in at short leg to Barnes, who hit a hook with all his great strength. Edrich received the ball inside the knee and went down like a log. Hardly anyone but Edrich, who seems to be made of iron and rubber, would have absorbed that blow and resumed his cricket, but after some rubbing he did go on—temporarily as it proved. Hammond crossed over to the hot spot in his stead. Ten minutes later Edrich had to hobble off and Hardstaff fielded for him for the rest of the day.

After fifty minutes' play Morris was l.b.w. to Bedser. Thirty-two for one. So to Barnes and Bradman, the alliance which had contributed 405 in the previous test. Voce was immediately brought back instead of Wright, and the high-kicking no-ball with which he reopened was tickled by the Australian captain for four. In a quarter of an hour Bradman, scoring 14, had passed the score of Barnes, who had been in more than an hour. From one over by Bedser he took two twos and a three. Yet his opening did not look safe. He spooned one ball from Bedser over Ikin's head at short-leg, and though there were no actual chances there were two or three might-have-been-outs.

Bedser, whose stamina was always a feature of our bowling, wa taken off after a good opening spell of eight overs for 24 runs and one wicket. Wright again, and a more convincing boundary to Bradman, followed by a lifted ball which would have given silly-mid-off a catch if such a fieldsman had existed. Lunchtime—71 for one; Bradman 30, Barnes 20. We feared trouble.

Soon after lunch Voce became a casualty and left the field—the first time, he told me, he had ever had to do so in a test match. A strained groin muscle was the cause of the trouble. Fishlock became a "thirteenth man," while Smith and Gibb were mobilised for duty as fourteenth and fifteenth if necessary.

Bedser and Wright, the only two front line bowlers left to us, were kept hard at it, and after Bradman and Barnes had added 76, a ball from Bedser which kept low had Barnes l.b.w. One hundred and eight for two. With Hassett in, a Bradman whose batting had sobered reached his 50.

Yardley came into the bowling economically to relieve first one then the other of our front rankers. Hassett was slow and drew fire from the barrackers. After staying fifty-three minutes for 12 he played forward to Wright and was well caught low down by Hammond at short slip. One hundred and forty-three for three.

Barely had Miller arrived than there came the sort of interruption I have never seen outside Australia. A gentleman with white shirt hanging loose outside his dark trousers climbed the fence and strolled out for a chat with anyone who would listen. Fishlock, on whom he first lighted, gravely exchanged a diplomatic handshake with him. Attempts at further conversation were interrupted by Umpire Borwick, reinforced presently by the police, who removed the man from probably the only limelight he has ever enjoyed. He had held up the game for about three minutes.

Feminine shrieks—usually aroused by a sharp run between wickets—are a lively feature of every Australian cricket ground. Which, of course, doesn't mean that there are women not knowledgeable about cricket. With the majority, I fear, knowledge is skin deep. They raised two choruses that afternoon—one when Hutton did not catch Bradman, the other when Fishlock caught Miller. Both efforts were off no-balls. Presently Compton in the outfield, running as he can on the Arsenal wing and throwing himself forward for the ball, did all he knew to make a catch at Miller's expense where no catch was. He failed by a foot. At teatime the Bradman-Miller partnership remained unbroken at 164 for three—Bradman 73, Miller 13. Yardley up to that point had bowled seven overs for only 14 runs and had well fulfilled his mission as relief man.

After tea it was twenty minutes before Bradman increased his score, but Miller was more active. It was Yardley who broke this stand of 45 by bowling Bradman, who, leaning forward for a forcing shot, played on to his wicket a ball which kept lower than he expected. Johnson was l.b.w. first ball to the same bowler, and so our crippled attack had five Australians out for 188. Yardley at the time was bowling his ninth over and his analysis read two for 19. Bradman had been in for two hours fifty minutes for 79— not one of his best innings by any means. There were only two fours, one of them off a no-ball.

Four runs after this double reverse to Australia Miller was out in trying to chop down hard on a ball from Wright. He hit the ball with the top edge and gave Evans a catch. One hundred and ninety-two for six.

The rest of the day's story is not so good. McCool and Tallon, excellent batsmen both, stayed together for more than an hour and had added 63 at close of play. It was the old story of inability of our bowlers to follow up a winning advantage. They can hardly be blamed, for we had not half a dozen bowlers, as Bradman usually had, able to relieve each other and so keep fresh. With both Voce and Edrich away, Yardley at 200 had to use the new ball with Bedser—a rôle he hardly expected in a test match. At "stumps" McCool was 28, Tallon 35. Bedser by then had bowled twenty-two eight-ball overs, Wright 21 and Yardley 18. If we had had enough bowling that day to keep up the pressure our evensong would have been more cheerful. Each of the three had two wickets.

SECOND DAY—GOOD AGAIN

Here again we did well—Australia all out 365, England 147 for the loss of Hutton's wicket.

Edrich, who overnight had been having his knee bruise "cooked" under electricity, came out with the rest of the side, twirled his right arm towards the spectators with that mannerism of his when about to bowl, and with the first ball of the morning had Tallon caught by Evans. Here was a return indeed. Two hundred and fifty-five for seven. Voce was still unable to take the field.

McCool, now joined by Lindwall, was nearly run out—Washbrook's return from cover just missed the stumps. The new pair put on 17 and then Lindwall was bowled by Bedser, who got under his defences.

Two hundred and seventy-two for eight, with McCool then 36 and Dooland and Toshack to come. There followed one of those late stands which often enabled the Australians to turn a moderate score into a better one. We had not enough reserve of bowling to seize our opportunities. Now Dooland, who is by no means a negligible batsman, came out with orders to hang on and let McCool make the runs. Hang on he did, for three-quarters of an hour and a stand of 83, of which Dooland contributed a modest 19. Towards the first 50 these two put on, the Adelaide slow bowler gathered 9. As these runs took only forty-four minutes the inference that McCool was travelling fast is obvious. He showed some lovely free strokes, quite the most attractive of the Australian innings. Just after McCool had reached his century Dooland was caught by Hammond at first slip off Edrich. Toshack provided the crowd with a little fun and snicked a four before the innings closed for 365 with the fall of his wicket. McCool, left not out for 104, had served his side magnificently at a crisis. The total, 365, was lower than we had expected when the innings began, but higher than seemed probable half-way through. The recovery shows how precious all-rounders are. Four of them in the Australian side—Miller, McCool, Tallon and Lindwall—are all capable of making centuries.

Wright, who often lost his length, was expensive at two wickets for 124, even though they were those of Hassett and Miller. Bedser had three for 99; Edrich three for 50; and Yardley two for 50, including the wicket of Bradman.

The wicketkeeping of Evans calls for special mention. Again he did not let a bye go past him, and as the same thing had happened in the Australian innings of 659 during the second test at Sydney here was an incompleted bye-less aggregate of 1,024. An extraordinary athlete is Evans, as well as a fine cricketer. His trim figure seems to be mounted on springs and he is quite tireless, with the same neat energy at the end of a long day as at the beginning.

McCool, we were told, was to be presented with £1 a run for his innings by a Melbourne sportsman. He deserved it, and good luck to him. But I dislike personally these individually bestowed bounties for test cricketers. In McCool's case duty to his side obviously coincided with personal gain, but there might arise cases conceivably where the two would not tally. And in a team game the picking out of individuals is invidious.

Our batsmen began just before three o'clock, and after the loss of Hutton with the score only eight did not lose a wicket for the rest of the day. Hutton scored two singles in a quarter of an hour, then played a forward defensive stroke to Lindwall and was caught by McCool at first slip. His test scores up to date had been 7, 0, 39, 37 and this 2. Much better was to come for the rest of the tour. Lindwall had been working up a fine turn of speed and Tallon, the wicketkeeper, had been taking post about a third way back to the fence. We must find an English counterpart to Lindwall.

Edrich once denied to me that shortness of stature was any disadvantage to him in playing fast bowling. Certainly what he lacks in inches Edrich makes up in quickness of eye and foot. Now he faced Lindwall confidently enough, driving him for two in front of the wicket, and in the same over turning a no-ball to leg for the first four of the innings. He and Washbrook saw out the first all-fast attack, lasting half an hour. Then Bradman replaced it with Toshack and McCool. Toshack has an appeal to the umpire of Duckworthian volume. Presently he cleft the sky with an l.b.w. supplication against a rather uncomfortable Washbrook, and seemed disappointed at its rejection. For the time being the attack was uppermost. Bradman, who to the outside observer is a much more conversational and consultative captain than Hammond, was often giving advice to his young bowlers and there was a general air of eagerness in the field.

Edrich was the faster as well as the more confident scorer. He twice hit Toshack to the boundary and at teatime, when the total was 48 for one, he had scored 28 and Washbrook 18.

After tea Washbrook was more assured, and Edrich no less so, so in the hour and three-quarters before the close 99 runs were added. Dooland joined the attack, but Edrich reached his 50 in eighty-five minutes, with no fewer than eight fours. When 47 he gave a sharp chance to Barnes, squatting on his heels in the silly leg position to Toshack's bowling.

Bradman apparently has great faith in Toshack. Five of Edrich's boundaries had come from him, but Bradman retained him for eleven overs, yielding 39 runs. Johnson became the sixth bowler of the day, but Edrich twice hit him to the screen. A quarter of an hour from the end Washbrook arrived at a 50 which had taken him two hours and thirty-five minutes and included only one boundary. After a hazy beginning he had appeared safe if slow.

THIRD DAY—"DIMINUENDO"

We ought to have gained a first innings lead of 200. Look at us at the end of that third day—14 behind on the first knock and Australia 33 for no wicket in the second.

The first hour was the worst. In it, Edrich, heading confidently for his second hundred of the series, Compton, Hammond and Washbrook were all out for the addition of a mere 32 to the overnight total. These reverses broke the back of our innings.

Eight singles off Lindwall and Dooland formed the sedate opening of the day's play under grey clouds. Then came an l.b.w. decision by Umpire Scott against Edrich and in favour of Lindwall that became more discussed than any other such verdict of the tour. Edrich, who the previous over had only half-stopped a ball from Dooland, played forward to Lindwall and the umpire's hand went up after the ball had hit his pads.

Players are not allowed in theory to discuss details of the cricket with newspaper men, but it is impossible to live among them without hearing the sort of bush wireless which disseminates what has happened as seen in the middle. Edrich did not talk to me about the incident, or at least if he did it was off the record! But it is well known that the batsman was convinced he hit that ball, and hit it quite hard. Umpire Scott and others have accused journalists who criticised that decision of claiming to see the unseeable from the distant ringside.

Weeks later, after the series was completed, Scott announced his retirement from test umpiring "because a few English writers had unfairly criticised some of his decisions."

"Critics," he said, "sit in a pavilion 250 yards away and side-on to the wicket, and from there tear an umpire to pieces. I was pilloried and lampooned by certain critics merely because I did my duty fearlessly. Some critics claim that Edrich hit the ball on which I gave him out l.b.w., but I saw daylight between bat and ball."

Now, while it is true that a writer cannot see as well as an umpire, and so cannot set his personal judgment against him, many of us knew that this particular decision had been received resentfully by the English team. It had come at an unfortunate moment, for it had been followed by disastrous failures that without it might not have occurred. Since it is the duty of a reporter to report what he hears as well as sees—or he would not be doing his duty by his newspaper—there is no need for surprise that this decision came under the microscope. No conscientious writer could let it pass without reference. What was written in the English and some of the Australian papers was based on better evidence than that of a glimpse 150 yards away.

It is, I know, distasteful and inadvisable to attack umpires as a matter of daily routine as angry football spectators boo a referee. Usually there is small evidence on which to base such attacks. But I deny that every decision by any umpire ought to be allowed to pass, whatever the circumstances, without comment. The umpire may not always be right, and if there is strong evidence of error, then any informed report of the match ought to mention it. My own account of the incident confined itself to mentioning that between what happened as the umpire saw it and what happened as the batsman saw, and felt, it there was a wide gulf. Which of them was right I do not pretend to say, for I was not near enough to see.

When Edrich was out he and Washbrook had added 147 to the total in nearly three hours' batting. One hundred and fifty-five for two was still a fair score. But 12 runs and eighteen minutes later Compton, who had opened quite happily, was out l.b.w. to Toshack.

This decision also met with criticism. Let me quote what Scott said about it later and leave it at that:

"A straight ball from Toshack caught Compton unawares. Compton bent his knees and the ball hit his pads—right in front of the middle stump. I gave Compton out and he did not seem to like it. But Washbrook, who was batting at my end of the wicket, said to me, 'What's the matter? That ball would have hit his middle stump'."

But suppose, as Compton thought, that the ball came in from the leg side?

Hammond opened his innings in the grand manner. He swept Toshack for four to the leg boundary. Then he planted him for three through the covers. But Dooland, bowling with Toshack, gave him a ball which he tried to drive without quite getting to the pitch of it. He drove it hard back to the bowler, who took the catch. One hundred and seventy-six for four. Three runs later Washbrook, playing forward to Dooland, touched the ball to the wicketkeeper. He had added only eight singles to his overnight 54 and had been nearly four hours in the middle.

Yardley, who began with a three, four and two against Dooland, and Ikin added 14 before lunch—193 for five. Ikin had been missed by Barnes—a difficult chance near the end of the bat.

I sympathised with these two batsmen during this series of tests. Too often they had to pull our innings together instead of being able to play their natural game. They had that task now, half an hour before lunch, and very well did they tackle it, staying until nearly teatime and adding 113. Yardley had five lively minutes immediately after the interval—a four and a three in one over from Johnson and a four from Toshack. These runs brought the 200 total, the new ball and the fast bowlers. Ikin, very quiet hitherto, took seven off Miller's opening over. Once Umpire Scott rejected an appeal by Tallon against Yardley. He might have appealed with more effect five minutes later if he had held on to a ball which that batsman appeared to turn to leg off Lindwall.

Our pair seemed happy enough against the fast bowlers and when Toshack replaced Miller Ikin cut him twice for four each time. Dooland came back and there was a loud appeal to Umpire Borwick against Ikin for a catch at the wicket. This, too, was negatived.

Soon there appeared to be a fighting chance of a first innings lead, even though there was not much batting left when this red-and-white-rose partnership was broken. Ikin in particular was batting better than in any previous tests, with more strokes and less scratching. He exemplified again this more confident mood by driving Toshack through the covers for a fine four. Toshack, with figures none for 76, came off for McCool. Off this new bowler Yardley completed his first 50 in a test match. He had one slice of luck when he snicked Dooland uncomfortably near first slip for three runs—a mishit which completed the 100 partnership. Just before tea he was out—bowled in trying to slam McCool round to leg. Two hundred and ninety-two for six, which soon became 298 for seven when Ikin was out too. He swung round to Dooland and hooked him hard, but Miller, fielding in the middle distance, took a good catch above his head.

Voce managed to bat, or rather to make a one-minute attempt at batting. He was l.b.w. to Dooland first ball. Bedser saved the hat-trick and Evans showed signs, as he always did, of being a batsman. Thus far he had played only six innings during the tour in three months. Now he and Bedser added 26 before Evans was bowled by McCool.

Bedser, while not possessing the lissomness of Evans, is by no means negligible with the bat. Now he and the last man, Wright, collected 27 runs. One off-drive in particular from Bedser would have done credit to anyone. This was at Dooland's expense, and when Bradman replaced him with Toshack Bedser added two more specimens of the same sort. Bradman, during the half hour this stand lasted, made several bowling changes. Wright, having entered double figures for the third time during this series, tried to hit Johnson and was bowled. Bedser had made 27 exemplary runs. Our total, 351, was only 14 behind, but how much better it ought to have been.

Voce was again out of the field when Australia began the second innings. In a quarter of an hour Barnes and Morris had scored 21 against Edrich and Bedser, at which stage there was an appeal by Barnes against the light. It was difficult to see why, and the umpires were unsympathetic. Barnes got a touch against Bedser on the leg side at which the agile Evans hopefully dived, but the ball was beyond his reach. In half an hour 33 were on the board at close of play.

FOURTH DAY—MORRIS A CENTURY

Day number four—a Saturday bringing 72,022 people—ended with the Australians 307 ahead, with six wickets in hand, including that of the opener Arthur Morris with 132 to his credit. Obviously the chances of winning this match had become hopeless. The start of the day was not discouraging. True, runs came for a while to Australia in an easy flow, but then Barnes was caught by Evans off a ball from the invaluable Yardley which popped rather high.

Meanwhile Evans's long run of bye-lessness had ended when a ball from Wright on the leg side evaded him and went for four. One thousand and eighty-two runs had been scored in Australian innings since the last bye had happened. These four runs indeed were then the only byes past Evans in his brief test career.

Morris, who combines with as sound a defence as any on earth very strong hitting powers, had been batting freely; he had hit a fresh Bedser for four and three in front of the wicket in the manner of a number five batsman anxious to push the score along.

Yardley, who had taken Barnes's wicket with commendable promptitude with the third ball of his first over, now had Bradman hazy for awhile. Twice Yardley had taken his wicket. Now Bradman produced two faulty strokes off him, one of them an intended drive which went for a single through the slips. Nor did Bradman look happy against Wright, to whom Hammond strengthened his slip field. Bradman when 3 swung round for a hook but missed the ball and the bowler appealed for l.b.w. Later the same over he tried another hook without connecting, then lifted the ball over mid-on for a single. A single to Morris brought Bradman back to face Wright and he hit two twos before being beaten but not bowled by the last ball of an eventful over.

Morris, however, continued confidently enough. Presently he hit the fourth four of his innings and brought up his own 50. Bradman was given a no-ball by Wright which he turned into four runs and at lunchtime Australia—112 for one; Morris 52, Bradman 19— were moving into a winning position.

We learned during the interval that the view of Umpire Scott over the Bradman l.b.w. appeal was that the ball would have gone over the top of the stumps.

After lunch came some more Bradman versus Wright, with Morris and Yardley as frequent interveners on the two sides. Bradman, after that bad half hour of his before the interval, was now playing the Kent man with rather more confidence, though he still could not make very much of him. A quarter of an hour of this duel and Hammond replaced the slower bowlers with Edrich and Bedser—Voce was again absent all day. Against Edrich, Bradman flashed out with two of his old-style hooks for four each in the same over. They were the first strokes of the innings to make us realise that indeed Bradman was batting.

When his score was 44 there came an appeal by Ikin in the gully as the ball sped low past the bat to the wicketkeeper. It was in vain, for Evans did not hold the ball and we never knew whether there was a chance or not. Anyhow, it did not matter, for just when the crowd were ready to acclaim the Don's 50 Yardley took his wicket for the third time running in these tests. This time Bradman came forward to drive him and gave the bowler a catch. Bradman had been batting ninety-nine minutes for his 49—a better innings, despite early uncertainties, than that of three days before. Yardley was now two for 25 and this wicket, like that of Barnes, was taken in the first over of a new spell. At 159 for two the Australians held a lead of 173, with lots of good batting to come. Hassett survived early l.b.w. appeals from the bowling of Wright and of Yardley. After he had scored only 9 in twenty minutes Wright got a well-deserved wicket at last. Hassett was late in trying a cut and was bowled. One hundred and seventy-seven for three now.

Miller, however, became a nuisance to us, though I have known him a much worse one. This time he stayed with Morris for eighty minutes while the total advanced by 65, of which Miller's share was 33. They included seven off Hutton, bowling, immediately before tea, his first over in this series. During this partnership a new ball came along, but Morris and Miller removed the shine from it without misadventure. Half an hour after tea Morris reached his century with an off-drive from Bedser for three. Though it had taken him 265 minutes his innings had been more entertaining than in previous efforts against us. Hooks and drives were his most fruitful strokes—his hooking is especially powerful. There was relatively little from him behind the wicket. Just afterwards he swung round to drive Yardley to leg and Edrich, leaping sideways, just got the tips of his fingers to the ball without being able to hold on.

Again it was Yardley who broke the partnership, aided by a good slip catch from Hammond after Miller had tickled the ball instead of driving it. Morris was then 107 and Yardley's figures were three for 45.

Our fieldsmen were standing up well to their task, with Washbrook prominent as usual at cover. It was quite a relief from monotony when at last he let one through. Wright was having too much running for a bowler at the deep third man position where he usually fields. This side of ours was short of out-fielders and Hammond has been criticised for placing Wright there. The reason is that Wright likes it.

There followed a partnership which, this day and the next, put an end to any lingering hopes we had of snatching victory. The new batsman was McCool and in the fifty minutes before close of play he and Morris took the score from 242 to 293 without being separated. McCool had his early uncertainty. He snicked Bedser through the slips and later put another near enough to Edrich in those regions to make that fieldsman dive optimistically. We badly needed Voce at this stage, for whether he had taken wickets or not he would have been able to share the bowling burden throughout a tiring day. Our four bowlers, Bedser, Edrich, Wright and Yardley, were sadly overworked; Wright bowled twenty-three eight-ball overs that day.

FIFTH DAY—551 TO WIN

This was Lindwall's day—as a batsman. He scored 100 in 109 minutes in a successful effort to leave his side time to win.

In the morning things went well with us. Rain looked likely to interrupt Morris's progress towards his 150. Indeed there was a light shower as the Englishmen, including the injured Voce, took the field, but the only effect of the rain was to make the ball slippery for the bowlers. In half an hour Morris and McCool, playing the right game for their side, scored 35 against Bedser at one end and Edrich and Voce at the other. Morris achieved his 150 after batting six hours for it, but a minute later he tried to turn Bedser to fine leg and was bowled. Three hundred and thirty-three for five. Five minutes later Johnson, usually a very good bat, achieved his pair of spectacles.

He was over-hasty in trying to run the single which would get him off the mark—and Washbrook is the last fieldsman against whom to take risks. Washbrook threw down the wicket promptly without the intervention of Bedser, the bowler. Three hundred and thirty-five for six now. Six runs afterwards McCool snicked a catch off Bedser to the wicketkeeper. Three hundred and fifty-five for seven and Bedser that day two for 24. Voce had bowled four overs for only 8 runs, but it was obvious that he could not let himself go in swinging over for his delivery of the ball.

Now began the Tallon-Lindwall partnership, which yielded 154 in eighty-eight minutes. Soon after they joined forces it became evident that if we were to win we should have to break our fourth innings record in tests against Australia, which is 411. Even the usually economical Yardley had twelve hit off one over. The new ball was treated much as the old one had been, and no one was able to dam the spate of runs. Thirty-seven came off three overs—one each by Yardley, Bedser and Voce, the last two with the new ball. Tallon's 50 came in sixty-five minutes and Lindwall was scoring with similar freedom. The 100 partnership took a mere fifty-eight minutes, the last 50 having been made in twenty minutes. Once Lindwall, hooking Wright, gave Ikin the chance of a picture catch near the ground, but failure to take it was fully excusable. Hutton was again brought on and off him Lindwall took an enormous six to long-on into the rejoicing crowd. Eight runs short of his century, Tallon spooned at last an easy caught and bowled to Wright. His runs, which included ten fours, had taken him 105 minutes.

Lindwall was then 66 and after being joined by Dooland began hitting at everything. He struck three successive balls from Bedser for boundaries, all of them past the bowler. Dooland, trying to hit too, gave Compton a catch in the deep off Wright. At the incoming of an unreliable last partner in Toshack, Lindwall still needed 19 for his hundred. Toshack managed to hang on for a quarter of an hour until the 100 came with another drive by Lindwall over Bedser's head to the screen.

Then Bedser at last took Lindwall's wicket as the batsman tried another grand slam and gave Washbrook a catch. In eighty minutes after lunch the so-called Australian tail had added 151 in eighty minutes. Lindwall, who had scored one previous century in first-class cricket, hit a six and 13 fours. We were faced with the hopeless task in a fourth innings of making 551 to win in just over seven hours.

Fast bowlers as a rule do not make centuries in test matches. I believe Jack Gregory, in the Melbourne test of 1920, was the last before Lindwall. Larwood, at the end of the "bodyline" tour of 1932-3, made 98 in the fifth test at Sydney, and, such are the vagaries of Australian crowds, I believe that everyone there was disappointed when he was caught—by "Dainty" Ironmonger of all fieldsmen—two short of the century.

Our bowling had looked good early that day. Later Edrich, who had eighty-six wicketless runs hit off his bowling, Bedser, three for 176, and Wright, three for 131, suffered heavily. Yardley, three for 67, was the only bowler with a respectable analysis.

A quarter of an hour after taking off his pads Lindwall was opening the Australian bowling against Hutton and Washbrook; he gets his stamina from Rugby League football. Our openers made 18 runs quite happily and there was a pause in the game, heralded by a note sent out to Bradman. The Duke of Gloucester, whose term in Australia as Governor-General was ending, came out on to the field and greeted the two sides. The Duchess accompanied him.

Hutton and Washbrook were not parted in nearly two hours that evening. Washbrook does not usually outstrip his comrade. This time he did, for he scored 60 to 25. He gave McCool a chance at short slip off Dooland—a difficult ball wide to the fieldsman's left hand and shoulder high. The hook was the stroke that mainly kept Washbrook ahead. It was entertaining to watch Bradman's attempts to make him pay the penalty by deepening the net set for Toshack's bowling after Washbrook had planted the ball over the fieldsmen's heads. Twice, in spite of this rearrangement, Washbrook eluded the leg field for more fours. It was these strokes that brought the Lancashire batsman to his 50 while the Yorkshireman was only 19. A six—off Toshack—and 5 fours had helped him to the half-century with extraordinary rapidity for an opening batsman—only 84 minutes. Ninety-one for none at the close was a good start towards that unattainable total.

SIXTH DAY—WE MANAGE TO DRAW

We had hoped to make an honourable draw of the match. In fact we just managed to avoid defeat. For saving the game Norman Yardley and the rain were chiefly responsible. At the end we were 240 runs behind with the wickets of Yardley, Evans, Voce and Wright alone uncaptured. Of the 300 minutes possible for play, rain, which four times stopped cricket for short periods, lost Bradman forty-six minutes in trying to force a win.

Melbourne in its climate will give London a start and a beating for changeability. When play was resumed Hutton was batting in a sweater, although the season was midsummer in a hotter land than ours.

Washbrook again made most of the running. When the score had been taken to 100 he had scored 69 to Hutton's 27. Most of the runs came from Lindwall, the fast bowler, for at the other end McCool opened with four maidens. Bradman again called on Toshack early, probably hoping that Washbrook's liking for the hook would lead him into trouble. To have a chance of winning, Bradman needed to break this troublesome stand before lunch. In three-quarters of an hour five bowlers were tried, and even McCool, who had bowled six overs for five runs, had to come off. Barnes, at his usual position of silly short leg, had a ball from Dooland driven by Washbrook almost down his throat. I often feared for the life of this fieldsman, so close did he stand to the bat: indeed, as now, he sometimes was too close even to sight the ball.

Half an hour before lunch Hutton was out. Trying to hit Toshack over the bowler's head he lifted the ball high, and Bradman, running from deep mid-off, had a comfortable catch. Hutton, for once, had been outshone by his partner. His 40 had taken him three hours—though time scarcely mattered—and when he was out Washbrook was 90.

Edrich, after playing a nice cover-drive for four, nearly shared the fate of Hutton, but the ball fell just short of the hard-running Bradman. Then with a lovely late cut for three Washbrook reached the only century he has scored thus far for his country. It had taken him three and a quarter hours, which is reasonably fast in the circumstances, and had hit eight fours and a six. Edrich stayed only twenty minutes and was then out l.b.w. for the second time in the match. One hundred and sixty-three for two.

Compton, in just before lunch, also had a brief stay. He snicked one four past short slip and off-drove another—in each case against the off-spinning Johnson. At the other end he was lucky not to be stumped off McCool, for when he was out of his ground Tallon appeared to miss the bails as his hand swept forward with the ball. Twenty minutes after the resumption, driving Johnson to deep cover, Compton started for a run which Washbrook refused. Miller's return to Tallon beat his attempt to regain his crease and he was run out. This at a time when runs were of no special value, but wickets and time meant everything. It was a cricketing tragedy. One hundred and eighty-six for three.

With rather more than three hours left for play Hammond arrived. He opened by sweeping McCool to leg for four. But not long afterwards he lost Washbrook, who was beaten while playing forward to Dooland and bowled. Washbrook had been in more than four hours for his 112—easily his best innings in the series.

Now the two Australian leg-spinners, McCool and Dooland, were in full cry—as troublesome as mosquitos in Brisbane. Occasionally Hammond, whom Ikin had joined, showed us strokes, but Ikin, scratching and scraping at the other end, looked likely to get out at any time.

Then the rain took its first hand. Hammond stood his ground as the shower accelerated, as though determined he would not take the initiative of leaving the ground, and it was on Bradman's appeal that everyone scampered off. This interruption lasted only a quarter of an hour. Then Bradman put on his new-ball bowlers, and off Miller Ikin spooned up a simple catch to Hassett at short mid-on. He had not been happy; indeed the chief merit of the innings was that it had lasted thirty-two minutes.

Yardley drove Miller straightway to the boundary and snicked another four high over the slips. At tea, with an hour and three-quarters for play and more clouds gathering, Hammond and Yardley were still there—240 for five, Hammond 22 and Yardley a rapid if rather chancy 17.

Hammond had been batting better than in any previous test except perhaps for his efforts on the rain-soaked wickets of Brisbane. But soon after tea he tried to off-drive Lindwall and was beaten by the pace and bowled. He had been in an hour and a quarter for his 26. Two hundred and forty-nine for six, and an Australian victory more likely than not, for an hour and a half remained. Bedser snicked a four through the slips and then heavy rain came to the rescue.

This interruption also lasted about a quarter of an hour. Then Yardley and Bedser settled down to an hour's partnership which saved the match. Bedser twice off-drove Dooland for fours which Kennington Oval would have rejoiced to see. The stand was twice interrupted near its end by more rain, after which Bedser was l.b.w. to Miller. There was now only a quarter of an hour left, and Evans, shielded as much as possible by Yardley, stayed in until the end for a sturdy nought not out. Yardley, after his streaky start, had batted in exemplary fashion for an hour and a half for a 53 which saved us from crushing defeat.

This was the first test match drawn on the Melbourne ground for 65 years, and only the third draw in test history out there. All these draws have occurred at Melbourne—the two previous ones back in 1881-2. The reason, of course, for the long intervening series of finished games is that Australia has only just emerged from a long period of timeless tests. In England, where we have usually insisted on time limits, twenty-nine tests have been drawn. Better that than the drab monotony of playing everything to a finish.

Barnes hits Edrich, at short leg, the blow on the knee which deprived England of his bowling on the first day of the third Test Match.

Hammond lets off, hitting to leg in the Melbourne Test Match. Fieldsmen: Edrich (left), Evans, Hammond.

Photo: Melbourne Herald.

AUSTRALIA

FIRST INNINGS		SECOND INNINGS	
S. Barnes lbw b Bedser	45	c Evans b Yardley ..	32
A. Morris lbw b Bedser	21	b Bedser	155
D. Bradman b Yardley	79	c and b Yardley ..	49
A. L. Hassett c Hammond b Wright	12	b Wright	9
K. Miller c Evans b Wright ..	33	c Hammond b Yardley	34
I. Johnson lbw b Yardley	0	run out	0
C. McCool not out	104	c Evans b Bedser ..	43
D. Tallon c Evans b Edrich ..	35	c and b Wright ..	92
R. Lindwall b Bedser	9	c Washbrook b Bedser	100
B. Dooland c Hammond b Edrich	19	c Compton b Wright ..	1
E. Toshack c Hutton b Edrich ..	6	not out	2
Extras	2	Extras	19
Total	365	Total ..	536

Fall of wickets: 32, 108, 143, 188, 188, 192, 255, 272, 355, 365.

Fall of wickets: 68, 159, 177, 242, 333, 335, 341, 495, 511, 536.

BOWLING	O.	M.	R.	W.		O.	M.	R.	W.
Voce	10	2	40	0	Voce	6	1	29	0
Bedser	31	4	99	3	Bedser	34.3	4	176	3
Wright	26	2	124	2	Wright	32	3	131	3
Yardley	20	4	50	2	Yardley	20	0	67	3
Edrich	10.3	2	50	3	Edrich	18	1	86	0
Hutton	—	—	—	—	Hutton	3	0	28	0

ENGLAND

FIRST INNINGS		SECOND INNINGS	
L. Hutton c McCool b Lindwall ..	2	c Bradman b Toshack	40
C. Washbrook c Tallon b Dooland	62	b Dooland	112
W. Edrich lbw b Lindwall ..	89	lbw b McCool.. ..	13
D. Compton lbw b Toshack ..	11	run out	14
W. Hammond c and b Dooland ..	9	b Lindwall	26
J. Ikin c Miller b Dooland ..	48	c Hassett b Miller ..	5
N. Yardley b McCool	61	not out	53
T. G. Evans b McCool	17	not out	0
W. Voce lbw b Dooland	0		
A. Bedser not out	27	lbw Miller	25
D. Wright b Johnson	10		
Extras	15	Extras	22
Total	351	Total (7 wkts.) ..	310

Fall of wickets: 8, 155, 167, 176, 179, 292, 298, 298, 324, 351.

Fall of wickets: 138, 163, 186, 197, 221, 249, 294.

K

BOWLING					BOWLING			
	O.	M.	R.	W.		O.	M.	R.	W.
Lindwall	20	1	64	2	Lindwall	16	2	59	1
Miller	10	0	34	0	Miller	11	0	41	2
Toshack	26	5	88	1	Toshack	16	5	39	1
McCool	19	3	53	2	McCool	24	9	41	1
Dooland	27	5	69	4	Dooland	21	1	84	1
Johnson	6.5	1	28	1	Johnson	12	4	24	0

This test match was a fine money spinner. The English share alone was about £15,000 in Australian money, or four-fifths in sterling.

Immediately after the third test the same two umpires, Jack Scott and George Borwick, were reappointed for the fourth at Adelaide, though it was not due until a month later. This was the first time during the series that the umpires had been announced before the Australian team. The inference was obvious—that Hammond had raised no objection. It does not follow that he was in agreement with the decision of Scott in the Edrich or Compton case.

I don't want to labour this distasteful subject, but here is an opinion worth quoting because it is that of an Australian. Writing in the Melbourne *Sporting Globe* during this third test match a well-known cricket writer, Hector de Lacy, said:

"Once again unfortunate umpiring decisions have upset what might be termed the natural outcome of a big cricket game. If this were unique it might be passed over as the natural rub of the game, but since the English tour opened almost every game has been influenced by decisions that were admitted, even by the side receiving the benefit of the decisions, to be wrong.

"Yesterday Bill Edrich was given out leg before wicket to a ball which hit on to his pads. I saw the incident through a pair of binoculars which would make it possible to lip-read what players are saying in the centre. The Compton decision I won't comment on except to say that Compton's every attitude suggested that the ball was pitched outside the leg stump. . . . He made no attempt to play the ball.

"These decisions have again wrecked the whole atmosphere of the Test, coming as they do on others which have been disputed not only by the Englishmen but by Australian players too. . . .

"There is an impulsiveness about Australian umpiring through the length and breadth of the land. In one game the umpire had a finger up for a l.b.w. before an appeal was made.

"Two suggestions have been made: First, that we appoint neutral umpires for tests; secondly, that Australia's young umpires go to England, where they could earn up to £20 a week umpiring in county matches and improve their experience.

"I don't for a minute suggest that Australian umpires are other than impartial. Our present umpires do not get sufficient experience. They have been almost without big cricket for eight years and are rusty.

"Whatever the remedy I would hate to see another test series played under such a cloud of questionings as this has been. Only the good nature of players has prevented serious repercussions."

Such outspokenness from an Australian shows that the so-called "squealing" has not been entirely on our side. At the same time I don't want to over-emphasise the topic. Australia won the tests because she produced better cricketers than we.

CHAPTER XX

RUSH THROUGH TASMANIA

WE spent nine days in Tasmania. On six of them there was cricket, one was a Sunday and one was taken up in travel. So there was not much time to see this beautiful island, one of the loveliest in the world. Norman Yardley, speaking there, said the only trouble about the visit was that it was so short. How right he was. True, a cricket tour is not arranged for players to go sight-seeing; but Tasmania, with its cool climate, very like that of England, would have been a first-class training ground for the Adelaide test match. Instead of taking advantage of it the team's itinerary rushed the men off to Adelaide for a "rest period" of several days, which they had to spend in the stifling heat of a South Australian January. Really the M.C.C. and the Board of Control between them were not very clever in planning this part of the programme.

More attention indeed ought to be paid by planners of long tours to the staleness which always threatens a side after several months of travel and cricket. I have been in Australia with three English sides, and at close quarters with Australian teams on tour in England. Always the players, and for that matter the accompanying writers too, feel the accumulating strain when the tour passes the half-way stage. I firmly believe that the remedy is to allow the party to break up for a week or ten days of individual holiday. Let every man not only stop playing cricket but go away among his friends where-ever he wishes—out of the cricket atmosphere and in different company. There would be no lack of hosts for this holiday. Put up the shutters on cricket for a week and set everyone free.

Cricket executives, with an eye on finance, would reply that while the expenses of the tour would still be mounting the incomings would cease. So they would, but sometimes expense should be allowed to go hang. The tour just over was so lucrative financially that the strain could easily have been borne.

Our cricketers were a happy crowd, with no quarrels, so far as I know, either on or off the field. But it is a strain on good temper to come down to breakfast week after week, month after month, in ships, trains and hotels to "the same old faces." A holiday away from it all is essential. If the programme had been differently arranged the players could have taken it amid the fine mountain and river scenery, the fishing and shooting of Tasmania.

There was time for one official attempt there to give the men a view of something away from a main road. The way back from Hobart, in the south of the island, to Launceston, in the north, was planned to take the party past the Great Lake, which C. B. Fry and myself had visited ten years earlier. But the motor coaches in which the cricketers and press party travelled showed signs of reluctance to carry men and baggage up the hills, and we all beat a retreat to the main road to Launceston, leaving about forty uneaten high teas somewhere on the mountain way.

There were two matches in the island, both of three days, and ranking as first class. The first, on the lovely Hobart ground with its view of the harbour on the one side and Mount Wellington on the other, was against a Combined XI, with the Island players strengthened by four test stars from the other island—Lindsay Hassett, Keith Miller, Sid Barnes and Ian Johnson. As everyone played the game in free holiday spirit Hobart saw cricket as attractive as any on the tour—a good deal more attractive, indeed, than some of the tests.

We won the toss and had our usual batting crisis—four wickets down for 52, the first three of them victims of one Julian Murfett, a fast bowler working in a local tourist office. This is typical of Australian cricket; everywhere one meets competent local players holding even the most eminent opposition in no awe at all. At thirty-one Murfett had done nothing more notable in the game than play for Tasmania, yet here were Gibb, Hardstaff, and Compton falling rapidly before him. Fishlock, with 52, and Edrich 82, were together while 106 were added, of which Edrich made 80. In one period of that partnership Edrich scored 36 while Fishlock, with little of the strike, was making one. At home Fishlock compares well with Edrich in rate of scoring. Here he was feeling his way—the difference between one man who has had an unlucky tour and another who has had a good one.

Later in the innings Bedser made his only 50 of the tour—an affair of a six and six fours. He and Evans put on 70 in fifty-two minutes, and as Wright made a show also at number ten our total mounted to 278. Combined XI replied with 374, including a gay 70 by Miller and a not-out 94 from Gardiner, who went in at number nine and laid about him with Miller and then with Clark. If anyone could have stayed with him Gardiner would have completed, against the English test bowling, his first century in first-class cricket. Yet I was told that his place in the side as wicket-keeper had been in doubt in the selectors' minds.

Our second innings was distinguished by a partnership of 168 between Compton (124) and Hardstaff (60) and though later five wickets fell in a hurry to J. Laver, a leg-spinner, we were able to declare at 353 for nine. Laver, who bowled only four overs and two balls for 26 runs and five wickets, had figures flattered because our later batsmen did not need many runs.

The Tasmanians and their mainland guests, left after lunch on the last day with 258 to make for victory, showed signs of going for the runs by opening with Miller and Hassett, but when these two were out the task became hopeless. Still, with Johnson not out 80 at the close in a score of 145 for two, we had had the worst even of this drawn game at Hobart.

Hammond had not come to Tasmania. Inevitably he came in for some press criticism for his absence—though why any Australian newspaper should concern itself with the matter I cannot think. Certainly no English paper would criticise Bradman if, while captaining an Australian side in England, he decided that he did not want to play cricket in Scotland. Rupert Howard, the manager, asked to reply to this attack, pointed out that Hammond had played in nine out of the last ten matches, including three tests, and needed a holiday.

The Launceston match—against Tasmania unaided—was easier for us. Even so it was drawn, chiefly because rain on the second day limited play to seventy minutes. Our only innings, totalling 467 for five declared, yielded the biggest English partnership of the tour— 282 by Compton and Hardstaff. They thoroughly enjoyed themselves—Compton for three hours in making 163 and Hardstaff for nearly four, while collecting 155, his only century, unhappily, of the tour. Murfett and Laver, bowling successes of the previous match, were both in the nought-for-plenty class this time.

Edrich, Ikin, Voce and Hutton got the Tasmanians out for 103 and their second innings became a rare race between our bowlers and the clock. About two and a quarter hours were left for batting, and twenty-two minutes from the end Tasmania had lost six wickets—four of them to Ikin. But Wilkes and Clark hung on.

Tasmania is a hospitable as well as a beautiful state. I personally have pleasant memories of entertainment by Mr. Gordon Rolph and his family at his beautiful home on Tamar's banks, where Yardley, Edrich, Howard and myself found Mr. "Bob" Menzies, leader of the Commonwealth Liberal Party and an ardent cricket follower, an entertaining fellow guest; and by Mr. Harold Bushby, manager of a former Australian cricket side in England.

We left Launceston on a Saturday, spent that night in a ship on the Bass Straits, the inside of Sunday in Melbourne and the following night in a train—in order to be in Adelaide in good time for a match against South Australia the following Friday. The intervening three days were the cricketers' mid-tour "rest period"— spent, as anticipated, in an oven. I hope that between them the M.C.C. and Board of Control will think of something better next time.

CHAPTER XXI

HAMMOND ONE HUNDRED AND EIGHTY-EIGHT

NEARLY three weeks in Adelaide are well worth the spending, even though the city and its heat are not the best of preparations for a test match. True, Adelaide is not "gay." Lovers of night life will find little enough of it there; drink restrictions seem heavier here than elsewhere, or is it that Adelaide enforces them more severely? But better Adelaide with its primness than Sydney with its sophisticated smartness. It has no harbour, no bridge; its only river, the Torrens, is a mere park ornamental water, which whatever Swinburne may say, does not wind somewhere safe to sea. But Adelaide's street lay-out is far superior to Sydney's rather tortuous and grubby jumble; its parks and gardens are second to none in Australia. Anyhow, as the Yorkshireman said, you "can't live on t'view." There is something about the spirit and temperament of Adelaide that I specially like.

We had three days of swimming at Glenelg and nearby places before cricket began with the return match against South Australia. Almost needless to say, the match resulted in the inevitable draw. Four days were not enough for all the runs the easy wicket was capable of fostering. The match was of some importance as a guide to test prospects. Some of the English and Australian papers had been suggesting that Hammond's crop of runs in the three previous tests—32, 23, 1, 27, 9 and 26—had been so meagre that he might stand down. He had not batted since the Melbourne test; could he regain form?

His answer in the sweltering heat was an innings of 188, his fourth century of the tour and his second in first-class matches. Hutton, with 88, made us feel he was in form for the bigger event and Fishlock brought himself into the reckoning with an innings of 57. But it was the partnership between Hammond and Langridge which built up the total to a massive 577. Together they put on 243 for the sixth wicket and Langridge scored his only hundred of the tour.

He is an unlucky player. In the search for all-rounders the selectors had turned their minds in his direction. It was hoped he would make some runs and keep an end going economically when required to bowl. But during fielding practice he had strained a groin muscle, which had put him out of the Tasmanian matches.

He ought not to have played at Adelaide, but, keen to win at forty his first appearance in an England versus Australia test match, he took the risk for the sake of practice.

It was evident during his long innings that he could hardly run, and when, next day, he tried to bowl he broke down and had to leave the field after only one over. The injury was worse than ever, and he did not play again for the rest of the tour.

South Australia, apart from Dooland, is not a strong bowling state, so the huge total may have been rather illusory. All the same it was warming to the heart to see our men really piling on the runs at last against a Sheffield Shield side.

Our innings extended to the morning of the third day, and the South Australians, despite the loss of Bradman for 5, were able to make a comfortable draw without having to follow on. Ron Hamence won his place against us in the fifth test by playing one of the loveliest innings of the whole tour. Nearly every one of his 145 runs was supremely worth watching. Ridings and James, less graceful and free but equally stubborn, played big parts, too, in the total of 443. The rest of the match became merely batting practice for Hutton, Hardstaff and Fishlock, for there was no chance of a result.

Remember Hamence. If he does not delight you next summer in England I shall be astonished.

By the way, Hardstaff in the latter part of the Australian innings, had one of his rare spells of bowling and took three wickets for 24, probably turning Paul Gibb green with envy.

One entertaining question of umpiring practice arose during this match. Paul Gibb and Umpire Scott, of the tests, were the principals. Gibb had gone out to field as twelfth man instead of the injured Langridge. As he wears glasses he took with him a cap for use in fielding against the sun. Finding himself on the shady side of the ground, he tried to hand his cap to Scott, who refused to take it.

Gibb, rather flummoxed, retired to the outfield cap in hand and placed it on the grass in front of him. Here he came under the jurisdiction of the other umpire, who warned him that "you can't do that there here"—or its equivalent. Hammond briefly joined in the discussion. So Paul, very much the centre of the picture, stuffed the cap into his trousers pocket and went on fielding.

There is nothing in the rules of cricket to compel an umpire to be a clothes horse, but there is a well-recognised practice. When I thought of the two or three sweaters with which an English umpire burdens himself on a chilly day I wondered at the fuss over one cap. Scott at the time was carrying the bowler's cap during alternate overs—and that appeared to be all. One cap more would not have hurt him.

Scott told me at the first interval that if everyone brought caps on to the field for him to carry his pockets would be crammed over-full. We were informed a little later that player and umpire had talked things over in the dressing-room and the whole incident was closed. We gathered that they were now as David and Jonathan. But which had given way we never ascertained, for Gibb returned to the field capless.

Incidentally another umpire of long experience told me that he would never have told a fieldsman to pick the cap up; instead he would have awarded five penalty runs to the batting side if the ball had hit it. There is no law covering the contingency specifically, but the umpires are the "sole judges of fair and unfair play." So I suppose the "pick it up" request was in order. What a silly storm in a teacup.

CHAPTER XXII

FOURTH TEST

N o w to the fourth test, in many ways the most interesting of the five. First we thought it would be known evermore as "Lindwall's match," for he took three wickets in four balls; then "Compton's match," for in scoring two centuries he saved us from defeat. Finally Morris, with exactly the same very rare feat, claimed a share in the label for posterity.

The match, for a change uninterrupted by rain, was played throughout in the hottest spell of weather we struck during the tour. It is important to remember this, for heat in Australia plays quite a part in cricket. Bowling and fielding all day in such conditions are a tremendous strain even on the home side. Adelaiders told us that, while they often had higher temperatures than the 100 degrees then prevailing, they seldom had the humidity as well. All those six days we were walking waterfalls.

FIRST DAY—GOOD IN PARTS

It was grateful and comforting, then, to win the toss that last day of January, when you in England were beginning the record freeze. We had a satisfactory morning and afternoon, but an unhappy evening—the outcome of it all being a slow harvest of 239 runs for four wickets. At lunch we were 58 for none: at tea 149 for one—Washbrook being out a quarter of an hour before that interval—and then came the loss of the wickets of Edrich, Hutton and Hammond for inadequate additions to the total. The work of the six Australian bowlers—Lindwall, Miller, Toshack, McCool, Johnson, Dooland—was uniformly good, for the wicket was made for runs.

England played a batsman instead of a bowler by including Hardstaff—playing his first test of the series—instead of Voce. The change threw practically all the bowling on to Bedser, Edrich, Wright and Yardley. Australia were without Barnes, who had been attacked by that enemy of cricketers, fibrositis, which years ago we used to call backache. In his place Mervyn Harvey, of the six cricketing brothers of Melbourne, became the opening bat. The bowling was unchanged.

Hutton and Washbrook provided the sort of opening one expects in any well-conducted test—14 runs in the first half-hour. Once Hutton drove Miller in front of the wicket for four; Washbrook, trying to hook the same bowler, had the breath knocked out of his body. We had in use the newly designed stumps, the bails sitting on a domed top to ensure that they fall if hit: happily they were not put to the proof.

Lindwall, Miller, Toshack, McCool were all tried without result before lunch. There were what the weather people call bright intervals, during one of which 8 runs came off the swarthy left-hander, Toshack, in one over. But in the main the cricket was as dour as the score indicates. This time our two openers were running neck and neck. Doubts had been cast of late at Hutton's ability to play fast bowling. That morning there seemed no reason to doubt.

After lunch Umpire Scott said no to a whole-hearted appeal against Washbrook with Lindwall bowling. The running between wickets was not always of the safest, and once Washbrook must have only just been in when Bradman shied at the wicket from cover and broke it. The scoring was no faster than in the morning; only now and then came a full-out shot such as Washbrook achieved in driving McCool to the off-boundary. Hutton now was rather the faster scorer, and when he reached his 50 in just over two hours his partner was only 38.

Hutton and Washbrook reached their hundred partnership that day after 133 minutes' batting they had done it for the second time running. No Australian pair had achieved the feat at all, though Morris and Harvey were to follow suit in this match and Morris and Barnes in the fifth test.

Washbrook's 50 came ten minutes after Hutton's, although his boundaries numbered five to two. Thereafter a race developed between them. Washbrook caught his partner at 62 each, but McCool gave Hutton a long hop which enabled the Yorkshireman to lead again. Dooland, who had bowled eight excellent overs for 20 runs, at last broke the partnership when Washbrook, trying to drive him, edged the ball to the wicketkeeper. One hundred and thirty-seven for one—one short of the Melbourne stand by the same partners. Washbrook had batted three hours—an innings not quite as interesting as Hutton's, but foursquare as his own sturdy figure, rather reminiscent of Maurice Leyland's years ago. Edrich made four runs before tea and all seemed set fair for us.

So it still seemed immediately after tea, for Edrich, looking thoroughly happy, twice drove Dooland for four, Then, in trying to do so again, he was caught and bowled way out to the off-side. One hundred and seventy-three for two. Hammond, greeted by 23,746 people as though he were Bradman himself, took three through the slips off the first ball from Dooland.

Half an hour after Edrich was out Hutton fell, when six short of his century. Bradman had brought on McCool for Dooland, chiefly, I expect, because Hammond does not like him. Pushing forward to the new bowler Hutton missed and was l.b.w. One hundred and ninety-six for three. Hutton had played his best as well as his highest innings thus far this series. He had been safe all through, and had shown that fluency of stroke we admire at home. He had batted nearly four hours. Hutton's previous best in these tests was 40. He had shown his liking for the Adelaide Oval by successive scores of 136, 88, 77 not out and now 94.

Compton next. The stroke with which Hammond brought up the 200 was a hook off McCool which sailed so quickly past Lindwall that he had not time to raise his hands for a catch. But with the total —202—unaltered, Hammond, playing forward to Toshack, was beaten and bowled. This total was very moderate on such a perfect wicket.

On Compton and a not-very-safe-looking Hardstaff the task of pulling the innings together depended. The batting was thrown on the defensive apart from an occasional smite at a loose ball, such as boundaries by Hardstaff off McCool and Dooland and by Compton off Johnson.

Bradman changes his bowling more frequently than Hammond, for the good reason that he has more bowling to change. He rang the changes often that evening, but Hardstaff improved and Compton, while not his audacious self, was competent. The pair stayed until the end—239 for four.

SECOND DAY—BRADMAN A DUCK

Our innings was completed for 460—not quite good enough— and the Australians lost two wickets, including that of Bradman, for a duck, for 24 runs.

When play was resumed Bradman could have had the new ball to play with immediately. He preferred to give McCool a couple more overs. In the first of them Hardstaff swatted hard at one ball without hitting it, but for the rest the batsmen played him well enough. So the new ball arrived and Lindwall and Miller pounded it down under a sun hotter than that of the previous day. Hardstaff, who has practised much at the nets with Larwood and Voce, was happier against the fast than the slow stuff, and turned Miller prettily to leg for four. In half an hour 26 runs came. There followed a quarter of an hour with only one single against Johnson, who had succeeded Miller. That superb fieldsman Lindsay Hassett must have saved four boundaries at least at extra cover to Johnson, but at last Compton found a way past him. When Hardstaff reached

50 by gently persuading a ball between the umpire's legs he had been batting two hours all but nine minutes. Compton for once had been outstripped: he had been in twenty-three minutes longer for 34.

Ten minutes before lunch the 100 partnership was completed and at the break the total was 308 for four—Hardstaff 63, Compton 43.

Compton—resuming his innings clad in a "lucky shirt" whose tear down the back Hardstaff playfully extended—hooked Miller for a four which was the most Compton-like stroke yet made. His 50 had taken him two and a half hours. At 118 Hardstaff attempted to hook Miller too, and played the ball hard down on to his stumps. His 67, scored out of 118 in two and a half hours, justified his place in the side.

Ikin, coming in for once with a fair score in the book, took two rapid fours off Johnson, and as Compton became faster this partnership became the liveliest thus far of the innings. Ikin added a third boundary and Compton two others and in forty-five minutes the pair added 61. Then Ikin, trying to drive Dooland, was caught at mid-off by Toshack. Three hundred and eighty-one for six.

Toshack soon appealed vociferously against Yardley and did not look too pleased when the verdict went against him. It took Compton twenty minutes to advance from 90 to 100, and once Yardley sent him back at 99 when he started a chancy single. At last a two off Toshack brought him to his first century of the series, his previous best being his 54 at Sydney. He had taken his time—four hours all but eight minutes—and had mixed a strong dose of prudence into that engagingly eager temperament.

The Australians were facing their own hot sun with their faces daubed by an anti-sunburn mixture. That sun was still strong after tea, when Compton, with Yardley as a reliable partner, let himself go a little. They added 61 together, of which Yardley's share was 17. Frequently now Compton came out boldly to the slow bowlers almost in R. W. V. Robins manner. Once, running out to drive Dooland, he found the length unsuitable and changed the stroke into a saucy cut for two, plus an overthrow. In the half-hour after tea he kept up a run a minute rate while Yardley was scoring 8.

It was too good to last. Just before five o'clock Lindwall came on in preparation for the new ball. His first ball was fatal to Compton, who played forward to it and gave Lindwall an easy caught and bowled. Compton had been in for four and three-quarter hours and his innings was a mixture of early ca' canny and late aggression. Towards the stand of 74 for this wicket Yardley had made 17.

With Bedser in play was interrupted for a minute by a cat which wandered out from the fence and amused the crowd. From then on Yardley could find no one to stay with him. Bedser and Evans were bowled by successive balls from Lindwall, showing so much speed that the batsmen mistimed him. Wright, the last man in, nearly completed the hat trick, for he tried to touch his first ball without quite succeeding. Next ball he was bowled neck and crop. Lindwall had ended the innings with four wickets for 2 runs, the last three of them in four balls.

Far out where the ball had trickled there developed a struggle among Australian fieldsmen for its possession. Miller and Johnson were nearest, and Miller brought down his comrade with a Rugby tackle while the crowd laughed. But Johnson kept possession. The ball in any case was destined to go to the bowler, who received it, inscribed with the details of his performance, from the South Australian Cricket Association, together with a watch.

Four hundred and sixty was not a high enough total on such a wicket. The collapse of our tail immediately Compton left was disappointing, for Yardley looked well able to make runs. The seventh wicket had fallen at 455; the last three all five runs later.

Australia that day had half an hour's batting. In it things happened. With only 18 scored Bedser bowled Harvey, and then, without addition to the score, Bradman. This happened during nine balls and his figures at that moment were two for 9 in four overs. One wondered whether, after all, Lindwall, had done his side good service by causing them to bat that evening.

Bradman was not happy during the eight balls he played from Bedser in two overs. To judge from the way he shaped at the ball which bowled him, it was an inswinger. It beat the bat as he played late. Despite the enormous innings Bradman has achieved in tests he is no stranger to ducks. Bowes bowled him first ball in the 1932-3 series and he had two more during the tour captained by G. O. Allen four years later.

THIRD DAY—TOIL AND TRIBULATION

Not until four-thirty that evening of a hot and humid day did another Australian wicket fall. Then Hassett was out after helping Morris to take the score from the overnight 24 to 207. Morris, too, was out before the end of the day, but Australia, with 293 for four and lots of good batting to come, were then in a strong position— only 167 behind.

The only Englishman who braved the sun hatless in the field that morning was Hardstaff; half a dozen of our men were in white wideawakes. Bedser and Wright were the opening bowlers to Morris and Hassett. Against them 28 runs came in the first half-hour, including a four and a three cover-driven by Morris off successive balls from Wright and later a hook for four by the same batsman off the same bowler. Edrich for Wright was the first change. Bedser needed careful watching, one over he bowled to Hassett being specially full of problems.

Bedser bowled five overs for 11 runs, but the wicket would not come and Hammond tried Wright at that end. Edrich was sending them down still from the other with fair economy but no success. Wright gave Morris a no-ball which the left-hander converted to six runs over the fence beyond mid-on.

Yardley for Edrich, but nothing happened. Bedser tried again before lunch and Morris, after remaining with his score 42 for a full quarter of an hour, advanced three runs further at last before the break—Australia 84 for two, Morris 45, Hassett 22. Sixty runs in an hour and a half.

A few drops of thundery rain fell during lunch without delaying the cricket. Soon Morris had his 50, scored in the leisurely time of two hours and twenty minutes. A strange cricketer this left-hand opening bat, whom you will no doubt see in England next summer. He has long spells of complete quietude with balls that could yield runs; then he gets in a tremendous clout, for no one can hit harder than he at times.

At the other end Hassett was playing another innings of un-Hassett-like cageiness. I have a theory that test cricket is often better to read or hear than to see. It was so then.

Hammond changed the bowling often, but the only false stroke one saw in hours was a snick through the slips, Morris off Edrich, and even that was safe enough. Wright gave Morris another of the no-balls of which some of our bowlers were guilty and the batsman turned it into a six. Just before tea Morris reached his hundred in 217 minutes, with two sixes and nine fours. Tea 181 for two, Morris 101, Hassett 62. As was to be expected, there had been a better scoring rate against tiring bowlers—97 in this hour and a half between meals.

Hassett, when 62, won the race for the first 1,000 runs out there that season in first-class cricket. He beat Miller, 998, on the post. Compton, Hutton and Bradman were close behind.

After tea the 200 came up as Morris hit Yardley hard to the boundary, and Hassett treated Wright similarly. We hardly expected a wicket to fall all day, but at four-forty, Hassett touched a leg-break from Wright to Hammond in the slips. Hassett had been in three hours, forty minutes for his 78 towards a partnership of 189 with Morris.

A quarter of an hour later Morris, whom Miller had joined, was out too. Bedser had come on for the new ball, without as yet having taken it. Morris played back to him and gave Evans a catch.

Three hundred and twenty-two now for four after Morris had batted for nearly four and a half hours for his 122. Two sixes, twelve fours. After these two quick wickets there was renewed eagerness about our fieldsmen, though they had stuck it well all that torrid day.

Ian Johnson, however, proceeded to show that that double duck of his at Melbourne was too bad to be true. He got rather nervously off the mark with a single, then pulled a ball high into the air near the square-leg umpire. Edrich running hard did all he knew to make a catch one-handed with the sun in his eyes.

Miller, big and buoyant, who is no pleasant batsman to have in opposition at five-thirty of a hot January day in Adelaide, leaned forward and smacked a tiring Bedser heartily through the covers for four. Another no-ball went for a boundary to Johnson. For this last half-hour, indeed, the batsmen took their toll of the tired bowling. One over from Wright yielded 14. The moral of it all was that three front line bowlers were not enough.

No-balls cost us many runs that day. Seven were called against Wright and five against Bedser. They cost thirty-one runs from the bat, including three sixes, plus four down in the analysis as extras.

FOURTH DAY—STILL ANYBODY'S GAME

Here was a day's cricket indeed. Hutton and Washbrook on our side, Miller on theirs, made it memorable. By teatime Australia's innings of 293 for four overnight had been increased to 487—a lead of 27. At close of play we had replied with 96 for no wicket.

Into the inclined plane of feminine bright summer dress there soared a six off the opening ball of the day. It was hooked by Miller off Wright, whose dragging foot had again brought a no-ball call from the umpire. This was the fourth six hit from no-balls in two days. Miller, on the look out for runs, took a three and a four from Edrich that sent up his 50. He is a joy to watch, this Miller, with his full swinging bat and hard-hit drives. He exudes personality. Three overs from Wright brought 18 runs. He came off for Bedser and Yardley replaced Edrich, so we had four bowlers deployed in half an hour.

Miller in this mood does not mind much who bowls against him. He hit Bedser for a soaring four past mid-on, and 20 came off this bowler in two overs. In the first forty minutes Miller had scored 51 and Johnson 11.

The 100 and the 150 partnership sped by like telegraph poles alongside a railway line. Then Johnson, having just passed his 50, was out. Wright, returning for Bedser, had him l.b.w. as he missed a hook. He and Miller had added 150 altogether in 118 minutes, but that day they had been faster—79 in fifty-five minutes.

A quarter of an hour later—with McCool now in—Miller, tossing his long hair back from his brow in a familiar gesture, tapped a single off Yardley which completed his 100. It had taken him no more than 150 minutes, with a six and five fours. Miller's 67 that day had been scored in seventy minutes.

I mentioned after Lindwall's century at Melbourne that he was the only fast bowler to distinguish himself thus with the bat since Jack Gregory's time. Well, Miller is undeniably fast; but he is more bat than bowler.

McCool did not stay. After taking twenty minutes for two he gave Bedser a very well-taken snap catch close in at forward short-leg off Yardley. Three hundred and eighty-nine for six, or 71 behind. At lunchtime 396 without further loss, Miller 104, Tallon 3.

After lunch we were reduced to three bowlers by the absence of Bedser, whom stomach trouble kept in the pavilion. Fishlock fielded for him. Even so we had success with the first ball. Tallon, usually a stylish bat, was bowled by Wright in attempting a very unstylish hit. Miller just afterwards hit Yardley hard past Fishlock at short-leg. The ball sped by shoulder high and apparently in reach, but the fieldsman was beaten by the pace.

Lindwall stayed with a much quieter Miller for half an hour and 27 runs before he was caught at the wicket off Yardley. Four hundred and thirty-seven for eight, and a tussle ahead for first innings lead. With Dooland in there was one exciting over from Wright during which Miller hit a four and two twos and was missed by Edrich far out behind the bowler. Edrich appeared to have made the catch after running under the ball, but he tripped, fell and failed to hold on.

Dooland, a much better bat than most number tens, defended stoutly whenever he had a chance to take the bowling and now and then made a good stroke.

Bedser had returned to the field when Dooland came in. Now he bowled a good over with the new ball to Dooland, who survived an l.b.w. appeal off Edrich at the other end. This partnership of 63 took the Australian total past ours. Then Bedser duplicated against Dooland the catch he had made at McCool's expense.

Toshack, the last man, was cheered for every ball he stopped. When Wright bowled to Miller he set a far-flung field—six men close on the fence. Miller, trying a grand slam, might have been stumped. It did not matter much, for a straight throw by Edrich at mid-off ran out Toshack when he and Miller were trying to turn a single into a two. The total was 487, a lead of 27. Miller, the best of whose innings had been played in the morning, had been batting six and a half hours for his 141 not out. His earlier display

L

was almost the finest exhibition of forcing batsmanship seen during the tour.

There was a peal of thunder as Hutton and Washbrook walked to the wicket after tea in a dull light; obviously someone was "catching it" somewhere, but despite zigzags of lightning the storm almost passed by Adelaide Oval.

Before Washbrook had even taken strike Hutton had scored 12; when Washbrook had received only one ball the Yorkshireman was 20. This is how it came about. Off the first over from Lindwall Hutton took a two and a single. Then he hit Miller for two fours and another single. The last ball of this over fell to Washbrook who stopped it. Then a twenty minutes fall of rain and—under a rainbow—Lindwall bowled to Hutton again. There were in this over two twos and a four. Twenty runs in all to Hutton, after which Washbrook at last scored a single.

In seventeen minutes' batting these two cleared off the arrears as though it were no trouble at all. Washbrook, like Hutton, treated Lindwall rough, first with a four hooked and then with a six hit to leg which carried past the fieldsman.

This became an odd race between our opening pair. After Toshack had come on for Miller, Washbrook scored 20 to Hutton's 2. Fifty were up in thirty-six minutes, Hutton 29, Washbrook 24.

This certainly was the sort of cricket any crowd likes. After Lindwall had yielded 37 Miller took over his end, the other being in the hands first of Toshack and then Dooland, who beat Washbrook without bowling him. Hutton reached his 50 in fifty-seven minutes, his partner then being 33.

The pace bowlers were presently superseded altogether by Toshack and Dooland and the scoring waned. Indeed, there was one period of ten minutes without runs. McCool had one over at the end of the day, when the total was 96, scored in eighty-two minutes—an arresting performance.

FIFTH DAY—IN TROUBLE AGAIN

Taking the narrow view, the outstanding feature of the last day but one of the match was the masterly nought not out by Godfrey Evans in the last three-quarters of an hour of the evening. Taking the broad one, let us note with regret that another English batting failure made such stone-walling necessary. At the day's end we were 274 for eight—or 247 runs ahead. All too little for forcing the hoped-for victory. Once again the game had gone Australia's way.

In the morning Hutton and Washbrook stayed together just long enough to equal a record. By scoring another 100 together they followed the precedent of Hobbs and Sutcliffe, in 1924 at Sydney, in making a century partnership in both innings of a test match. Moreover our opening pair had already put on a hundred together at Melbourne—thrice in a row, which is what Hobbs and Sutcliffe also did.

Two balls after the three figures had gone up the umpire's hand also went up after an appeal for a catch at the wicket against Washbrook by Tallon off Lindwall. This opening stand had taken no more than eighty-seven minutes.

Edrich though hitting powerfully—as bowler Johnson once realised when he took a ball on the chest—found extreme difficulty in evading the field set by Bradman. But he did get through the ring to the screen two fours from this bowler. He scored 21 towards a partnership of 37 with Hutton in fifty minutes. Then Hutton, playing back to an off-break from Johnson, was bowled, which made the total two for 137. No more was seen that day of the overnight fireworks which Hutton had given us, but so much was he at home that we had regarded a century from him as inevitable.

Hammond, like Edrich, found the field set so well that he was denied anything more than singles and twos until a piece of misfielding by Johnson near the boundary gave him his first four for an on-drive. Both Hammond and Edrich looked so well set that one regretted the luncheon break, taken with the score 164 for two, Edrich 33, Hammond 16.

I heard during lunch that Washbrook admittedly did hit the ball off which he was given out. Umpire Borwick had to decide whether it went straight to the wicket-keeper or bounced off the ground. During the interval Mr. R. G. Menzies, the Liberal Leader, told me that "it is a part of the eternal justice of things that Walter Hammond should play at least one great innings every test series." Unhappily it did not happen now.

Edrich turned his attenton after lunch to Johnson, slamming him for two fours, a two and a single in one over. But, trying to treat Toshack similarly, he skied a ball deep to mid-on and was caught by Bradman. He had batted an hour and a half for his 46. One hundred and seventy-eight for three.

Eleven runs later Hammond was out. He tried an all-out hit to leg off Toshack. Lindwall, waiting in the middle distance, brought off a high-speed catch. One hundred and eighty-nine for four, and two newly arrived batsmen, Compton and Hardstaff, trying to play themselves in. They had made 118 together in the first innings. Now they did not look capable of collecting the odd 18, so rocky did Hardstaff appear. Nor was Compton very contented at that stage and both were thrown on the defensive.

Hardstaff was there thirty-five minutes for 9 of the 19 added for the wicket. Then he leaned forward defensively to Toshack and played the ball on to his wicket. Two hundred and seven for five.

Ikin next, stopping a maiden over from Toshack and another from Johnson before scoring his only run. Then he played forward to Toshack and was l.b.w. So to-day Toshack was four for 30.

When Yardley faced this bowler he found two short-legs sitting almost on his bat and two others rather further removed. He pierced the ring for a quick four, and Compton treated a no-ball similarly.

In the hour and three-quarters between lunch and tea four of our wickets had gone and the chance of winning the match had gone too.

Toshack, continuing his long effort after tea, bowled in all twenty-one overs unchanged. But it was Lindwall, coming on just before the new ball was taken, who broke up the Compton—Yardley partnership of 35. With his first ball Lindwall had Yardley caught at the wicket.

Bedser came in with the obvious intention to play safe and let Compton have his head. This time, however, he did not last long: indeed Bedser is a better bat when going all out for what runs he can collect. Now he scored a single and a two before being caught at the wicket off Miller. Two hundred and fifty-five for eight.

This brought in Evans and the beginning of an astonishing partnership with Compton, who did all he knew to "farm" the bowling. After a preliminary consultation between the batsmen Compton proceeded to take three-quarters of it, though what balls did come his way Evans played very well. Two or three times he might have got off the mark, but refrained for tactical reasons. Evans might have been run out in scampering an end-of-the-over single, but Bradman fumbled the ball for his throw-in.

Once when a run was refused for a stroke which nearly hit the fence Bradman ironically trickled the ball gently back to the wicket-keeper along the grass. Perhaps he had forgotten that Australian batsmen have in their day adopted similar tactics.

Compton reached a 50 which had taken him more than three hours. All that three-quarters of an hour in the evening Evans held on—and there was more resistance coming on the morrow. In that time only 19 had been added, so that even Compton was hardly swift.

SIXTH DAY—ENGLAND DECLARE

A declaration by England, even of the nominal sort, was the last event we thought of that morning of the last day of the fourth test. Yet it happened, for the only time in the series. True, there did not seem the slightest hope of forcing a win, unless the Australians became reckless after runs.

Evans stayed on with Compton all morning and for one ball after lunch. Then Hammond called his batsmen in with the score 340 for eight, Compton 103 not out, Evans 10 not out. The Australians, set the task of making 314 in three and a quarter hours, scored 215 for one, Morris and Bradman not out respectively 124 and 56. So the match was drawn, greatly in Australia's favour.

The final day's play took place in the stickiest heat Adelaide has known for years. Even to watch was to swelter as one does in the Red Sea.

Compton was still taking all the bowling he could corner, but more of the strike fell to the Kent wicket-keeper that day than the previous evening. Early he played out a maiden over from Toshack as competently as Compton himself.

Until the last two balls of the over, when he closed his men in to prevent singles, Bradman set mainly a defensive field to Compton, designed to allow ones but cut off fours and twos. It was fun to watch the sneaking of these end-of-the-over singles, whose running was often a breath-taking scamper.

Bradman began with Toshack and Dooland, changed to McCool and Lindwall. Evans continued his runless record; even when Compton was taking strike scoring was not rapid. But in one over from Dooland he took a two, a four and a single, which was followed by what appeared to be a missed stumping chance as Evans played the last ball of the over.

In half an hour 15 had been added—Evans still nought not out. Presently we really thought he had scored when a ball from Dooland ballooned above McCool's head and passed through the slips for a two. But the umpire signalled leg-byes. Compton, running four exhausting runs at full speed for a leg hit, and following this stroke with a snick for another four, brought up the 300.

Then at last, Evans, after fifty-one minutes batting that day and ninety-five altogether, broke his distinguished duck—and I felt sorry it happened, for it destroyed the quaintness of his effort. The stroke was a two to leg off Lindwall. There were all sorts of fun and games now. Once Compton, dancing down wicket to Lindwall, of all bowlers, bent on a strategic single, turned the ball adroitly through the slips. Denis told me afterwards that he has adopted this way of running out to a fast bowler now and then because the bowler "never knows what is coming." I can well believe it.

Once he had become a scorer Evans continued to take a run or two and he had one boundary off Toshack through the slips. Compton treated Dooland to two off-driven fours in one over, though it looked as though the second of them was an over-hit

attempt at a strategic single. A third drive of the same sort brought
Compton to his 100 just before lunch. He had taken 274 minutes
for it, while that of Morris the same day was compressed into
125. But Compton's innings was played in entirely different circumstances. Moreover he would have been quicker to his hundred
if he had not been so keen on farming the bowling. He must have
sacrificed twenty runs or more in taking singles instead of twos,
and sometimes refusing to run at all. This innings, played all against
his own eager temperament, will always be a memorable one in
his career.

Before Compton—and later the same day Morris—only three
men had scored a century in each innings of an England versus
Australia test match. They were Warren Bardsley, Herbert Sutcliffe
and Walter Hammond.

I had always urged the claims of Evans to real batsmanship.
Records of the sport are hard to trace, but I believe that his score-
less ninety-five minutes was a record. Warwick Armstrong recalled
to me that the late Charles Kelleway, in the 1921 series, batted
seventy minutes with him before getting off the mark, even though
he was keen to do so.

One ball was played by Evans after lunch, and then the innings
was closed. The manœuvre gave the Australians a quarter of an
hour less for going for victory.

During their stand of 133 minutes for 85, of which Evans scored
10, Evans received ninety-seven balls to Compton's 179.

To make the runs the Australians had to score at the high
though not impossible rate of ninety-seven an hour. Opening batsmen
can hardly begin at such a rate; yet Morris showed some signs
that the task would be attempted. In half an hour he and Harvey
had 30, towards which Harvey made a modest 7; the 50, too, was
up in even time. But much better than this was now needed. Bedser
and Edrich had opened our bowling; they were followed by
Wright—who while setting his field was treated to impatient cries
from the crowd—and Yardley. Despite four swept to leg off Wright,
the total in an hour was only 61—36 short of requirements. If
Harvey could have kept pace with Morris there would have been
a real contest between players and clock. Morris at the tea interval
had scored 68 to 30 and the total was 99 for none.

In ten minutes after tea, Morris, to the bowling of Bedser and
Yardley, put on 16 to Harvey's one. He hit Yardley for two fours
in one over—an event that does not often happen.

At 116 the first wicket—English or Australian—to fall that day
became Yardley's. Harvey, trying to hit him to leg, turned the ball
into his stumps.

Our fieldsmen, as usual, concentrated on trying to prevent
Bradman from tapping his first single. He played a few balls quietly

from Bedser: then drove him for three to long-on. Soon afterwards Morris reached his second century of the match. It was indeed strange that a feat accomplished only thrice before in the history of test matches between England and Australia should now have happened twice in one match.

An hour before the end 147 were still needed. Bradman completed his 50 in an hour, but the Australians were still 99 runs short of winning at the close. When the last ball was bowled there was the usual souvenir scramble. Bradman secured a stump and tossed the ball to Bedser, who in the first innings had bowled him for a duck.

That test match cost the South Australian Cricket Association three new wrist watches—that already mentioned as having gone to Lindwall and others to Compton and Morris. Compton received his on the station platform as the M.C.C. party were embarking for Ballarat. My Adelaide colleague and friend Harry Kneebone commented on "Australia's uninspiring refusal to pick up the gauntlet which Hammond had thrown down by declaring the English innings closed. No attempt was made to score the 314 runs required and turn the ultimate tame finish into a thrilling climax."

I will not say "No attempt," for Morris showed signs during his innings of much greater hurry than he usually displays as an opener. But I think that instead of Harvey, playing in his first test match, Bradman might have risked the wicket of Miller, with Lindwall to follow. There was abundant batting to put up the shutters if the hitters had fallen.

The gross gate was a record for an Adelaide test, but this was due to increased charges rather than record attendance. Here is a comparison:

				£
1946-7	..	135,980	..	18,117
1936-7	..	172,016	..	17,495
1932-3	..	174,452	..	16,241
1928-9	..	134,894	..	12,491

The two middle attendances, much greater than the others, were attracted when the issue of the rubber was still open, which has led to feeling in Adelaide that the third test rather than the fourth ought to be allotted to South Australia.

This drawn game meant that we had lost all chance even of drawing the rubber.

ENGLAND

FIRST INNINGS		SECOND INNINGS	
L. Hutton lbw b McCool	94	b Johnson	76
C. Washbrook c Tallon b Dooland	65	c Tallon b Lindwall ..	39
W. Edrich c and b Dooland ..	17	c Bradman b Toshack	46
W. R. Hammond b Toshack ..	18	c Lindwall b Toshack	22
D. Compton, c and b Lindwall ..	147	not out	103
J. Hardstaff b Miller	67	b Toshack	9
J. Ikin c Toshack b Dooland ..	21	lbw b Toshack ..	1
N. Yardley not out	18	c Tallon b Lindwall ..	18
A. Bedser b Lindwall	2	c Tallon b Miller ..	3
G. Evans b Lindwall	0	not out	10
D. Wright b Lindwall	0		
Extras	11	Extras	13
Total	460	Total (8 wickets dec.)	340

Fall of wickets: 137, 173, 196, 202, 320, 381, 455, 460, 460, 460.

Fall of wickets: 100, 137, 178, 188, 207, 215, 250, 255.

BOWLING	O.	M.	R.	W.	BOWLING	O.	M.	R.	W.
Lindwall	23	5	52	4	Lindwall	17.1	4	60	2
Miller	16	0	45	1	Miller	11	0	34	1
Toshack	30	13	59	1	Toshack	36	6	76	4
McCool	29	1	91	1	McCool	19	3	41	0
Johnson	22	3	69	0	Johnson	25	8	51	1
Dooland	33	1	133	3	Dooland	17	2	65	0

Miller bowled 2 wides.

AUSTRALIA

FIRST INNINGS			SECOND INNINGS		
M. Harvey b Bedser	..	..	12	b Yardley	..	..	31
A. Morris c Evans b Bedser	..	122	not out	..	..	124
D. G. Bradman b Bedser ..	..	0	not out	..	..	56
A. L. Hassett c Hammond b Wright	78			
K. R. Miller not out	..	..	141		
I. Johnson lbw b Wright ..	..	52		
C. McCool c Bedser b Yardley	..	2		
D. Tallon b Wright	..	..	3		
R. Lindwall c Evans b Yardley	..	20		
B. Dooland c Bedser b Yardley	..	29		
E. Toshack run out	..	..	0		
Extras ..	..	..	..	28	Extras	..	..	4
Total	..	..	..	487	Total (1 wicket) ..	215

Fall of wickets: 18, 18, 207, 222, 372, 389, 396, 423, 486, 487.

Fall of wickets: 116.

BOWLING					BOWLING			
	O.	M.	R.	W.		O.	M.	R.	W.
Bedser	30	6	97	3	Bedser	15	1	68	0
Edrich	20	3	88	0	Edrich	7	1	25	0
Wright	32.4	1	152	3	Wright	9	0	49	0
Yardley	31	7	101	3	Yardley	13	0	69	1
Ikin	2	0	9	0					
Compton	3	0	12	0					

Bedser and Wright each bowled two no-balls, and Edrich two wides.

Match drawn.

CHAPTER XXIII

IN WINELAND

In every capital city of Australia all the states have their tourist bureaux, whose job it is to boost the scenery and attractions and help holiday-makers. None of these organisations showed much interest in the presence of fourteen English journalists, many of them with interests beyond cricket. Now and then private concerns were more enterprising. So it happened that during a break in the Adelaide cricket the *Advertiser* newspaper and Messrs. B. Seppelt and Sons invited us to see the wine-growing district of South Australia.

A wonderful day it was, a revelation to those who had not been to Seppeltsfield before, a vivid reminder to some who had. Mr. John Bonython, a director of the newspaper, and Messrs. Walter and Ian Seppelt were our conductors.

Though Victoria used to be the largest wine-growing state in the Commonwealth, South Australia now produces about four-fifths of the total output. Australia to-day ferments annually about 18,000,000 gallons of wine, of which it normally exports over 4,000,000. This is relatively small in the world scale of production, but a substantial industry even at that. Vine-growing and wine-making employ thousands of workers.

This particular great firm, with wineries and cellars scattered over a wide area within comfortable motoring distance of Adelaide, had a remarkable beginning. Its founder, Mr. J. E. Seppelt, arrived in Australia in 1849 to grow tobacco. Two years later he began cultivation, but found that the tobacco would not mature well enough for smoking purposes, so he turned over to the vine. The first grapes were processed in Mrs. Seppelt's dairy, an underground cellar beneath the present office. It is still used—as a repository for recipes for liqueurs.

Next year the crop was increased, a shed was built for bottling and further excavations were made. Now—with permission—one can wander through seemingly unending cellars at Seppeltsfield, Chateau Tanundra and other places in the district. In these temples of the vine, as silent and solemn as any cathedral, are scores of vast casks and barrels filled with this and that maturing brew (the wrong word, I know) of brandy, wines and liqueurs. Even vinegar is a product there. Within these thick walls the temperature was almost cold compared with the fierce heat outside.

Now the fourth generation of the Seppelts family is active in the enterprise; a fifth is growing up to take over in turn. We were told that the products of this and other Australian firms compare well with those of the European homes of the wine industry. So, in taking samples that day, I thought myself. Australians are drinking with their meals more of their own wine than they used, but still not as much as they might. I was informed that the average home consumption is no more than a gallon per person every year. In France the figure is forty-five gallons: yet the French are a temperate people. This may sound interested pleading, but there is sense in it all the same.

We paused during that taking of samples. I fell into conversation with a foreman who had been employed in the cellars ever since boyhood. He pointed out an enormous cask, almost a vat in volume, with a small hole not big enough, one imagined, to admit a full-sized man. Yet he told me that when the cask is emptied a man squeezes through to clean it.

"In fact," he said, "I believe I have been inside in my time, every cask in this cellar—and there are dozens of them."

The whole countryside round Seppeltsfield is one of orderly vineyards, with their vines in neat rows up and down the hill sides. Unfortunately, we were too early in the year to see the harvest or watch the processing. Standing idle until March were machines which crush 500 tons of grapes each day. So begins the wine-making and maturation process which will give Australians and— I hope—us in England the 1947 vintage—in two years in the case of light hock or claret and in ten or twelve in that of heavy sweet port. Many methods have been used to quicken the maturing process, but with varying success. The time-honoured system of long storage is still maintained by most wineries. It makes the spirity harsh young wine softer to the taste.

We lunched that day in the Community Hotel at Nuriootpa. Reckoning the champagne served at current prices in England our meal was one for millionaires.

The fourth test match and our second and longer stay at Adelaide ended almost simultaneously. I suppose that our stronger English touring sides of normal years would have regarded the match which followed—against a Victorian Country side at Ballarat— as an anti-climax. Actually it became quite a struggle. Ballarat, batting first, made the respectable total of 268. Our men had to struggle hard to exceed it by a mere twenty. Two of our first three men—Fishlock and Edrich—were out for ducks to the local fast bowler R. McArthur, but Gibb and Compton ran into the sixties and Evans came late to the rescue of the side with 82, the top score. English prestige was restored somewhat in the Victorian second innings—70 for five, with Smith two for 10 and a wicket to Evans, set free by Gibb from wicketkeeping duties. How wicketkeepers do like to show they can bowl. Leslie Ames, Kentish forerunner of Evans in the English side, used to love to toss down his slows in country matches.

This was the last appearance of Hammond in a cricket field in Australia. After fielding for part of the Victorian innings he retired with the fibrositis which had begun to attack him during the Adelaide test, and took no further part in this or any future game until the side reached New Zealand.

Since before the war Hammond has been subject to this back trouble. Nearly every season it assails him—and he never knows whether the enemy will stay a day or a month. This was one of the longer attacks which, while allowing him to walk, ruled out cricket even in the fifth test match more than a fortnight later. Meanwhile there was in the newspapers a perpetual "Will he play?" query. Sydney would have liked to see a final appearance on the ground where many of his greatest innings have been played. But Hammond could only watch the match.

Victoria was the one Sheffield Shield state we had beaten, although it is the strongest of the four. Now in mid-February we were due to play the Victorians again; in the meanwhile they had confirmed their strength by winning the current Shield competition. This time we had the worst of another of those wearisome draws. We gained a lead of 28 on the first innings—355 to 327—but were all out for 118 in the second. There was no time for Victoria to bat again, for play on the third day had been limited by rain to an hour and a half.

Our first innings was distinguished by an innings of 93 by Compton, who towards the end of the tour could do nothing wrong, 51 by Fishlock, 71 by Ikin—his highest of the tour—and 41 not out by the invaluable Evans. Evans had a hand in dismissing the first four Victorian batsmen to go. Two of them were "stumps" off fast-medium bowling, Meuleman's wicket being credited to Pollard and Miller's to Bedser. I cannot recall a parallel to this dual feat. Three wickets were down for 32, but Hassett and a young player who, if I mistake not, is destined to cricketing greatness, came to the rescue. He is eighteen, a left-hander, Neal Harvey, brother of Mervyn and one of six brothers all of whom play cricket in the same Melbourne club. His innings of 69 towards a stand with Hassett of 120 was the best effort by a very young batsman during the tour. Hassett three days later—Sunday and the rain-spoilt Monday having intervened—made his own score 126, and Tribe, the bowler, afterwards hit for eighty minutes and 60 runs. This young left-hander travelled to England in the same ship as myself to go into Lancashire League cricket. Tribe ought to do well, for they like all-rounders in Lancashire, and they like their scoring bright and brief. One cannot blame any young Australian cricketer for going where the money is, but one regrets at the same time that young players should feel impelled to depart from the main stream of the first-class game. Tribe, in the view of Denis Compton, who ought to know, was the best of the Australian spin bowlers. He may return to Australian first-class cricket in the autumn.

Why our second innings should go to pieces as it did is hard to discover. One hundred and eighteen in the circumstances was an entirely discreditable total. It looked as if the prospective drawn game had destroyed the concentration of our batsmen; and I can well believe that if a result had been likely the total would have doubled. But these sorry efforts do matter, even if a match is not imperilled. They go down in the records, are bad for the morale of a side, and give readers and listeners unaware of the circumstances a bad impression.

Tribe, who in test matches had made little dent in our batting, now took six wickets for 49 and the only double-figure batsmen were Fishlock with 11, Compton 10, Hardstaff 26, Ikin 12 and Yardley 28. There was at one time a distinct possibility that Tribe and Ring would get us out early enough to force a Victorian victory, but Bedser hung on with his captain for twenty minutes while 22 were added and the match was saved. It is fashionable to call such an effort as Yardley's a "captain's innings." If the cliché is permissible—though it makes me shudder—I will attach it to this piece of determination. It is a pity that some of the others earlier in the innings did not make this last-ditch resistance unnecessary.

So on to Sydney again for the last two matches of the tour—the New South Wales return and the final test. We were not at all sorry. We had had more than enough of cricket, and in addition terrifying news was being splashed all over the front pages of the newspapers about the desperate plight of a snow-buried England. With cold, hunger and unemployment in England, here were we playing cricket in the sunshine and eating eggs and bacon, with plenty of etceteras, for breakfast. We felt, not without reason, that the folks at home had ceased to care about our mock battles. Letters from wives and friends worried us too. One, for instance, from my own wife which told of a fireless room; another from a friend who had to climb 179 steps twice a day because her office lift had ceased to work; one from my sister which told of work by candle light in the cold of that bleak February. But what would you? The show had to go on; we couldn't do anything about it.

The *Melbourne Argus* about this time published the following letter from a correspondent who had received it from a friend in England. It displays the same undaunted sense of humour as did the World War One soldier who on the way up to the Flanders trenches one bleak February night audibly thanked God "there's no wasps about." Here in cricketing language was this Englishman's summing-up of the situation at home:

ENGLAND v THE REST

Pipes c Burst b Frost	8 days
Water retired	8 ,,
Bathroom b Flood	3 ,,
Boiler st Fuel b Ration	5 ,,
Electricity b Shinwell	7 ,,
Father c Cold b Flu	6 ,,
Mother not out	10 ,,
Junior c Chilblain b Snowball ..	4 ,,
Butcher run out	7 ,,
Milkman st Snow b Over ..	1 day

To bat: Plumber. It is doubtful whether he will be available to-morrow.

All very well, this sort of joking, but the state of England those dreadful days was very much in everyone's minds out there. Except, perhaps, the dock strikers.

However, summer—and cricket—are back in England and the story becomes more readable now.

We drew, then, this return match against New South Wales. There might have been a pleasing and exciting result if rain again had not intervened. The scores—N.S.W. 342 and 262 for six declared, M.C.C. 266 and 205 for three—give no hint of the last-day thrills.

Towards the N.S.W. first innings total our friend of the Australian Forces side D. K. Carmody, E. Lukeman and R. Lindwall were chief contributors. Among our bowlers Peter Smith had his biggest bowl of the tour, with nine wickets for 121—a performance which put him into the fifth test match. Dick Pollard, in duty bound, had taken a wicket in mid-innings, and probably wished he hadn't, for then Smith would have had a chance of getting all ten. This feat unusual though it is, has been accomplished fifty-two times in the long history of first-class cricket. Eddie Watts of Surrey—ten for 67 against Warwickshire in 1939—is the latest bowler logged for such a performance. Frank Smailes, of Yorkshire, the same season had ten for 47 against Derbyshire.

Compton, continuing his good break, headed our first innings score with 75 and Smith followed up his bowling with his top score but one of the tour, 33. In their second innings the New South Welshmen were saved by a slow but invaluable 80 not out by another eighteen-year-old left-hander, R. Kissell. His innings in my opinion did not compare well with that of young Harvey against us at

Melbourne, but any State or Country side would be proud to have him. "Ginty" Lush, the home captain, declared and left the English-men 339 to win in four hours playing time.

Hutton in the first innings had been struck by a ball from Lush and now played with plaster over the chin and two stitches in the wound. That this had not affected his nerve he showed by scoring 72 fast runs before being l.b.w. to Johnson. Edrich gave us a swift 34 and it became obvious that our men were really going out for runs. The first 100 took only eighty-one minutes, the 150 just 101. In other words the last 50 had come in twenty minutes, which is travelling indeed with bowlers of the calibre of Lindwall and Toshack in action. The fourth 50 was up in thirty-two minutes more.

After Hutton, Washbrook and Edrich were out, Compton became the main hope of victory. He scored 74 not out, full of his most likeable strokes; and Fishlock, 11, was settling down nicely with him when it was all over. At teatime our total was 205 for three, but then the rain washed out further play. At that time we needed 134 to win in 105 minutes. We had been beating the clock hand-somely. Now the best finish of the tour was dissolved from the clouds.

CHAPTER XXIV

FIFTH TEST—HUTTON b. TONSILITIS

Three days later we were in the toils of the fifth test, one of cruel luck and lost opportunities. We lost it after leading on the first innings for the first time in the series. The ill-luck lay in the illness of Hutton, who scored 122 not out before tonsilitis laid him low, and was unable to bat in the second innings.

Here are the totals: England 280 and 186, Australia 253 and 214 for five—a victory by five wickets.

For the first—but probably by no means the last—time in his cricketing career, Norman Yardley captained an England side, and he captained it very well, his Yorkshire fighting qualities tempered by a very likeable personality. It was no fault of his that we lost a match which we had a very fair chance of winning.

Hammond was absent through fibrositis; and Hardstaff, who had played in the Adelaide match, was out of the running now because of a knee injury. The newcomers were Fishlock, playing for the first time this series, and Smith, who had played in the second test but not since. This meant that we had sacrificed a batsman for a bowler. There was in any event little choice, for illness and injury had depleted our reserves.

Australia had three changes—Barnes (back after illness), Hamence (his first test) and Tribe for Harvey, Johnson (injured) and Dooland. The omission of Dooland was discouraging to this fine bowler who had been expensive in the Adelaide match, but had bowled well all the same.

FIRST DAY—BAD AFTER GOOD

Yardley won the toss—which made it 3-2 to England in the series—and the day produced uneven batting by his side. From a score of 151 for two England degenerated to 237 for six at the end of the day. Another of our many disappointments: we just could not hold on to a strong position.

Sydney had received lots of rain on the days before the match and the groundsman had been impeded in his preparation of the wicket; I wish this could happen every time, then we should have livelier matches with moderate scores and more fun. The morning breeze had completed the drying process and Yardley had no serious doubts about deciding to bat.

After four minutes and a single tapped by Hutton we had a

Miller's drive. Edrich, Evans, Hammond, Bedser all watch it. So does the invisible bowler, during the third Test Match.

Hutton is caught by McCool for two off Lindwall in the third Test Match. Fieldsmen, left to right: Miller, Johnson, McCool, Tallon, back to camera, Barnes.

disastrous opening. Washbrook, brought to the end where he faced Lindwall, survived one ball and then was bowled by a real beauty that might have taken anyone's wicket. One for one. Edrich next, and slow repair of the damage. It was fully half an hour before the total reached 10—eight singles and a two, which Hutton managed.

Then to the slower bowlers. Tribe was hit by Edrich for three and next ball by Hutton for four, but it was noticeable that the slow left-hander was able to turn the ball from the word go and he needed careful watching. Toshack, with his usual leg-field, bowled two of his inevitable maidens; indeed one of his chief assets is his ability to keep batsmen quiet. Hutton, however, deflected him for a two and a four.

Sometimes even test cricketers can be human while the solemn rite goes on. Miller, scrambling to stop a ball, arrived on all fours close under Edrich's nose. Edrich meditatively applied the bat to his hind quarters.

Towards lunch the scoring rate quickened a trifle. Sixty-eight for one was the result of the morning hour and a half—Hutton 40, Edrich 21.

In the afternoon Bradman had to call up all his bowlers against a partnership which went from strength to strength. Hutton achieved his 50—I have seen better as well as not so good half-centuries from him—in two hours. The 100 total took the sedate time of 130 minutes, and the double figure stand followed immediately.

Each batsman had an escape. Hutton might have been caught in the slips off Miller's first ball after lunch; Edrich gave Tallon a sharp chance low off Lindwall. But luck was with the batsmen. Hutton continued to score at almost twice the rate of his partner until Edrich developed a liking for driving Toshack, whom he sent to the fence thrice in quick succession. He reached his 50 with a straight drive which, in theory at least, was a chance, but so fast was the ball travelling that McCool sensibly withdrew his hand from the warm offering, and the ball sped to the boundary. Though this half-century had taken two and a half hours it included seven fours, showing that when Edrich intended to hit 'em he really did so.

A high bouncer from Lindwall proved fatal to Edrich after his three hours stay. He pushed his bat to the ball and was caught at the wicket. He and Hutton had added 150—our highest for the second wicket during the series. Fishlock, not Compton, rather surprisingly was sent in at this stage. He saw Hutton give a chance, very sharp and low to Barnes at forward short-leg. Tea 162 for two—Hutton 88, Fishlock 2.

Miller was bowling bouncers, sometimes as many as two or three an over, and frequently had Hutton ducking. Off one of them Fishlock was caught by Tallon on the leg-side, but the batsman was given not out, apparently because the umpire judged that ball came off arm rather than bat. At which Miller did not look grateful. He sent down another bouncer or two and Fishlock gave a confirmatory rub of the arm. Hutton's century came after three and a half hours. It had contained some very fine strokes and a few bad ones.

Fishlock struggled on for forty minutes before being bowled by McCool. One hundred and eighty-eight for three. Compton stayed with Hutton for another forty, and we were full of hopes about him when he was treated to four successive short balls from Lindwall. In standing back to play the last of these he trod on his wicket. His only boundary was a sweet cover-drive off Toshack. Two hundred and fifteen for four.

No sooner was Yardley in than he appealed against the waning light, on the ground that Miller's arm was over the screen. The appeal was refused. Two wickets fell soon afterwards. Yardley was caught in the slips off Lindwall at the opposite end with the score 215 and Ikin bowled for a duck with the score unchanged. Then Evans remained with Hutton until the close—237 for six.

You can "argie, argie, argie" all day about the rights and wrongs of the bouncing fast bowling which the Australians had turned on with success that day. Our batsmen had no grouse about it, but there were certain regrets that Harold Larwood, past the age of test cricket, was even then keeping a shop in Blackpool instead of bowling at Sydney. "Bodyline" this bowling was not, in the sense that we saw it under Jardine's captaincy fifteen years earlier. There was no close leg-side field—nor for that matter was there the fine accuracy that made Larwood so great a bowler. Yet intimidatory this bowling was in a sense—and be it noted that the new rule does not say anything about the presence of a packed field; it leaves a wide discretion to the umpires, who can apply it quite irrespective of where the fieldsmen are standing.

Since the Australians were the instigators of this new rule and protested so hotly about dangerous fast bowling they should be extra careful now. At the moment they have the fast bowlers and we have not. It will not always be so—and we don't want the ancient wrangle revived.

The dismissal of Compton in that unlucky way had been the turning point of the innings. But Hutton, with 122 against his name, was still in.

SECOND DAY—BLANK SATURDAY

Why Sydney's rain should so frequently arrive on a Saturday is one of the mysteries of its climate. In the previous test there, play on that day was limited to an hour and a half; Saturday and Monday were complete blanks during one of the matches against New South Wales; and now the second day of the fifth test was a complete washout. Sydney can look as gloomy as Manchester. It did so that day.

About the region of deep third man there were growing half a dozen mushrooms of button size. Lindsay Hassett, ever a humorist, told me in the pavilion that the previous day in the outfield he had spotted one for himself, and had covered it up with loose grass until it reached consumable size.

That morning Hutton had come down to breakfast complaining forebodingly of a sore throat. Everyone thought that a Sunday's rest would put him right. It did not.

Twice Sunday saved Australia in these tests. After this Saturday downpour, as after the last, the idle Sabbath was fine and dried the wicket nicely for the Australian batsmen. At Brisbane, where we had had "stickies" for both our innings, there was no Sunday in between.

THIRD DAY—EVANS AGAIN

On the Monday morning Hutton, with a temperature of 103, was packed off to hospital. In his absence our tail added a useful 43 runs on a wicket which rolled out easy. The chief contributor of the morning was Godfrey Evans, who after losing Smith quickly to Lindwall became senior partner in a bright stand of 25 with Bedser. He produced in one over from Tribe two sweet cover-drives for four each and a less praiseworthy snick through the slips for three. He fell trying to hit Lindwall. Success to Godfrey with the bat is a rather heady wine. Wright was soon caught at the wicket and the innings ended for 280. Lindwall was the outstanding bowler with five for 46, including the wickets of Washbrook, Edrich, Compton, Yardley and Ikin—a fine performance which he will be very apt to repeat in English conditions next year.

The afternoon crowd that Monday was a big one—probably because an innings from Bradman was in the offing—and Bradman is still a big draw in the Sydney where he used to live. For a long time it looked as if Barnes and Morris would crowd him out that day, for they settled down to a long opening stand. In an hour before and after lunch they had 50 up. The scoring was slow against Bedser and Edrich, but against Smith Barnes had four, four and two off one over, and against Wright a four and a three, plus four in leg-byes. There was one puzzling over by Smith to Morris; otherwise the batsmen were on top of their world.

Through generations of English cricketers the position of first slip has been invariably filled by Hammond. He has hardly ever fielded anywhere else except when the field-placing abolished slips altogether. Now, when not bowling, Edrich was there. It seemed like the passing of a cricketing epoch.

The second fifty of the partnership would have been quicker than the sixty-three minutes it took but for the accurate sealing of one end by Yardley and the strengthening of Wright's attack. Wright beat Morris without bowling him, and just afterwards it looked as if Evans might have stumped Barnes when the batsman had just passed his 50. Yardley bowled, with the aid of a strong leg-side field, five overs for a mere 8 runs. Our fielding had earned very nearly full marks—especially Washbrook, Compton, Bedser and Fishlock.

Not until a quarter of an hour after tea did a wicket fall. Then, with the total 126, Barnes, trying to late cut Bedser, snicked the ball to the wicketkeeper. He and Morris had been together two and a quarter hours.

Bradman, who received the same sort of greeting always given to Hammond, opened with a sharp single which was turned into three by an overthrow. He followed by hitting Wright past point for three; then a stroke for two sailed high between slip and gully. As Morris entered his fifties we wondered whether he would make cricket history by scoring his fourth successive test century against us. But he was beaten by a good ball from Bedser and was l.b.w. One hundred and forty six for two.

This revival of our fortunes became more heartening still when Bradman was out at the same score. He advanced to a ball from Wright to turn it into a toss, missed and was bowled after making 12 in half an hour. Bedser's figures since tea had now become 4—2—9—2. So Hassett and Miller came together. Miller immediately had one very anxious over from Wright. He usually gets on with the job in hand—the making of runs—but this time twenty minutes passed with no score and the two batsmen both at zero. At last Hassett managed to poke a single off Bedser. Then came an over from Wright which yielded 10 runs, including the first full-out drive by Miller.

All manner of shadows lay across the ground as the day's cricket was dying, for in early autumn the Sydney sun is low in the sky by five-thirty. One of the shadows was a moving one—that of a flag fluttering on top of a stand—and Miller was bothered by the image on the pitch. An umpire ran to the fence and desired the flag to be struck.

About four minutes from the end Wright turned and popped a ball which had Miller caught in the gully by Ikin. The umpires had refused an appeal for bad light. Miller and Hassett had stopped the rot by adding 41, but at 187 for four the Australian total was poor.

Hamence, in his first test match, came in with three nervy minutes to go and played an anxious last maiden over—quite an ordeal for any batsman in such circumstances.

FOURTH DAY—ONE FOR THE BOWLERS

Twelve wickets fell that Tuesday, the fourth day of the match, on a wicket now taking all the spin a slow bowler could give it. We achieved a lead of 27 and at the close were 171 ahead with four wickets in hand, including that of the still-absent Hutton. Wright in the morning, McCool in the afternoon, both gathered harvests on this favourable soil. Wright did his best feat of the tour with five for 42 that day, or seven for 105 altogether. McCool finished his day's work with four for 32.

This was a real sporting day's play—the best to watch in any of the tests. A pity it was that it was reserved for the fifth match; had the rubber still been open the crowd would have been in raptures.

Wright, bowling more slowly, or rather less fast, than usual and giving the ball more air, showed in his very first over to Hamence that he was out for blood. Every ball of this maiden set the batsman queries about its disposal. Never since the tour began had the English bowlers attacked with more zest than in this first hour. Bedser, while not as puzzling as Wright, kept both Hassett and Hamence quiet and runs came at a mere crawl. Our fielding was keen too, but there was one slip. When Hamence, who had not scored overnight, had made 7, that fine fieldsman Ikin failed to take a chance in front of him in the gully.

But after fifty minutes and 29 reluctant runs, Ikin, in the same position, flung himself sideways to achieve a superb catch dismissing Hassett. The batsman had shown fine judgment in knowing what to leave alone. Two hundred and eighteen for five.

McCool stayed with Hamence for only nine minutes, during which he struck only one blow. Then he was out in similar fashion to Hassett, but this time it was Yardley, Ikin's neighbour in the slip ring, who bent to the catch. Two hundred and thirty for six, Australia still 50 behind.

Without a run more Tallon tried to hook Wright and skied the ball more or less straight to Compton at deep square leg. Wright that day had now three for 28. Lindwall, like Tallon, had a duck. After seeing Hamence score 3 he tried to drive Wright and was caught very well indeed by Smith at extra cover.

With seven wickets down for 233, Tribe, the little left-hander, tried to hit Wright off his length but did not get very far towards his object. He struck two fours and a single in one over, but when

Wright bowled to him again he slammed a ball to deep long-on, where Fishlock had an awkward sideways run for the catch. Toshack struggled through an exciting over before lunch in which he was twice nearly caught and once was actually caught—off a no-ball. Finally he did a cow-shot over the bowler's head for two.

Wright at the interval had five for 41 that morning. At one stage he took the wickets of McCool, Tallon and Lindwall in nine balls for three runs.

Only eight Englishmen have taken eight wickets against Australia in one innings of a test match. Wright lost his chance of becoming the ninth when Toshack was run out. Four Australians have accomplished the feat; one of them, A. A. Mailey, indeed, took nine wickets. But Wright's seven for 105 is memorable for all that. It gave us a lead of 27, which as matters turned out was all too small. Hamence had every reason to feel proud of his first test innings. He had batted an hour and twenty minutes for his 30 not out and had behaved like a veteran.

Fishlock, assuming the place he habitually occupies in the Surrey side, went in first with Washbrook in the absence of Hutton. He was l.b.w. to Lindwall first ball of the innings. It came through low and fast so that the bat was too late. Edrich, again virtually an opening bat for the second time in the match, snicked the second ball hazily through the slips for four. Eleven came off that over, including a five for an overthrow in Washbrook's favour.

With Wright's achievements fresh in mind Bradman turned over to an all-slow attack after half an hour, with the left-hander Tribe at Wright's old end and the right-hander McCool at the other. By then Washbrook and Edrich had scored 25 very well, and they continued to handle the bowling competently if without show. Edrich hit Tribe for one boundary and Washbrook McCool for another. It seemed for the time being that neither bowler could get the same snap off the pitch as Wright in the morning and the partnership reached 42 in fifty minutes. Then Washbrook was bowled by a leg-break which passed from pad into wicket. Forty-two for one.

Tribe's uncertainty of length helped Compton happily on his way and Toshack was brought on in his stead. Compton swung and turned him hard to the leg boundary twice in his first over. This Middlesex partnership was showing signs of doing us proud when Edrich ran out to hit McCool, missed and was stumped. Sixty-five for two.

Ikin had an unhappy two balls. The first he drove to mid-off —and started to run. Compton refused, Ikin fell, scrambled up and threw himself back just in time. The effort probably unsettled him. Anyhow he tried to drive the second ball without connecting and was stumped. So spectacles were his—the first and last on our side all the series. Sixty-five for four.

McCool at that stage had done better than Wright with three for 11. Yardley, again given his frequent chance of stopping a rot, held on with Compton until teatime—68 for four, Compton 18, Yardley 2. They added 17 rather careworn runs after the interval and then Yardley was bowled round his legs by McCool—now four for 14.

Evans was lucky enough to receive a rare long-hop from McCool, and, hitting it round to leg with all his might, scored a bullseye on Barnes close in. Barnes showed his toughness after this bang by coming on to bowl three overs as a leg-spinner opposite McCool, and Evans drove him for two threes. Presently up came the hundred. Compton was slow but sound, watching every ball carefully on to the bat before committing himself late to his stroke.

This new partnership defied even McCool, who was taken off with his figures four for 26. It was broken by Miller, who bowled Evans after the pair had added 35 in forty minutes. Evans had proved himself again a real help in time of trouble. A quarter of an hour before the close McCool returned, but Smith struck two or three good blows—and one bad one—and remained with Compton half an hour until the end. Compton, whose score stood at 46 for a quarter of an hour, hit McCool for a four which brought him to 50 in the last over. He had been batting 132 minutes with only two fours. One hundred and forty-four for six at the close.

FIFTH DAY—DEFEAT OUT OF VICTORY

Almost on the tick of time on the fifth day—with a whole day to spare—we lost a match which might so easily have been won. There were two big disappointments—one the continued absence of Hutton, the other the missing of Bradman by that usually safe and brilliant fieldsman, Bill Edrich—such things will happen in the best-regulated families. Bradman, then two, made 63 and saw his side well on the way to victory.

We had hoped, against all medical advice, that Hutton would be able to crawl to the wicket that morning and achieve the same sort of miracle as did Eddie Paynter in the Brisbane test of fifteen years earlier. Eddie, battling against a bad throat, emerged bandaged from hospital, and at a crisis in our fortunes scored 83 and won the Ashes for us. Hutton had been forbidden by his doctors to leave bed, but he told me later that when no one was watching he crawled out and tried to stand. The room was swimming round him, and he just had to crawl back. So all we had from Hutton that match was one incomplete innings. That it realised 122 runs indicates that he would have had power to add to the number.

Hutton had played his last innings of the tour. He did not go to New Zealand, and, still looking far from well, returned home by air for a tonsils operation.

Our innings that morning lasted only another fifty minutes, for the addition of 42 runs. Smith, who hit for four a full-toss from Tribe, scored 10 to Compton's 2 before being caught at the wicket off Lindwall for a more that useful 24.

When Bedser arrived Compton opened out, one over from Lindwall yielding a four and three threes to the two batsmen. But Compton himself was out soon afterwards, caught at fine leg by Miller off a ball from Toshack which popped up so vaguely to the fieldsman that many thought the decision was leg-before. Umpire Borwick told me later that the ball hit the bat, travelled to the wicket-keeper's pad—probably the "roll" near the knee—and thence to Miller. Which was hard luck indeed.

Bedser went soon afterwards—stumped by Tallon off McCool —and the Australians were left with 214 to make for victory, with as good as all eternity in which to make them.

The shine on the ball—usually so carefully preserved by bowlers and fieldsmen at the opening of an innings—was unwanted to-day, and our men took no pains to prevent the ball from hitting earth. After the formality of one over from Edrich—and I don't write thus in disparagement of him as a fast bowler—Wright was brought on at the end whence he wrought so much destruction the day before. Unfortunately he was not destined to repeat that perform-ance.

Round one of the fight went the Australians' way. They scored quite briskly for half an hour, Wright's second over yielding 10 runs, including two square cut boundaries by Barnes. Bedser at the other end bowled tight—three overs for only four runs.

Everything was going against us when, at 45, Morris was run out. This was due to a fortunate fumble by Compton at deep leg from a stroke by Barnes. It tempted the batsmen into trying a third run, and Compton, recovering himself, pelted the ball back to the wicketkeeper.

Bradman next—and the catch which went astray. He had scored two when he touched the ball from Wright close to Edrich at first slip. It was about shoulder high and within reach of both hands— the sort of chance that Edrich would absorb greedily and with gratitude ninety-nine times in a hundred. This was the hundredth time, for the ball passed through the fieldsman's hands.

We hoped again when Bedser, allied to Evans, took Barnes's wicket in the next over—a fine catch on the off-side. Fifty-one for two.

At this crisis in the match Bradman and Hassett waited till the clouds rolled by. They made 13 runs in the first fifty minutes of their partnership. But Wright and Bedser could not bowl for ever. When the one had bowled ten overs for 28 and the other twelve for 29 and a wicket Yardley replaced them with Smith and Edrich. Nine came in Edrich's first over, and Yardley, who had not many runs to play with, replaced him himself after one over. Smith bowled only two overs for 8 and on came Wright again. Yardley bowled economically, but it was off him that Bradman punched the four to the off-boundary which brought up the 100 in 132 minutes. At teatime half the Australian task had been accomplished, with only two wickets gone. An omen was that in the last over before the break Hassett hit a tiring Wright for two fours.

After tea came the death flurry. Compton was tried for an over before Wright and Bedser resumed a task by now almost hopeless. Wright was still unable to make the ball lift and turn as on the day before. Two fours off him in one over brought Bradman to his 50 in ninety-seven minutes. But once he beat the Australian captain and missed the stumps by the thickness of a Commonwealth threepenny bit. Bradman and Hassett added 98 in nearly two hours, and had put their side within hail of victory when Bradman, trying to drive Bedser, gave Compton an easy catch at extra cover.

The Australians had now 65 to make with an hour of that day to go, and the only interest in the match lay in the question whether it would last till the morrow. Seventy-eight runs had been hit off Wright before he took his first wicket of the day—that of Hassett, whom Ikin caught acrobatically in the gully near the ground. The umpire consulted his colleague before allowing the catch. One hundred and seventy-three for four.

Our fieldsmen stuck to their work as though they believed they had a chance of winning, and Wright was now bowling better than earlier in the day. Presently a ball from him curled off the edge of Hamence's bat and was taken by Edrich in the slips. One hundred and eighty for five.

Miller and McCool knocked off the remaining 35 runs in just under twenty-five minutes. Both made their quick contributions. Compton was put on just before the end and a three hit off him by McCool completed the Australian task. Miller the irrepressible completed the running of that three carrying a souvenir stump, snatched as he turned. Technically, I suppose, he had "obstructed the field" by breaking the wicket, and could have been given out, but nobody bothered in the whirl of excitement which always follows the last ball of the fifth test, no matter who wins. We had lost by five wickets.

There were no after-the-match speeches at the ground, but later Hammond and Bradman "talked." Bradman thought that if Hutton had remained well his batting might have turned the result the other way. He suggested that cricket administrators might consider wickets which, like the one in this match, gave the bowlers a chance. How right he was. On the abolition of over-easy wickets depends the whole future of test and county cricket; these long drawn out struggles with their obstinate defence and frequent lack of batting enterprise must sooner or later disgust the cricket-following public.

Hammond felt that Australia would possess a strong side for several years to come, but he felt also that by the time her men came home in 1948 English cricket ought to be able to offer a strong challenge again.

So of the five test matches we had lost three and drawn two very much in our own disfavour. Three days later, for the first time in cricket history, an English side took off on a long overseas flight from Rose Bay, Sydney's water airport, to Auckland. Even in New Zealand this team did not have all their own way.

We must admit that they were not up to their task. Never has any side had better excuses for failure than this one, with its long years of wartime inactivity ageing the men and taking toll of their skill and stamina.

Perhaps the despatch of a team ought to have been delayed another year. And yet I don't know—the goodwill aspect of the tour was very apparent, whatever may be said or written to the contrary. Never have seventeen men been better liked than the seventeen who failed to win a test match. If any cynic says that popularity in Australia goes in inverse ratio to success then don't believe him.

Scores in the fifth test match are appended:

ENGLAND

First Innings				Second Innings		
C. Washbrook b Lindwall	..	0		b McCool	.. ..	24
L. Hutton retired ill	.. ..	122		absent ill	.. ..	0
W. J. Edrich c Tallon b Lindwall	..	60		st Tallon b McCool	..	24
L. Fishlock b McCool	.. ..	14		lbw b Lindwall	..	0
D. Compton b Lindwall	.. ..	17		c Miller b Toshack	..	76
N. Yardley c Miller b Lindwall	..	2		b McCool	.. ..	11
J. Ikin b Lindwall ..	.. ..	0		st Tallon b McCool	..	0
T. G. Evans b Lindwall	.. ..	29		b Miller	.. ..	20
T. P. B. Smith b Lindwall	..	2		c Tallon b Lindwall	..	24
A. V. Bedser not out	.. ..	10		st Tallon b McCool	..	4
D. V. P. Wright c Tallon b Miller		7		not out	.. ..	1
Extras ..	.. .. ..	17		Extras	.. ..	2
		---				---
Total	.. .. ..	280		Total	..	186

Bowling					Bowling			
	O.	M.	R.	W.		O.	M.	R.	W.
Lindwall	22	2	63	7	Lindwall	12	1	46	2
Miller	15.3	2	31	1	Miller	6	1	11	1
Toshack	16	4	40	0	Toshack	4	1	14	1
McCool	13	0	34	1	McCool	21	5	44	5
Tribe	28	2	95	0	Tribe	14	0	58	0
Barnes	—	—	—	—	Barnes	3	0	11	0

Fall of wickets: 1, 151, 188, 215, 225, 225, 244, 269, 280.

Fall of wickets: 0, 42, 65, 65, 85, 120, 157, 184, 186.

AUSTRALIA

First Innings		Second Innings	
S. G. Barnes c Evans b Bedser ..	71	c Evans b Bedser ..	30
A. Morris lbw b Bedser	57	run out	17
D. G. Bradman b Wright ..	12	c Compton b Bedser ..	63
A. L. Hassett c Ikin b Wright ..	24	c Ikin b Wright ..	47
K. R. Miller c Ikin b Wright ..	23	not out	34
R. A. Hamence not out	30	c Edrich b Wright ..	1
C. V. McCool c Yardley b Wright ..	3	not out	13
D. Tallon c Compton b Wright ..	0		
R. Lindwall c Smith b Wright ..	0	Did not	
G. Tribe c Fishlock b Wright ..	9	Bat	
E. R. Toshack run out	5		
Extras	19	Extras	9
Total	253	Total (5 wickets) ..	214

Bowling					Bowling			
	O.	M.	R.	W.		O.	M.	R.	W.
Bedser	27	7	49	2	Bedser	22	4	75	2
Edrich	7	0	34	0	Edrich	2	0	14	0
Wright	29	4	105	7	Wright	22	1	93	2
Smith	8	0	38	0	Smith	2	0	8	0
Yardley	5	2	8	0	Yardley	3	1	7	0
Compton	—	—	—	—	Compton	1.2	0	8	0

Fall of wickets: 126, 146, 146, 187, 218, 230, 230, 233, 245, 253.

Fall of wickets: 45, 51, 149, 173, 180.

Australia won by five wickets.

CHAPTER XXV

HIGH FINANCE

So ends this story of the Failure of a Mission, for failure in a cricket sense it certainly was. This time I did not see the brief but pleasant prolongation of the tour in New Zealand. I heard about it only in radio snatches aboard the homeward-bound *Largs Bay*, in which three members of the side travelled home with the heavy baggage. One of them, Paul Gibb, may have reflected during the long voyage home that he was quite capable of piloting the fine Sunderland flying-boat, named for civilian purposes the *Sandringham*, which took thirteen of the players quickly from Sydney to Auckland. Didn't Gibb command a Sunderland in many a wartime expedition over the Bay of Biscay?

Some of us watched the flying-boat depart one early morning from her base at Rose Bay, Sydney. Overhead was a signpost, at once like and strangely unlike our roadside directions at home. It said:

> Darwin 2,247 miles.
> Singapore 4,386 miles.
> Karachi 7,639 miles.
> Cairo 10,016 miles.
> London 12,410 miles.

A long way we had travelled for cricket—30,000 miles to, from and in Australia alone. The whole journey would have been completed by everyone in the ancient rail, road and sea manner but for the post-war difficulties about transport. So for the first time an M.C.C. side undertook an overseas journey by air—first to New Zealand and back, then home from Sydney by flying-boats. All the players should have had this experience. They ought to have gone home as a team, even if the £50,000 profits of the tour had been diminished by a few hundreds. To send three players home in a more economical manner than the rest savoured of cheese-paring—a frequent operation in England these days.

This brings me naturally to the financial side of the tour, which was by no means a failure. The figure mentioned, £50,000, is a rough one, for the details are in the pavilion at Lord's. The sum is Australian currency, only four-fifths as valuable as sterling. I understand that from it has to be deducted the payments of professionals and the expenses of sending the side out, which cannot amount to much under an average of £1,200 sterling a man. Payments to professionals, of whom there were fourteen in the party, are a minimum of £550 a head, with bonus which may amount to another £200; in addition there is a small allowance to amateurs and professionals for out-of-pocket expenses, though this does not cover the men's outlay by any means.

In round figures, the net profits may amount to £20,000 sterling, which sounds a lot, but when divided in allotted proportions between seventeen first-class counties, the M.C.C. and the minor counties and universities does not mean a fortune for anyone. It is good, anyhow, that the profits of these tours are "ploughed back" into the game. The money is sorely needed.

Division of the spoils in Australia, as in England, is based on payment to the visiting side of half the "outer" gate, less entertainment tax. Attendances in the tour just over were not a record, but receipts—and tax too—exceeded those of earlier tours because prices of admission were substantially increased. Here are figures for the five test matches:

	Attendance	Takings
		£
Brisbane	77,344	14,515
Sydney (second test)	196,253	26,544
Melbourne	343,675	44,063
Adelaide	135,980	18,117
Sydney (fifth test) ..	93,011	12,619
Totals ..	846,263	£115,858

About a quarter of this is given to the tax collectors. Various aspects of these figures are worth comment. Firstly we pay, in England and Australia, rather heavily for allotting Brisbane a test match. If it be pointed out that the Brisbane takings exceeded those of the second game at Sydney the explanation is that the latter fixture—played after Australia had won the rubber—had a blank Saturday and was over in four days of cricket.

Melbourne, though smaller than Sydney by a quarter of a million people, upholds its reputation as the bigger provider of crowds. On the second day of the test there we had anticipated a record of nearly 100,000. In fact the gates were closed on only 70,863, not, we were informed, because the stands were full, but because certain passages had become congested. Sydney and Melbourne alternate in having two matches. In 1950 it will be Melbourne's turn again.

In 1936-7, when we won the first two tests and Australia the next three, and public interest was naturally greater, 960,794 saw the matches, or 114,531 more than this time, but the £87,840 they paid is smaller by £28,018 than now.

The good returns from the tour as a whole are surprising, considering our lack of success and the rain-ruined Saturdays. In Sydney alone three wet Saturdays for state and test games cost an estimated £10,000 at the gates. The Australian public were obviously eager to welcome cricket back to its old position in sport. But if the game is to retain that position there will have to be an end to the drab series of draws in matches against the states.

The previous best takings by the M.C.C. were £40,427 (Australian) during the 1928 tour, even though on that occasion A. P. F. Chapman's side won the series by four matches to one. But money then was worth more than now.

By many of the English counties, their usual hard-up state aggravated by the need of after-the-war reconstruction, the share-out will be awaited with eagerness. The sum, relatively small though it is, means to some the difference between solvency and bankruptcy. In Australia the State Associations which take their share will find the money hardly less welcome.

It cannot be said that the players, English or Australian, who are the actors in the cricket entertainment take more than their share of the proceeds. The reward of the Australians playing at home is about £60 a test match; our own players, as already mentioned, may make £700 to £750 from the tour. This plum can be awarded only to the very few among the scores of professionals employed by our county clubs. As recognition of the highest ability it compares badly with the sums earned by the best boxers, golfers and American baseball players. The ordinary "professor" playing in one of the less well-endowed county sides in England is fortunate to earn from the game more than a net £7 or £8 a week throughout the year. The answer to complaints is always that it is impossible to take out of a game more than the cricket public put into it.

As for the Australian cricketers, they are apt to fall between two stools. There is not enough first-class cricket out there for the formation of a class of whole-time professionals. But there is enough play, even when there is no visiting side from overseas, to break the continuity of a young man's job and make employers look askance at him. Not unnaturally the young man likes to pursue an occupation at which he excels rather than settle down to a humdrum job where he is merely one of many; hence uncertainty about employment and offers from the Lancashire League.

Australian newspapers have often urged the Board of Control to do something for the men who keep first-class cricket going—and I think there is every reason for the agitation. It ought to be possible to ensure that a man learns a lucrative trade or profession under a sympathetic sport-minded employer, so that when his cricket is over he can feel his future assured.

Now that Western Australia has been admitted to the Sheffield Shield competition the problem becomes even more serious. In the normal Australian season each state side will have to play eight matches of four days each, and for half of these long journeys are necessary. No sooner does a player return to his work than he has to ask for time off again. He ought not to be left to face this problem unaided.

One institution which ought to have been brought to England from Australia years ago is still unknown here—the tell-all giant scoreboard which keeps the most unenlightened spectator in touch with the game. On the test match grounds the board gives all the facts anyone wants to know, including an electric flash against the name of any fieldsman touching a ball. Australians laugh at our antiquated scorecards. Even on the minor Australian grounds— Hobart for example—more details are given on the board than at Lord's.

Dwellings are more important than cricket scoreboards, so in England the innovation will have to wait even longer. In any case it can hardly be adopted by counties which, like Kent, spread their matches over several towns. But at least we might have an up-to-date board on all English grounds where test matches are played. Let the M.C.C. question their most conservative-minded members who have seen the Australian boards. I think they will find many converts among them.

We people who go often to cricket and know the players by sight, and often personally, cannot appreciate the fog in which the once-or-twice-a-season spectator sits during a cricket match. He can identify the batsmen, bowlers and wicketkeeper; for the rest he must trust to his knowledgeable neighbours for more or less reliable guidance. It may take him hours to identify the fellow standing just across the fence at deep third man. In Australia the information will be there directly this fieldsman runs for a ball.

It is just in matters like these that the casual onlooker can be made to feel he is wanted at cricket matches and encouraged to come again.

I cannot end this book without acknowledging the wonderful welcome the English party—players and journalists alike—received right through Australia. We fourteen writers and broadcasters were helped immeasurably by our colleagues in the press box in such all-important details as the allocation of seats and so forth. And once, when hotel accommodation was "sticky" down in Tasmania, Tom Goodman, of the Sydney *Morning Herald*, spent time he could ill spare in stirring up things in that island. I hope that when some of these cheerful colleagues come to England in

1948 with their Southern Cross neckties they will receive, from cricket executives and English newspapermen, the same consideration and facilities we had in Australia.

Finally, there is "Fergie," otherwise William Ferguson the scorer, whose twenty-eighth trip for this or that cricket power has now ended barely in time for the twenty-ninth—that of the South Africans in England—to begin. Next northern winter he will be back in Australia with the Indians. Then he returns to England with the Australians. And—I hope—so on for many more tours. When I tell you in this book that so-and-so scored a hundred in 219 minutes the fact is from "Fergie's" watch, not mine, which is just as well. In Australia the scorers are not cloistered in a remote box of their own. They preserve, for the minute-to-minute use of all concerned, a running record of the factual side of the game. "Fergie" is the prince among them. I think that every cricketing country should run a benefit match for him. In the inner world of cricket he is better known than most players, for while they last only a few years he has lasted many.

Failure of a mission? Yes and no. This M.C.C. side, while losing its matches, was as well liked as any ever to visit Australia. Test cricket is on its legs firmly again, even though we placed it there a season too soon for winning our matches.

But what is the matter with our old friend the barracker? He isn't what he used to be. The Hill at Sydney has become almost respectable. Which perhaps is just as well for the next lot to go South.

Bradman bowled by Bedser for a duck in the fourth Test at Adelaide.

Photo : Krischock Studios, Adelaide.

Photo: Telegraph, Sydney.

Douglas Wright in action in the fifth Test at Sydney. Non-striking batsman is Sid Barnes.

APPENDIX

RECORDS OF THE TOUR

BELOW are the scores in all matches except the tests, which are dealt with in their appropriate order in the book. One and two-day matches do not count as first-class.

v. Western Australian Country XI at Northam, 2nd and 3rd October. Won by an innings and 215 runs.

Northam (first innings): J. Tetlaw lbw b Smith 34; M. Madew c Edrich b Voce 0; N. Allnutt c Evans b Edrich 5; G. Solomon b Voce 0; B. Lawrence c Edrich b Voce 32; L. Solomon c Edrich b Ikin 1; W. Slater b Smith 26; M. Sanders st Evans b Smith 1; G. Hay c Langridge b Smith 4; L. Havercroft not out 9; H. Phillips b Smith 4; Extras 7. Total 123.

M.C.C.: L. Hutton lbw b G. Solomon 51; C. Washbrook c Slater b G. Solomon 47; L. Fishlock c Slater b Havercroft 2; D. Compton b Phillips 84; W. R. Hammond retired 131; J. Ikin c Tetlaw b Phillips 30; W. J. Edrich not out 38; J. Langridge not out 10; Extras 16. Total (six wickets) 409. Innings declared.

Northam (second innings): Tetlaw b Smith 29; Madew b Edrich 1; Allnutt c Evans b Edrich 0; Lawrence c Ikin b Smith 16; Slater b Edrich 1; G. Solomon b Smith 6; L. Solomon b Edrich 0; Sanders b Edrich 0; Havercroft b Edrich 0; Hay not out 12; Phillips lbw b Smith 2; Extras 4. Total 71.

Bowling: England—Voce 3 for 11 and 0 for 17; Edrich 1 for 12 and 6 for 20; Smith 5 for 55 and 4 for 18; Ikin 1 for 38; Langridge 0 for 12. Northam—Phillips 2 for 61; L. Solomon 0 for 41; Allnutt 0 for 50; Havercroft 1 for 68; G. Solomon 2 for 54; Hay 0 for 26; Sanders 0 for 55; Slater 0 for 28; Madew 0 for 10.

v. Western Australian Colts at Fremantle, 7th October. Drawn.

M.C.C.: Washbrook lbw b Alderman 25; Gibb c Sparrow b Rigg 51; Fishlock b Fisher 50; Hardstaff lbw. b Rigg 10; Ikin not out 31; Yardley not out 7; Extras 23. Total (four wickets declared) 197.

Colts: B. Rigg lbw b Pollard 1; F. Sparrow c Yardley b Voce 6; W. Langdon c Voce b Langridge 48; L. Letchford b Wright 8; I. Dick b Wright 30; W. Alderman b Langridge 18; T. Outridge not out 22; V. Fisher not out 3; Extras 2. Total (six wickets) 138.

Bowling: Colts—Dunn 0 for 49; Alderman 1 for 38; Fisher 1 for 33; Rigg 2 for 49; Langdon 0 for 5. M.C.C.—Voce 1 for 18; Pollard 1 for 14; Wright 2 for 52; Bedser 0 for 31; Langridge 2 for 21.

191

v. Western Australia, at Perth, 11th, 12th, 14th October. Drawn.

Western Australia: H. Rigg c Edrich b Smith 34; A. Edwards c Hardstaff b Smith 43; G. Robinson c Wright b Smith 36; A. Barras c Washbrook b Wright 10: D. Watt lbw b Wright 85; M. Herbert c Hammond b Wright 53; W. Langdon lbw b Wright 19; G. Kessey not out 44; C. Puckett b Voce 0; T. O'Dwyer b Voce 14; K. Cumming b Smith 10; Extras 18. Total 366.

Bowling: Voce 2 for 75; Edrich 0 for 78; Smith 4 for 132; Wright 4 for 55; Ikin 0 for 8.

M.C.C.: Washbrook c Barras b Cumming 17; Gibb lbw b Puckett 20; Ikin run out 66; Hardstaff lbw. b O'Dwyer 52; Hammond b Puckett 208; Edrich c Watt b O'Dwyer 10; Yardley b Puckett 38; Smith lbw b Cumming 46; Evans lbw b Puckett 7; Voce b Puckett 5; Wright not out 0; Extras 8. Total 477.

Bowling: Cumming 2 for 108; Puckett 5 for 126; O'Dwyer 2 for 140; Herbert 0 for 60; Barras 0 for 21; Langdon 0 for 14.

v. Combined Team at Perth, 18th, 19th, 20th October. Drawn.

Combined Team: K. Meuleman c Pollard b Ikin 16; A. Edwards run out 45; S. G. Barnes c and b Ikin 45; G. Robinson c and b Ikin 8; D. Watt run out 157; M. Herbert b Edrich 28; I. Johnson c Hutton b Langridge 87; G. Kessey not out 34; B. Dooland c Langridge b Pollard 10; C. Puckett c Yardley b Bedser 2; K. Cumming b Ikin 13; Extras 17. Total 462.

Bowling: Pollard 1 for 68; Bedser 1 for 86; Edrich 1 for 20; Langridge 1 for 85; Ikin 4 for 172; Compton 0 for 14.

M.C.C.: Hutton b Cumming 10; Washbrook lbw b Dooland 80; Fishlock c Kessey b Puckett 11; Compton st Kessey b Dooland 98; Edrich st Kessey b Dooland 1; Ikin c Dooland b Johnson 2; Yardley c Johnson b Dooland 56; Gibb run out 1; Langridge not out 30; Bedser c Barnes b Johnson 1; Pollard b Johnson 0; Extras 12. Total 302.

Bowling: Puckett 1 for 77; Cumming 1 for 41; Johnson 3 for 76; Dooland 4 for 88; Barnes 0 for 8.

v. South Australian Country XI at Port Pirie, 22nd and 23rd October. Won by an innings and 308 runs.

M.C.C.: Hutton c Veal b McLean 164; Gibb lbw b Corrie 19; Fishlock c and b Adams 98; Compton c Corrie b McLean 100; Hardstaff not out 67; Yardley c Corrie b Veal 12; Langridge c White b Davis 5; Smith not out 17; Extras 5. Total (six wickets declared) 487.

Bowling: Davis 1 for 90; Corrie 1 for 66; Hutchinson 0 for 126; Adams 1 for 63; Paterson 0 for 34; Giffen 0 for 14; McLean 2 for 44; Veal 1 for 34; Tuck 0 for 11.

Country XI (first innings): J. A. J. Horsell c Hutton b Smith 27; C. V. White b Wright 32; G. Tuck lbw b Smith 4; C. B. Giffen c Gibb b Wright 0; L. Veal c Hutton b Wright 1; D. W. McLean c Hutton b Smith 0; L. H. B. Patterson b Smith 1; M. D. Hutchinson c Compton b Smith 3; L. Corrie c and b Wright 7; D. Davis lbw b Wright 5; D. H. Adams not out 2; Extras 5. Total 87.

Bowling: Voce 0 for 22; Bedser 0 for 4; Smith 5 for 16; Wright 5 for 40.

Country XI (second innings): Horsell lbw b Wright 0; White c Gibb b Wright 25; Tuck c Hutton b Wright 30; Giffen lbw b Smith 2; Veal b Smith 7; McLean not out 8; Paterson c Hutton b Smith 0; Hutchinson b Langridge 8; Corrie c Fishlock b Langridge 2; Davis b Langridge 0; Adams b Langridge 0; Extras 10. Total 92.

Bowling: Wright 3 for 38; Smith 3 for 27; Langridge 4 for 17.

v. South Australia at Adelaide, 25th, 26th, 28th, 29th October. Drawn.

M.C.C. (first innings): Hutton c and b Dooland 136; Washbrook c Englefield b O'Neill 113; Compton c O'Neill b Mann 71; Hammond st Englefield b Dooland 9; Edrich st Englefield b Dooland 71; Yardley not out 54; Ikin not out 35; Extras 17. Total (five wickets declared) 506.

Bowling: O'Neill 1 for 104; Noblet 0 for 54; Ridings 0 for 57; Mann 1 for 65; Dooland 3 for 142; James 0 for 20; Gogler 0 for 27; Craig 0 for 20.

South Australia (first innings): R. J. Craig c Evans b Pollard 14; P. L. Ridings b Langridge 57; R. A. Hamence b Smith 0; D. G. Bradman c and b Smith 76; R. James b Langridge 58; K. G. Gogler b Smith 19; B. Dooland lbw. b Smith 12; K. O'Neill c Evans b Smith 8; J. L. Mann b Langridge 3; J. Noblet b Edrich 8; W. Englefield not out 6; Extras 5. Total 266.

Bowling: Pollard 1 for 66; Edrich 1 for 38; Smith 5 for 93; Langridge 3 for 60; Ikin 0 for 4.

South Australia (second innings): Craig b Pollard 111; Ridings c Hammond b Compton 20; Hamence st Evans b Compton 7; Bradman c Edrich b Pollard 3; James run out 15; Gogler c Compton b Langridge 1; Dooland c Hammond b Langridge 16; O'Neill b Edrich 3; Mann not out 62; Noblet not out 25; Extras 13. Total (eight wickets) 276.

Bowling: Edrich 1 for 37; Pollard 2 for 23; Smith 0 for 70; Langridge 2 for 73; Hammond 0 for 8; Compton 2 for 46; Hutton 0 for 6.

v. Victoria at Melbourne, 31st October, 1st, 2nd, 4th November. Won by 244 runs.

M.C.C. (first innings): Hutton b I. Johnson 15; Washbrook c Barnett b W. Johnston 0; Gibb b Ring 22; Compton c Harvey b Ring 143; Hardstaff lbw b Freer 15; Yardley c and b Tribe 70; Ikin not out 31; Langridge lbw b Tribe 0; Voce c and b I. Johnson 21; Bedser run out 22; Wright b Tribe 0; Extras 19. Total 358.

Bowling: W. Johnston 1 for 68; Freer 1 for 62; I. Johnston 2 for 79; Tribe 3 for 88; Ring 2 for 42.

Victoria (first innings): G. Tamblyn c and b Wright 5; K. Meuleman c Yardley b Voce 2; M. Harvey c and b Wright 21; K. Miller c Hutton b Wright 32; L. Hassett c Bedser b Ikin 57; I. Johnson c Gibb b Voce

31; B. Barnett not out 17; F. Freer c Ikin b Voce o; D. Ring c Gibb b Wright 1; G. Tribe lbw b Wright 4; W. Johnston b Wright o; Extras 19. Total 189.

M.C.C. (second innings): Hutton not out 151; Washbrook b Tribe 17; Gibb c Tribe b Ring 16; Compton c Tribe b Ring 18; Hardstaff lbw. b Johnson 21; Yardley lbw b Johnson 20; Ikin st Barnet b Johnson 21; Voce c Freer b Johnson 7; Extras 8. Total (seven wickets declared) 279.

Bowling: Johnson o for 66; Freer o for 45; Tribe 1 for 70; Johnson 4 for 38; Ring 2 for 52.

Victoria (second innings): Tamblyn b Hutton 24; Meuleman run out 14; Miller b Langridge 8; Harvey c Ikin b Bedser 57; Hassett c Compton b Wright 57; Johnson c Ikin b Wright o; Barnett c Ikin b Bedser 3; Ring b Wright o; Freer c Hardstaff b Bedser 14; Tribe c Hutton b Wright 13; Johnston not out 7; Extras 7. Total 204.

Bowling: Voce o for 14; Bedser 3 for 40; Langridge 1 for 33; Ikin o for 12; Compton o for 17; Hutton 1 for 8; Wright 4 for 73.

v. An Australian XI at Melbourne, 9th, 11th, 12th, 13th November. Drawn. Rain-ruined. Match should have started on 8th November, but rain prevented play and an extra day was arranged. No play on 12th November.

M.C.C. (first innings): Hutton c Freer b McCool 71; Washbrook b McCool 57; Edrich lbw b McCool 4; Compton st Saggers b McCool 24; Hammond c Miller b McCool 51; Yardley b McCool 11; Ikin b Puckett 15; Evans c Ellis b Freer 18; Smith b Ellis 28; Voce c Freer b McCool 15; Pollard not out 11; Extras 9. Total 314.

Bowling: Ellis 1 for 47; Puckett 1 for 58; Freer 1 for 60; Pettiford o for 26; McCool 7 for 106; Miller o for 8.

Australian XI (first innings): M. Harvey c Ikin b Smith 22; A. Morris c Evans b Yardley 115; D. G. Bradman c Pollard b Compton 106; A. L. Hassett c Hutton b Smith 28; K. Miller c Evans b Smith 5; J. Pettiford not out 27; C. McCool not out 22; Extras 2. Total (five wickets) 327.

Bowling: Voce o for 98; Pollard o for 69; Smith 3 for 111; Ikin o for 13; Compton 1 for 26; Yardley 1 for 8.

v. N.S.W. at Sydney, 15th, 16th, 18th, 19th November. Drawn. Play limited by rain to two and a half hours on first day and three hours on fourth. Second and third days blank. Hammond won toss and put N.S.W. in.

N.S.W. (first innings): K. Carmody c Edrich b Bedser 7; A. Morris not out 81; S. G. Barnes c Yardley b Edrich 1; J. Pettiford b Wright 24; R. Saggers b Bedser 3; W. Alley not out 43; Extras 6. Total (four wickets) 165. Declared

Bowling: Wright 1 for 71; Edrich 1 for 13; Pollard o for 27; Bedser 2 for 48.

M.C.C. (first innings): Hutton run out 97; Washbrook c Grieves b Lindwall 13; Gibb not out 37; Compton not out 1; Extras 8. Total (two wickets) 156.

Bowling: Lindwall 1 for 20; Beath 0 for 36; Alley 0 for 35; Toshack 0 for 23; Powell 0 for 19; Pettiford 0 for 15.

v. Queensland, 23rd, 24th, 26th, 27th November. Drawn.

Queensland (first innings): R. Rogers c Gibb b Bedser 66; G. Cook not out 169; W. Morris run out 4; D. Tallon c Gibb b Bedser 26; C. McCool c Gibb b Yardley 26; K. McKay c Gibb b Edrich 13; K. Archer c Edrich b Wright 18; A. Young c Compton b Wright 53; V. McMahon b Smith 10; L. Johnson b Yardley 8; J. Ellis hit wicket b Yardley 3; Extras 4. Total 400.

Bowling: Bedser 2 for 83; Edrich 1 for 74; Wright 2 for 137; Smith 1 for 58; Compton 0 for 14; Yardley 3 for 19; Ikin 0 for 11.

M.C.C. (first innings): Hutton c Tallon b McCool 42; Washbrook st Tallon b McCool 40; Gibb st Tallon b McCool 16; Compton b Johnson 55; Ikin c and b Johnson 37; Hammond st Tallon b McCool 8; Edrich not out 64; Yardley c and b McCool 14; Smith b Johnson 15; Bedser c Young b McCool 13; Wright b Johnson 0; Extras 6. Total 310.

Bowling: Ellis 0 for 80; Johnson 4 for 53; Cook 0 for 19; McCool 6 for 105; Young 0 for 25; Mackay 0 for 13; McMahon 0 for 9.

Queensland (second innings): Rogers b Smith 29; Cook b Smith 11; Morris b Wright 30; Tallon lbw b Smith 35; McCool b Wright 0; Mackay not out 33; Johnson c Compton b Wright 75; Archer not out 7; Extras 10. Total (six wickets declared) 230.

Bowling: Bedser 0 for 21; Edrich 0 for 24; Smith 3 for 93; Wright 3 for 63; Compton 0 for 14.

M.C.C. (second innings): Washbrook c Tallon b McCool 124; Gibb c Rogers b Cook 6; Edrich b McMahon 71; Ikin st Tallon b McCool 11; Compton c Ellis b McCool 13; Hammond b Young 1; Yardley not out 5; Extras 7. Total (six wickets) 238.

Bowling: Ellis 0 for 9; Cook 1 for 7; McCool 3 for 78; Johnson 0 for 51; McMahon 1 for 23; Young 1 for 24.

v. Queensland Country, at Gympie (two days—7th-9th December). Drawn.

Queensland Country (first innings): J. Cockburn st Evans b Voce 12; J. Barnes b Voce 2; H. Zischke hw b Smith 32; T. Allen c Fishlock b Smith 53; C. Stibe c Evans b Smith 5; N. Wright hw b Compton 22; L. Johnson b Langridge 40; W. Tallon c Hardstaff b Smith 11; K. Gartrell not out 9; A. Semgreen b Smith 5; T. Ball c Pollard b Langridge 0; Extras 17. Total 208.

Bowling: Voce 2 for 34; Pollard 0 for 47; Langridge 2 for 21; Smith 5 for 80; Compton 1 for 3; Ikin 0 for 6.

M.C.C. (first innings): Fishlock b Johnson 62; Gibb run out 31; Hardstaff b Ball 64; Langridge c Wright b Cockburn 42; Compton c Barnes b Ball 4; Ikin b Johnson 1; Yardley c Stibe b Johnson 33; Smith b Ball 24; Voce not out 2; Evans b Ball 1; Pollard b Ball 1; Extras 17. Total 282.

Bowling: Ball 5 for 69; Johnson 3 for 51; Cockburn 1 for 50; Tallon 0 for 73; Allen 0 for 10; Semgreen 0 for 12.

Queensland Country (second innings): Cockburn c Ikin b Langridge 41; Barnes b Pollard 6; Zischke c Voce b Smith 31; Allen c Compton b Ikin 40; Stibe lbw b Compton 75; Wright c Compton b Gibb 32; Johnson c Voce b Compton 16; Tallon c and b Compton 10; Gartrell not out 52; Semgreen c Pollard b Hardstaff 1; Extras 7. Total (nine wickets) 311.

Bowling: Voce 0 for 24; Pollard 1 for 25; Langridge 1 for 48; Smith 1 for 49; Compton 3 for 47; Ikin 1 for 46; Hardstaff 1 for 39; Gibb 1 for 26.

v. Northern Districts N.S.W. at Newcastle, 21st-23rd December.

M.C.C. (first innings): Hutton c and b Hinman 42; Washbrook c de Courcy b Pickles 9; Fishlock b Hinman 110; Hammond st Felton b Hill 142; Compton c and b Hill 6; Hardstaff c Sullivan b Hill 1; Edrich not out 59; Langridge c Hill b Mannix 21; Gibb b Hinman 0; Voce lbw b Hinman 1; Pollard b Hinman 1; Extras 3. Total 395.

Bowling: Sullivan 0 for 76; Pickles 1 for 35; Hinman 5 for 92; Mannix 1 for 58; Hamilton 0 for 30; Hill 3 for 101.

Northern Districts (first innings): M. Hinman b Pollard 46; C. Johnston b Voce 7; J. Mayes c Gibb b Langridge 22; R. Camps b Pollard 12; J. de Courcy c Hammond b Voce 30; K. Hill c Compton b Voce 14; W. Pickles c Hammond b Langridge 5; J. Mannix c Washbrook b Hutton 32; K. Sullivan b Voce 0; M. Felton lbw b Hutton 11; C. Hamilton not out 4; Extras 19. Total 202.

Bowling: Voce 4 for 45; Pollard 2 for 62; Edrich 0 for 26; Langridge 2 for 46; Hutton 2 for 4.

M.C.C. (second innings): Hutton b Pickles 5; Washbrook lbw b Pickles 9; Fishlock b Pickles 0; Hardstaff b Sullivan 16; Compton not out 75; Langridge lbw b Pickles 0; Gibb lbw b Sullivan 0; Hammond not out 30; Extras 11. Total (six wickets) 146.

Six wickets were down for 40 runs.

Bowling: Sullivan 2 for 26; Pickles 4 for 29; Hill 0 for 18; Hinman 0 for 24; Hamilton 0 for 17; Mannix 0 for 21.

v. Southern Districts N.S.W. at Canberra, 27th and 28th December. Drawn.

M.C.C. (first innings): Hutton c Hourigan b Johnston 133; Washbrook c Potts b Patterson 115; Fishlock c Fisher (sub) b Patterson 11; Hammond c Patterson b Stevens 42; Compton c Hanson b Stevens 76; Ikin lbw b Bennett 35; Langridge run out 15; Smith not out 8; Evans lbw b Bennett 6; Bedser not out 1; Extras 23. Total (eight wickets) 465. Declared.

Bowling: Bennett 2 for 80; Patterson 2 for 118; Johnston 1 for 105; Stevens 2 for 35.

Southern N.S.W. (first innings): Merchant b Pollard 0; Potts c Evans b Pollard 0; Longbottom b Pollard 1; Hourigan lbw b Pollard 4; Stevens not out 3; Goodfellow not out 0; Extras 3. Total (four wickets) 11.

Bowling: Bedser 0 for 6; Pollard 4 for 2.

Abandoned after rain.

v. Victorian County at Bendigo, 30th December. Won by six wickets.

Victorian County (batting twelve): N. Arthur c and b Smith 4; I. Phyland b Pollard 39; L. Harris st Gibb b Smith 25; H. Hease c Gibb b Voce 14; H. Day c Fishlock b Smith 2; H. Knight c Ikin b Smith 2; R. Nuttall c Ikin b Smith 8; E. Cleary c Voce b Wright 20; W. Mills c and b Ikin 20; R. Seelenmeyer c Gibb b Smith 4; J. Burchell c Ikin b Smith 1; A. Smith not out 7; Extras 10. Total 156.

Bowling: Voce 1 for 9; Pollard 1 for 20; Smith 7 for 43; Wright 1 for 26; Edrich 0 for 3; Ikin 1 for 18; Langridge 0 for 10; Hardstaff 0 for 17.

M.C.C.: Gibb st Smith b Burchell 49; Fishlock b Phyland 41; Hammond c Nuttall b Harris 9; Edrich c and b Knight 62; Langridge not out 30; Extras 9. Total (four wickets) 200.

Bowling: Harris 1 for 51; Phyland 1 for 31; Burchell 1 for 22; Knight 1 for 15.

v. Combined XI at Hobart, 10th, 11th, 13th January. Drawn.

M.C.C. (first innings): Gibb c Gardiner b Murfett 1; Fishlock lbw b Barnes 52; Hardstaff c Morrisby b Murfett 3; Compton c Morrisby b Murfett 11; Ikin c Gardiner b Johnson 5; Edrich lbw b Clark 82; Yardley b Clark 4; Bedser c and b Clark 51; Evans c Clark b Miller 34; Wright c and b Johnson 20; Pollard not out 2; Extras 13. Total 278.

Bowling: Murfett 3 for 89; Miller 1 for 35; Johnson 2 for 74; Clark 3 for 48; Barnes 1 for 19.

Combined XI (first innings): R. Morrisby b Pollard 16; R. Thomas c Edrich b Bedser 16; S. E. Barnes c Pollard b Wright 57; L. Hassett c Evans b Bedser 70; I. Johnson c Edrich b Compton 6; M. Thomas run out 1; J. Laver c Evans b Compton 30; J. Gardiner not out 94; D. Clark c Ikin b Edrich 27; J. Murfett c Evans b Edrich 9; Extras 13. Total 374.

Bowling: Pollard 2 for 124; Bedser 2 for 75; Edrich 2 for 40; Wright 1 for 48; Compton 2 for 58; Yardley 0 for 16.

M.C.C. (second innings): Gibb c Gardiner b Murfett 11; Fishlock c and b Johnson 46; Hardstaff c M. Thomas b Johnson 60; Compton c Barnes b Laver 124; Ikin c Clark b Miller 50; Edrich st Gardiner b Laver 22; Yardley b Laver 19; Bedser c Morrisby b Laver 5; Evans not out 4; Wright c Gardiner b Laver 0; Extras 12. Total (nine wickets) 353. Declared.

Bowling: Miller 1 for 52; Murfett 1 for 99; Hassett 0 for 21; Johnson 2 for 52; Clark 0 for 61; Barnes 0 for 30; Laver 5 for 26.

Combined XI (second innings): Hassett c Fishlock b Pollard 11; Miller lbw b Ikin 30; Johnson not out 80; M. Thomas not out 21; Extras 3. Total (two wickets) 145.

Bowling: Pollard 1 for 37; Bedser 0 for 21; Compton 0 for 17; Ikin 1 for 35; Gibb 0 for 14; Hardstaff 0 for 18.

v. Tasmania at Launceston, 15th, 16th, 17th, January. Drawn.

M.C.C. (first innings): Fishlock c R. Thomas b Richardson 20; Hutton c R. Thomas b Kilbey 51; Gibb st Gardiner b Clark 22; Hardstaff b Clark 155; Compton c Richardson b Clark 163; Edrich not out 30; Ikin not out 15; Extras 11. Total (five wickets) 467.

Hardstaff and Compton stand of 282 in 181 minutes.

Bowling: Murfett 0 for 108; Richardson 1 for 90; Kilbey 1 for 93; Clark 3 for 98; Laver 0 for 67.

Tasmania (first innings): R. Morrisby c Ikin b Voce 0; R. Thomas c Gibb b Edrich 8; M. Thomas c Yardley b Voce 4; A. Wilkes lbw b Ikin 13; D. Calvert c Gibb b Edrich 2; J. Gardiner lbw b Edrich 0; J. Laver c Gibb b Ikin 5; D. Clark c Pollard b Ikin 0; J. Murfett not out 46; C. Richardson st Gibb b Hutton 8; K. Kilbey b Edrich 12; Extras 5. Total 103.

Bowling: Voce 2 for 7; Pollard 0 for 19; Edrich 4 for 26; Ikin 3 for 17; Hutton 1 for 29.

Tasmania (second innings): R. Morrisby b Pollard 5; R. Thomas c Compton b Ikin 35; M. Thomas c and b Ikin 22; A. Wilkes not out 33; D. Calvert c Yardley b Compton 18; J. Gardiner c and b Ikin 3; J. Laver c Fishlock b Ikin 0; D. Clark not out 6; Extras 7. Total (six wickets) 129.

Bowling: Voce 0 for 8; Pollard 1 for 23; Ikin 4 for 51; Edrich 0 for 9; Compton 1 for 27; Yardley 0 for 1; Fishlock 0 for 3.

v. South Australia at Adelaide, 24th, 25th, 27th, 28th January. Drawn.

M.C.C. (first innings): Hutton c Vaughton b Gibson 88; Washbrook c Ridings b Dooland 21; Fishlock c Dooland b Oswald 57; Hardstaff c Bradman b Dooland 13; Hammond b Craig 188; Ikin lbw b Dooland 35; Langridge c Dooland b Craig 100; Evans not out 22; Voce c Vaughton b Oswald 21; Pollard st Vaughton b Oswald 6; Wright b Dooland 1; Extras 25. Total 577.

Bowling: Webb o for 71; Gibson 1 for 111; Ridings o for 68; Dooland 4 for 67; Oswald 3 for 182; Craig 2 for 39; James o for 14.

South Australia (first innings): R. Craig lbw b Wright 10; P. Ridings lbw b Voce 77; D. G. Bradman c Langridge b Wright 5; R. Hamence c Ikin b Wright 145; R. James b Hardstaff 85; R. Stanford b Hardstaff 31; R. Gibson b Hardstaff 4; R. Vaughton c Evans b Voce 20; B. Dooland not out 23; N. Oswald c Ikin b Voce 3; K. Webb b Voce 10; Extras 30. Total 443.

Bowling: Voce 4 for 125; Pollard o for 60; Wright 3 for 90; Ikin o for 60; Langridge o for 9; Hutton o for 45; Hardstaff 3 for 24.

M.C.C. (second innings): Hutton not out 77; Washbrook c Vaughton b Gibson o; Fishlock c Gibson b Oswald 26; Hardstaff not out 40; Extras 9. Total (two wickets) 152.

Bowling: Webb o for 21; Gibson 1 for 15; Ridings o for 22; Oswald 1 for 37; Dooland o for 23; James o for 12; Craig o for 13.

v. Victorian Country at Ballarat, 11th and 12th February. Drawn.

Victorian Country (first innings): S. Stephens c Gibb b Voce 40; V. Cahill lbw b Smith 31; C. Hopper st Gibb b Smith 8; K. Brown lbw b Compton 18; A. Meiklejohn c and b Ikin 34; D. Brown c Pollard b Voce 62; A. Simons b Voce 1; J. McIver b Pollard 34; J. Plummer not out 12; A. Brown lbw b Smith 11; R. McArthur b Ikin 1; Extras 16. Total 268.

Bowling: Pollard 1 for 52; Voce 3 for 28; Smith 3 for 70; Ikin 2 for 41; Edrich o for 18; Compton 1 for 43.

M.C.C. (first innings): Fishlock c Hopper b McArthur o; Gibb c McIver b Plummer 69; Edrich b McArthur o; Hardstaff lbw b Plummer 17; Compton b McIver 61; Ikin b Plummer 6; Evans lbw b A. Brown 82; Smith b Plummer 19; Voce c K. Brown b Meiklejohn 12; Pollard not out 3; Hammond absent o; Extras 19. Total 288.

Bowling: McArthur 2 for 70; Plummer 4 for 68; McIver 1 for 47; A. Brown 1 for 67; Meiklejohn 1 for 17.

Victorian Country (second innings): S. Stephens b Pollard o; V. Cahill st Gibb b Smith 35; C. Hopper b Pollard 1; K. Brown c Smith b Evans 24; A. Meiklejohn st Gibb b Smith o; D. Brown not out 3; J. McIver not out 2; Extras 5. Total (five wickets) 70.

Bowling: Pollard 2 for 7; Edrich o for 5; Hardstaff o for 20; Fishlock o for 21; Smith 2 for 10; Evans 1 for 2.

v. Victoria, 14th, 15th, 17th, 18th February. Drawn.

M.C.C. (first innings): Washbrook b Tribe 22; Fishlock c Hassett b Freer 51; Gibb c Johnson b Miller 17; Compton c and b Miller 93; Hardstaff c Tribe b Freer 9; Ikin b Tribe 71; Yardley b Miller 18; Bedser c M. Harvey b Tribe 11; Evans not out 41; Pollard lbw b Miller 9; Wright c Hassett b Ring 0; Extras 13. Total 355.

Bowling: Miller 4 for 63; Freer 2 for 77; Loxton 0 for 15; Tribe 3 for 143; Ring 1 for 45.

Victoria (first innings): Meuleman st Evans b Pollard 14; M. Harvey c Evans b Bedser 10; Miller st Evans b Bedser 6; Hassett c Fishlock b Yardley 126; N. Harvey c Evans b Wright 69; Loxton c Washbrook b Wright 2; Ring b Wright 0; Freer c Bedser b Pollard 22; Tribe c Bedser b Wright 60; Baker not out 13; Johnson absent 0; Extras 5. Total 327.

Bowling: Bedser 2 for 90; Pollard 2 for 72; Wright 4 for 108; Ikin 0 for 25; Yardley 1 for 27.

M.C.C. (second innings): Fishlock b Ring 11; Washbrook c Miller b Freer 0; Gibb lbw b Loxton 6; Compton c Freer b Ring 10; Hardstaff c Hassett b Tribe 26; Ikin lbw b Tribe 12; Yardley lbw b Tribe 28; Evans c Ring b Tribe 5; Bedser c and b Tribe 5; Pollard st Baker b Tribe 5; Wright not out 8; Extras 2. Total 118.

Bowling: Miller 0 for 2; Freer 1 for 9; Loxton 1 for 11; Hassett 0 for 5; Ring 2 for 36; Tribe 6 for 49; Meuleman 0 for 4.

Play on third day limited by rain to 40 minutes.

v. N.S.W. at Sydney, 21st, 22nd, 24th, 25th February. Drawn.

N.S.W. (first innings): Carmody lbw b Smith 65; Morris st Evans b Smith 44; Barnes c Voce b Smith 44; Lukeman b Smith 70; Kissell c Voce b Pollard 22; Lindwall c Pollard b Smith 45; Pettiford c and b Smith 6; Lush c Hardstaff b Smith 2; Saggers b Smith 21; Johnston not out 11; Toshack c and b Smith 5; Extras 7. Total 342.

Bowling: Voce 0 for 65; Pollard 1 for 74; Edrich 0 for 59; Smith 9 for 121; Hutton 0 for 16.

M.C.C. (first innings): Hutton lbw b Lindwall 40; Washbrook b Johnston 13; Edrich c Morris b Toshack 31; Compton b Pettiford 75; Fishlock c and b Johnston 0; Hardstaff st Saggers b Toshack 1; Yardley c and b Pettiford 25; Evans c Morris b Toshack 3; Smith c Morris b Lindwall 33; Voce c and b Johnston 28; Pollard not out 12; Extras 5. Total 266.

Bowling: Lindwall 2 for 54; Lush 0 for 20; Johnston 3 for 51; Toshack 3 for 88; Pettiford 2 for 48.

N.S.W. (second innings): Carmody c Evans b Edrich 26; Morris c Edrich b Pollard 47; Barnes c Evans b Smith 9; Lukeman c Yardley

b Smith 45; Kissell not out 80; Lindwall c Edrich b Pollard 28; Pettiford
c and b Smith 23; Extras 4. Total (six wickets) 262. Declared.

Bowling: Voce 0 for 54; Pollard 2 for 73; Edrich 1 for 34; Smith
2 for 97.

M.C.C. (second innings): Washbrook c Saggers b Lush 11; Hutton
lbw b Johnston 72; Edrich c and b Pettiford 34; Fishlock not out 11;
Compton not out 73; Extras 4. Total (three wickets) 205.

Bowling: Lindwall 0 for 43; Lush 1 for 33; Toshack 0 for 43; Pettiford
1 for 55; Johnston 1 for 27.

M.C.C. were set to make 339 to win in four hours. When 134 were
still needed in 105 minutes rain stopped play. Two hundred had been
scored in 133 minutes.

SUMMARY OF RESULTS
(in Australia only)

	Played	Won	Drawn	Lost
Test matches	5	0	2	3
Other first-class matches	12	1	11	0
Minor matches	8	3	5	0
Total (all matches)	25	4	18	3

ENGLISH AVERAGES

BATTING — TESTS

	Innings	Not out	Highest	Total	Aver.
Compton ..	10	1	147	459	51.0
Hutton ..	9	0	122*	417	46.3
Edrich ..	10	0	119	462	46.2
Hardstaff ..	2	0	67	76	38.0
Washbrook ..	10	0	112	363	36.3
Yardley ..	10	2	61	252	31.5
Hammond ..	8	0	37	168	21.0
Ikin	10	0	60	184	18.4
Bedser	10	3	27*	106	15.1
Evans	8	2	29	90	15.0
Gibb	2	0	13	24	12.0
Voce	3	1	18	19	9.5
Wright ..	8	3	15*	47	9.4
Smith	4	0	24	32	8.0
Fishlock ..	2	0	14	14	7.0

*Denotes not out. Note that if Hutton's 122, ended by illness, is regarded as a not out innings; his average becomes 52.1 and he goes to the top of the table.

BOWLING — TESTS

	Overs	Maidens	Runs	Wickets	Aver.
Yardley ..	114	15	372	10	37.2
Wright ..	240.2	23	990	23	43.0
Bedser	246.3	34	876	16	54.7
Edrich	115.3	12	483	9	53.6
Smith ..	47	1	218	2	109.0
Voce	44	12	161	0	—
Compton ..	16.2	0	78	0	—
Ikin	7	0	48	0	—
Hutton ..	3	0	28	0	—

BATTING—ALL FIRST-CLASS MATCHES

	Innings	Not out	Highest	Total	Aver.
Hutton	.. 21	~~2~~ 3	151*	1,267	66.6 70.4
Compton	.. 25	3	163	1,432	65.1
Langridge	.. 3	1	100	130	65.0
Edrich ..	.. 21	2	119	881	46.4
Hammond	.. 14	0	208	633	45.2
Hardstaff	.. 13	1	155	471	39.2
Washbrook	.. 25	0	124	891	35.6
Yardley	.. 23	4	70	614	32.3
Ikin ..	.. 24	3	71	590	28.1
Fishlock	.. 12	1	57	299	27.1
Evans ..	.. 16	5	41*	224	20.3
Smith ..	.. 8	0	46	154	19.2
Gibb ..	.. 14	1	37*	199	15.3
Bedser	.. 17	3	51	214	15.2
Voce ..	.. 9	1	28	116	14.5
Pollard	.. 7	3	12*	45	11.2
Wright	.. 16	5	20	76	6.9

*Denotes not out. If Hutton's 122 in last test match is regarded as a not out innings his average is raised to 70.4.

BOWLING—ALL FIRST-CLASS MATCHES

	Overs	Maidens	Runs	Wickets	Aver.
Hardstaff ..	14	1	50	3	16.6
Yardley ..	134.7	16	443	15	29.5
Smith ..	259.6	16	1,073	35	30.6
Wright ..	395.4	40	1,699	51	33.3
Ikin ..	107	8	481	13	37.0
Langridge ..	99	15	288	7	41.1
Edrich ..	215	26	949	22	43.1
Bedser ..	391.3	54	1,359	29	46.8
Compton ..	83.2	11	311	6	51.8
Pollard ..	233	45	735	13	56.5
Voce ..	174.4	33	660	11	60.0
Hutton ..	21	1	132	2	66.0
Fishlock ..	1	0	3	0	—
Gibb ..	1	0	14	0	—
Hammond ..	3	0	8	0	—

AUSTRALIAN AVERAGES

BATTING — TESTS

	Innings	Not out	Highest	Total	Aver.
Bradman ..	8	1	234	680	97.1
Miller	7	2	141*	384	76.8
Barnes	6	0	234	443	73.8
Morris	8	1	155	503	71.8
McCool ..	7	2	104*	272	54.4
Hassett	7	0	128	376	53.7
Lindwall ..	5	0	100	160	32.0
Tallon	6	0	92	174	29.0
Harvey	2	0	31	43	21.5
Johnson ..	5	0	52	106	21.2
Tribe	3	1	25*	35	17.5
Dooland ..	3	0	29	49	16.3
Hamence ..	2	1	30*	31	15.5
Toshack ..	5	2	6	14	4.6
Freer	1	1	25*	25	—

BOWLING — TESTS

	Overs	Maidens	Runs	Wickets	Aver.
Lindwall ..	122.1	20	367	18	20.4
Miller ..	122.3	15	334	16	20.9
Freer ..	20	3	74	3	24.6
Toshack ..	178.4	50	437	17	25.7
McCool ..	182	27	491	18	27.3
Johnson ..	124.6	35	306	10	30.6
Dooland ..	98	9	351	8	43.8
Tribe ..	95	9	330	2	16.5
Barnes ..	7	0	23	0	—